In loving memory of
Alan Steel Milward and Franco Bonelli,
giants who lent me their shoulders
to see my ignorance

A Europe Apart

History and Politics of European Monetary Integration

by Roberto Di Quirico Ph.D.

EUROPEAN PRESS ACADEMIC PUBLISHING
2020

This work was supported by the Open Access Publishing Fund of the University of Cagliari, with the funding of the Regione Autonoma della Sardegna - L.R. n. 7/2007

ISBN 978-88-8398-097-8

Florence, Italy
www.e–p–a–p.com
www.europeanpress.eu
Printed in Italy, UK and USA

A catalog record for this publication is available from the British Library

Library of Congress Cataloging in Publication Data

Contents

BEPGs	Broad Economic Policy Guidelines
EBA	European Banking Authority
EC	European Commission
ECB	European Central Bank
ECSC	European Coal and Steel Community
EDIS	European Deposit Insurance Scheme
EDP	Excessive Deficit Procedure
EEC	European Economic Community
EFSF	European Financial Stability Facility
EFSM	European Financial Stabilisation Mechanism
EGs	Employment Guidelines
EIOPA	European Insurance and Occupational Pension Authority
EIP	Excessive Imbalances Procedure
ELA	Emergency Liquidity Assistance
EMS	European Monetary System
EMU	Economic and Monetary Union
EPU	European Payments Union
ERP	European Recovery Program
ESCBs	European System of Central Banks
ESM	European Stability Mechanism
ESMA	European Securities and Market Authority
ESRB	European Systemic Risk Board Authority
EU	European Union
IMF	International Monetary Fund
LTRO	Long Term Refinancing Operation
MIA	Multilevel Inter-institutional Accountability
MR	Multilevel Responsiveness
MTOs	Medium-Term Budgetary Objectives
NEG	New Economic Governance
OCAs	Optimal Currency Areas
OCSE	Organization for Economic Co-operation and Development

OEEC	Organization for European Economic Cooperation
OMC	Open Method of Coordination
PIIGS	Portugal, Ireland, Italy, Greece, Spain (otherwise GIPSI or GIIPS)
SGP	Stability and Growth Pact
SRM	Single Resolution Mechanism
SSM	Single Supervisory Mechanism
TARGET2	Trans-European Automated Real-time Gross Settlement Express Transfer System
TSCG	Treaty on Stability, Coordination, and Governance

Premise

European monetary integration is a complicated process that touches many aspects of our lives and shaped the image of Europe we have in mind. Creating a common currency and an integrated continental economy profoundly influenced European and domestic politics, transformed national and international economies, imposed new rules and principles, modified the European societies, and, last but not least, changed the way in which European citizens perceived Europe and its founding values. Finally, the introduction of the euro was a historical milestone that changed the trajectory of European history, both reinforcing existing trends and disclosing new paths for the future. Such a profound impact generated many tensions and discontent. Many citizens perceived monetary integration as a menace to their lifestyles, welfare, and beliefs. Many others just did not understand the complexity of that process and instinctively refused the enormous challenge of transforming their societies drastically into something new, unknown, and inscrutable. Then, uncertainty, responsibility shifts, simplified or fake explanations, and retrenchment in the nation-states and societies became pivotal for the political debate and oriented both electoral programmes and citizens' expectations.

Monetary integration also challenged the traditional approaches used by those scholars who study Europe and European integration. The multiform influence of the common currency in many fields of European life made the mono-disciplinary approaches obsolete. Hence, after the introduction of the euro, especially after its crisis, no one could understand changes in European politics, economics, institutions, and society separately. Many scholars tried to do it and failed. Others quietly renounced accepting the relevance of monetary integration and its influence on their research fields and barely included simplistic or ideological explanations of the monetary integration process in their theoretical framework, sometimes adopting a misleading perspective appropriate for confirming their consolidated views.

Among all those scholars whose disciplines were touched by the effects of monetary integration, political scientists, historians, and theorists of European integration are the most challenged in their traditional interpretations. Since the early phases of European integration, both historical analysis and integration theories have favoured the political side of integration and saw economic integration as a second order level of integration or, at best, as the tool to boost further political integration; it means the most important field of integration. The turning point of the euro's creation discredited the political prevalence approach, and the impact of the euro crisis demonstrated how the near completion of monetary integration magnified the role of financial affairs in directing the whole process of European integration. On the other hand, studying monetary integration by paying no attention to its impact on all the other fields of research is nonsense. This is the reason I decided to address my research more towards the consequences of monetary integration on a broader range of topics than the monetary one and less towards monetary integration in itself.

European and member-state politics, EU institutional and economic structure, EU governance, and European identity itself have been touched undeniably and massively by monetary integration. The long-term trajectory of European history has been changed, as well as the societal values that emerged in Europe by World War II. The concept of the national state itself changed when a common currency started to circulate in Europe and, later, the consequences of the problematic interdependencies activated by monetary integration emerged. United Europe with a common currency prophesied by the early theorists of integration became a Europe for the common currency, a multi-layered and poorly coordinated complex of institutions and rules, indispensable but insufficient to face the impact of monetary integration. The euro, its problems, costs, and consequences became a central topic in everyday discussion in newspapers, political debates, and electoral programmes as well as on the new media where citizens' political participation grows quickly. As a political scientist and former economic historian, I aim to show that these changes had been caused by the common currency and explain why they are so relevant. I think it is an original and innovative approach to European integration, and I hope other scholars, as well as those who feel touched by my criticism of mono-disciplinary approaches, will appreciate my efforts.

Notwithstanding all errors and omission remain my responsibility, I appreciate very much the help and support received by many colleagues who discussed with me about the topics touched in this book. I am grateful to the forever friends Daniele Caramani and Leila Simona Talani who shared with me the "golden age" as PhD students and Jean Monnet Fellowship at the European University Institute and never ended debates on Europe. I also have a debt with Fabrizio Bientiesi, Marco Masini, Pompeo Della Posta, and Stefania Profeti who read parts of an early version of this book, and made valuable comments I used to ameliorate the manuscript substantially. I am also grateful to many others colleagues who discussed with me on different occasions some elements that became crucial for this book. Among them, all the Jean Monnet Professors who participated at the conference "EU a la carte" organized by the Jean Monnet Action in Malmoe (19-21 June 2016) where I discussed some findings of my research, Professors Mihai Drecin and Anca Stangaciu and the whole community of Romanian economic historians that usually join in the Oradea conference on Economic history and that discussed with me the monetary integration topics in unusual and stimulating perspectives, and those colleagues of mine in the Universities of Florence, Bath, and Cagliari who gave me suggestions and ideas about European integration during the periods in which I worked there.

My research benefited by the fundamental support of those institutions that in different times and ways funded my work. In particular, I am grateful to the Robert Schuman Centre for Advanced Studies and its former Presidents Yves Meny, Helen Wallace and Stefano Bartolini. The first two of them recruited me in their Centre where, almost twenty years ago, I started this research having as colleagues scholars as Frank Schimmelfennig, Ulrich Sedelmeier, Claudio Radaelli, and (again) Daniele Caramani. Later, Bartolini involved me in the debates carried on at the Robert Schuman Centre where I benefited of the critics and suggestions of Adrienne Heritier and Philippe Schmitter. Other institutions that supported me with funds and involvement in scientific debates were the Jean Monnet Action of the European Commission, the Italian Institute for Human Sciences (now part of the Scuola Normale Superiore) where I prepared the core of this work, and the University of Cagliari that funded the completion of this book.

Finally, last but not least, I am grateful to those scholars who played a relevant role in my education, and that addressed me toward the study of monetary integration in different moments of my research. Among them Gian Carlo Falco, Jaime Reis and Peter Hertner who helped me in the early phases of my career, Giorgio Natalicchi who introduced me to the theories of European integration, James Caporaso who contributed in a substantial way in my research about the impact of monetary integration on the European integration process, and Leonardo Morlino who taught me almost all I know about Political Science.

It is too late for thanking Alan Steel Milward and Franco Bonelli for their contribution to my education and work. However, I know they knew I would do it.

Cagliari (Italy), December 2019

Introduction

Many scholars suggest that European integration started in 1951 when the founding countries signed the Treaty of Paris and created the European Coal and Steel Community (ECSC). However, I prefer considering the creation of the European Payments Union (EPU) just a few months before as the first step toward economic integration in Europe and the establishment of the European Economic Community (EEC) as the decisive step; it was the moment in which "the choice for Europe" (Moravcsik 1999) was made. In fact, the EPU was the real engine of economic integration in Europe during the 1950s, granting non-tariff trade barrier protection to its members by using specific currency arrangements and inconvertibility[1].

In building the EEC, the founding six members maintained some of the advantages of the pre-existent European Payments Union, particularly a commonly defended internal market (Milward 1987). The EEC became a framework in which what remained of the EPU became an institutional structure successfully tested by means of the ECSC in the management of a limited number of economic sectors – coal and steel.

After the EPU creation, there were many attempts to obtain "an ever-closer union" in fields such as the military, currency, shared institutions, infrastructures, and many other policy areas. Some steps toward deeper integration succeeded, while others failed. Only one, monetary integration, resulted in the full integration of the founding member countries. Why?

[1] Tariff barriers among European countries had been very low since 1948. Consequently, an internal market appeared in the EPU area until its demission. On the European Payments Union, see Kaplan and Schleiminger (1989).

This is a very intriguing question but, unfortunately, it did not attract sufficient interest from those scholars who searched for a theory of European integration. They tried to explain monetary integration as part of the broader process of European integration, implicitly admitting that the same reasons and mechanisms determined integration in the currency field as well as in the other sectors[2]. I do not subscribe to this point of view.

In the first part of this book, I will try to explain the reasons for monetary integration and its completion. Probably the more challenging thesis of this book is that monetary integration has its logic, origins, and dynamics and that these are different from those at work in other sectors under integration. In other words, monetary integration followed a different path to full integration because it was for years an autonomous process intersected and supported by the integration of other sectors, but not originated by them. This independence of monetary integration makes monetary Europe "a Europe apart" that finally prevailed and shaped the evolution of European integration on the whole. In fact, since the 2000s, the needs of the Economic and Monetary Union's (EMU) governance increasingly oriented the EU politics and institutional structure toward aims and practices sometimes in conflict with the European values and ideals proclaimed for decades. As a consequence, the perception of European identity changed, and European ideals appeared to be betrayed by politicians and central bankers.

In the first part of this book, this thesis will be supported by showing that the monetary problems of Continental Europe arose many years before political integration became an option. Of course, the existence of plans and proposals for European integration since the early first post-war period

[2] This is the case of those neo-functionalists who see monetary integration as a spillover of market integration.

and the 1920s will not be denied. However, they were and remained plans and proposals while monetary problems and attempts to solve them were real, and the need to reconnect the international economy with a working monetary system was stringent. Besides, it is acknowledged that monetary, economic, and political integration are connected and influenced by each other. I suggest they are strictly related, and advancements in every one of these three fields affected the others. Nevertheless, they remain three separate pillars of a historical process that would be better called "European integrations". The convergence of these integrations permitted the completion of monetary integration, which at that point oriented the whole integration process.

1– Dismissing the political prevalence approach

The thesis proposed here implies that to understand the whole integration process, it is crucial to analyse the relationship between integrations, in particular monetary, economic, and political integration. This statement is not an original starting point[3], apart from the new assumption adopted here; it means the dismissal of the political predominance approach that had dominated for decades the theories of European integration. This approach suggests that political integration is the core of the whole process of European integration and that integration in other sectors had been functional to political integration. The latter is the real culmination of integration. We could find this concept in the famous saying of De Gaulle: *L'intendance suivra* (the logistics will catch up). Instead, this book will demonstrate that "*l'intendance*" was miles ahead already at De Gaulle's time.

[3] The concept of interaction between sectors had appeared since the early phases of European integration, in particular in the neo-functionalist literature. Later, interaction was connected to side payments in the intergovernmental approach.

Many factors contributed to generating this misunderstanding. Probably the most important one is the dialectic. The word "integration" was insistently used only after the creation of the European Coal and Steel Community to legitimise this innovation politically and also to create an idealistic framework in which the surrender of sovereignty and its costs could be justified with superior ideals. Therefore, integration seemingly started when politicians initiated speaking about it in public thirty years after the rise of the European currency problem.

Moreover, one of the leading innovations introduced by the founding fathers of Europe was a rhetorical framework capable of including almost every kind of cooperation among European countries. This framework, here named "European mythology", is revealed as a powerful tool to legitimise further cooperation, outflanking nationalism with a superior ideal such as the European unification one. Technical matters remained in the shadow. However, they determined the path of integration.

Another factor that explains the success of the political predominance approach is the scientific background of many scholars who had studied European integration since the 1950s. They were mainly political scientists concentrating on institutional aspects or international relations. Their focus was prevalently political, and their skills and interest in "technical" matters such as currency affairs were scarce or non-existent. Later, historians arrived, but they were mainly diplomacy and international relations historians who devoted their attention to European integration. Their backgrounds strengthened the political predominance approach because this kind of historian traditionally pays minor attention to systemic approaches and prefers concentrating on leaders' relationships. In the meantime, many other scholars worked on European financial relationships and currency problems as well as on international trade without referring to European integration as a suitable solution. In fact, the reconstruction and consolidation of an international monetary system remained their primary concern and analytical perspective, in spite of European monetary integration entering into the EEC agenda as a possible solution because of the upcoming collapse of the Bretton Woods system.

After the disastrous results of European currency management in the early 1970s, it was only in the early 1980s that European integration became a useful paradigm as well for economists, economic historians, and scholars of other disciplines usually concentrating on international matters. In fact, at the end of the 1970s, European integration also became a politically attractive solution for problems like currency instability and the obsolescence of the European industrial system. Hence, European institutions became the ideal box where many integrative processes could converge. The attempt to create a European monetary system that had failed in the early 1970s was relaunched, and the communitarian box became the working environment for pursuing new aims such as filling the competitive and technological gaps between Europe and its competitors (mainly the USA and Japan at that time). It was in this period that political integration became instrumental to economic and monetary integration, although the political discourse and the focus of many scholars remained on European political integration and unification. During the 1980s, the so-called gold decade of contemporary European integration, member states succeeded in the same tasks they had failed in during the previous twenty years. The European Monetary System became a practical reality; new communitarian policies faced common problems such as economic backwardness, market fragmentation, and environmental pollution. More generally, European integration became a one-size-fits-all solution for member states at least until the mid-2000s when the political costs of surrendering sovereignty became evident. However, since the early 1990s, the traditional "idealistic" view of academics, politicians, and citizens was challenged by the perception of the predominance of economic matters resulted in the convergence of many separate problems into a single communitarian container. Critics of "bankers' Europe", "neoliberal Europe", and "anti-democratic Europe" included both academics and politicians. Meantime, constraints on national policies and politics, risks for welfare and patronage systems, and the vanishing of the idealistic view of Europe that had been prevalent since the 1950s revealed the real nature of the "converging integrations of Europe" and the price to pay for an ever-closer union.

2– The Fight for Europe

During the last 30 years, historians and political scientists have dismantled the idealistic view of European integration as a pleasant walk of peers animated by superior ideals and cosmopolitan ambitions. A fiercely competitive environment emerged in which member states fought to impose their national priorities on the others, encapsulating their goals in the communitarian framework. Thus, the communitarian arena appears as a real arena in which national governments fight for their interests and prosperity by trying to keep themselves free from those external constraints that endanger their ability to manage domestic politics and policies. Their main aim was revealed to be safeguarding national interests and the structure of power in their countries, i.e., the network of relations and arrangements between elites and those sectors of the society that grant consensus and keep governments in charge. Meanwhile, they try to pass on the constraints and costs of convergence to the other members.

Paradoxically, with monetary integration, EMU countries accepted strict communitarian constraints to avoid international restrictions imposed by the globalisation process they were unable to manage or influence[4]. However, their choice was based on an estimated balance between international and European

[4] The case of France is the more evident (Helleiner 1994, p. 140-145; Howarth, 2000).

constraints to domestic politics that changed dramatically with the EMU, the global crisis of the late 2000s, and the introduction of a more stringent set of rules we call New Economic Governance (NEG). Consequently, monetary Europe and its troubles induced the reorganisation of the EU governance, creating a much more pervasive supranational power that challenged many of the remaining prerogatives of national governments in domestic politics. In addition, the EMU and its governance became the core of European supranational governance, dismantling what remained of the political prevalence illusion. Thus, European monetary integration could be described as a "retreat inside Europe" of those European countries that proved unable to manage the impact of international monetary turbulences on domestic politics since the early 1970s. Monetary integration arose as a strategy to regain sovereignty in monetary and economic fields. It was only in the late 2000s that monetary governance became so invasive as to be widely perceived as a dramatic loss of national sovereignty. This development profoundly affected the national structures of power as well as the citizens' perception of the real costs paid for integration. The conflicts previously contained at the European level extended to the domestic level, generating the Europeanisation of domestic politics that explains part of the transformation in the political systems of the EMU member states.

In this book, I will insist on the relevance of internal power structure in shaping the European policies of EMU member states, the asymmetries between governmental influence in shaping monetary integration and the new economic governance, and the second-best nature of European monetary integration. More specifically, the domestic power approach will be crucial for explaining member states' strategies, preferences, and attitudes toward European integration and the reason for the partial implementation of EMU rules. In particular, this book will focus on the predominance assigned to internal politics and elections by the EU governments and the influence of domestic matters as well as the national impact of integration on shaping member state governments' attitudes toward the EU policies. Besides, the concepts of influence asymmetries and structural interdependence will be crucial to explaining the prevalence of some national priorities and the acceptance of them by the other member states. In fact, it is evident that countries influence each other in their "choice for euro" and that this influence sometimes became pervasive and unavoidable. Thus, a mechanism of chained and constrained choices addressed some crucial collective decisions in Europe.

The prevalence of domestic politics, influence asymmetries, structural interdependence, and the "retreat inside Europe" metaphor suggest depicting EU politics as something more complex than intergovernmental negotiation or, worse, supranational governance addressed by neo-functionalist spillovers. The concept of "conflictual cooperation" better describes the real essence of EU politics that has emerged since the late 1990s. This concept fits well with the defensive nature of monetary integration and its essence as "second-best choice" compared with the creation of a stable international monetary system that was pursued since the 1920s. It also fits with the picture proposed in this book of competing nation-states compelled to cooperate but oriented toward diverging aims and economic cultures, constrained by interdependence, asymmetric influence, and limited choices apart from cooperation.

Adopting the conflictual cooperation paradigm results in at least two other theoretical implications. First, if cooperation is conflictual, it needs to be governed. Thus, governance is the crucial variable in the process. It does not necessarily mean that the EU needs a government. However, EU governance, particularly in the economic and monetary fields, is crucial to keeping the EMU and EU at work. Second, and as a consequence, one kind of governance among the many has to prevail over the others. This means that if we can identify a German, a French, an Italian, and many others models of governance, only one of them or a hybrid mainly inspired by one of them can be adopted and implemented. Hence, more in-depth and stable integration requires convergence toward a common European governance and the abandonment of national varieties of governance, capitalism, and structures of power in those countries that fit poorly with the dominant model of governance. This process is at the centre of the main conflicts in the EU today, as well as the most prominent obstacle blocking further integration and reactions to the European crisis.

3– The multiple crises of Europe

Explaining the rise of the euro as the prevalence of monetary matters in European integration connects the euro crisis with the broader crisis of the European construction emerged in the late 2000s and the early 2010s. Today the word "crisis" is widely used in the debate on European integration. In the newspapers and academic literature, there are many references to the economic crisis, the sovereign debt crisis, the euro crisis, as well as many other crises that touch the European Union. In particular, the debate focuses on issues such as European democracy and the welfare state, EU political institutions, and, more generally, the people's support for European integration and the fundamental values of "Europe" itself. All of them are core topics in the political and academic debate about European integration because these issues are strictly connected to the general crisis that affects the European Union since the late 2000s.

The general crisis may be interpreted as a result of the prevalence of monetary Europe on the other "Europes". In fact, the EMU was the most ambitious and challenging step in European integration, and its crisis became the crisis of the whole European construction due to the impact of monetary integration on member states' economies and politics. This relevance is a consequence of monetary matters influencing the integration process. In other words, the completion of monetary Europe, meaning the "Europe apart" I refer to in the title of this book, made the EMU the core of European integration and attracted to its orbit many other matters, imposing on them coherence with the working of the EMU, in particular budget constraints and financial stability. EMU problems became the main challenges for the EU and influenced both European national policy and citizens' attitudes toward EU institutions and further integration. This influence created three kinds of issues: economic, political, and identity problems.

On the economic side, the problems that affected the Eurozone just before the crisis were not those suggested by the opponents of the EMU who referred to the Optimum Currency Areas theory (see chapter 4). It was the outflow of cheap money from Northern Europe to Southern member states and Ireland (the so-called PIIGS – Portugal, Ireland, Italy, Greece, and Spain, later renamed GIPSI or GIIPS) where interest rates were slightly higher to create the condition for something similar to a balance of payments crisis. Moreover, some countries like Italy suffered from a structural crisis that undermined their economy's competitiveness. Thus, imbalances in both the commercial and capital sides of their balance of payments increased.

This mechanism put in danger the entire EMU construction. Cheap money inflow into GIIPS resulted in wage increases that exceeded productivity growth and speculative activities, as well as public debt increases. Cheap money boosted inflation rates, and the competitiveness of Southern economies declined further. Meantime, private debt rose, mainly in those countries where a real estate bubble pushed speculation and government poorly respected prescriptions by the Stability and Growth Pact (SGP) or disregarded them. Consequently, when the international crisis arose, distortions in the Eurozone made the crisis more profound and harder to face than in the American crisis.

The picture drawn above makes the reform of economic governance in the Eurozone the critical solution for redesigning, saving, and relaunching the EMU and integration in Europe. Unfortunately, damages caused by governance shortages in the 2000s made reforming the EMU much more difficult.

When the sovereign debt crisis became dramatic with Greece close to collapse, member states took note of the impossibility for EU institutions to face the crisis and decided to outflank the EU stalemate by intergovernmental actions. This strategy allowed introducing new rules, both as intergovernmental agreements or Communitarian regulations as well as new instruments to manage the Eurozone. These innovations were not enough to face such a deep crisis. It was only the aggressive action of the ECB that allowed the sovereign debt crises to stop and to prevent the imminent collapse of the Southern EMU. However, the solution adopted by the ECB to end the crisis made it a political actor that arrogated powers and tools it was not entitled to use. The ECB drew its power from and built its weapons on a debatable juridical interpretation of the treaties and its mandate, as well as on the blackmail power stemming from the full discretionary power it enjoys as the emergency lender of last resort. Hence, the ECB gained enormous power to manage "informal economic governance" in the EMU. However, informal economic governance is an emergency solution that cannot work forever.

The emergence of the ECB as a "government of last resort" was not the end of the euro crisis but just a turning point. Later, the problem became how to manage the EMU and who had to do it. The run to find a temporary and acceptable solution to the sovereign debt crisis redesigned the roles of three kinds of actors: the traditional EU institutions, the member states, and the Euro system (ECB plus national central banks). While the leading EU institutions seemingly gained power thanks to the New EU Economic Governance, member states (particularly Germany and France) and intergovernmental forums appeared as the key players in defining the future of the EMU and the common currency. However, the only player that proved to be robust and efficient as needed by the crisis was the ECB. Member states' actions are strictly oriented by national interests and national electorates that are becoming more and more hostile toward surrendering sovereignty, EU supervision, and the euro. As a result, EMU governments pay obsessive attention to internal constituencies and priorities and put at the back of the line supranational needs. On the other hand, EU institutions are only formally reinforced by the NEG, but their real power to sanction member states or to contradict their actions remains uncertain. Today, the future of the EMU depends on a lame-ducks triad where the Commission and the Parliament have the right but not the power, member states have the power but not the will, and the ECB has the power and the will but not the right.

On the political side, the external constraints imposed by the adoption of the euro and the reinforcement of these restrictions as a consequence of the euro crisis and the introduction of the New Economic Governance feed anti-Europeanism and the opposition to further integration and surrender of sovereignty. The euro became the preferred target for anti-EU parties and the fulcrum of the new anti-Europeanism. Compared to traditional anti-Europeanism based on the rejection of European values and sovereignty surrender, the new anti-Europeanism draws a solid background for its argumentations from the problems attributed to monetary integration. The EMU and the euro became the primary targets of anti-Europeanists who claimed them as the causes of European depression, national sovereignty dismantling, and the decline of democracy in Europe. On the other hand, the euro crisis restarted the debate about the sustainability of a single currency without a European state i.e., the need for a European state with a government to manage the Euro. However, today this debate is developing in a more hostile environment than before. The EMU troubles induced both opponents and supporters of European integration to depict monetary and political integration as two faces of the same problem. It remains unclear what the problem is. Was creating or joining the EMU the wrong choice for some member states, or was it a wrong decision to set up the euro without creating a European state? What is the better solution to this problem? Dismantling the EMU or building united Europe? This dilemma revealed a new cleavage in the European party system that added a new dimension to the traditional right-left axis: the pro-anti euro axis. This new dimension superimposed on the traditional cleavages that divided the European party families and reshaped or redefined their political programmes and their electoral priorities. In this way, the new cleavage dramatically changed the distribution of votes, both in European and national elections.

Monetary integration also created the main fracture inside the European Union: the division between EMU and not-EMU countries. Today, this fracture seems the most probable separation line in the case of the EU breakup. In fact, due to the centrality of monetary matters and the connected economic governance, being outside the EMU means marginalisation and diminished relevance in the European decision-making arena. Besides, membership in the EMU created inextricable linkages among those countries that adopted the common currency, augmenting the cohesion of this core group and differentiating the EU institutions' capabilities to impose EU rules inside and outside the EMU. Both Brexit and today's tensions between the European institutions on one side and Poland, Hungary, and Italy on the other side are examples of the process described above and evidence of the extensive impact of monetary integration on EU politics.

The most worrisome aspect of Europe's crisis is the "crisis of the European identity", which is the set of values and ambitions perceived as the core of the whole integration process. This crisis is widely different from the previous crises faced by the EEC during the 1960s and 1970s. In those cases, political tensions and poor coordination generated institutional crises that affected the political and economic cohesion of the EEC.

Today, it is monetary integration, its impact, and its crisis influencing the political side and the citizens' feelings toward Europe. Thus, the U-turn in the relationship between integrative sectors is completed, and monetary Europe today will have an impact on the fate of political Europe. As a consequence, it is not surprising that anti-European parties concentrate their criticisms on the single currency and the pervasiveness of EU economic governance in internal politics.

Many elements feed this crisis. Among them, the perception of the EU as a neoliberal construction was magnified by the introduction of the New Economic Governance and the austerity policies. The Greek crisis negatively impacted the image of the EU as a community of solidarity, another value perceived as crucial to legitimising European integration. The imposition of heavy burdens and constraints for financial assistance as well as the rejection of proposals and requests democratically decided in Greece created a picture of Europe as a German-led Leviathan and an undemocratic instrument of domination. This perception of the EU poses questions about the legitimacy of the EU and the real meaning of integration. In addition, the inefficiency showed on many occasions such as the sovereign debt crisis and the recent immigration crisis make doubtful the utility of the EU as a problem-solving arena. All these doubts about the nature, fundamental values, and usefulness of European integration created a "crisis of the idea of united Europe" – an identity crisis that risks driving the EU to collapse.

4– Monetary integration and democracy in Europe

Another aspect that makes crucial the relationship between monetary and political integration regards the transformation of member state democracies induced by monetary integration. New rules, treaties, and the European monetary policy reshaped the member states' regimes. Stricter supranational supervision of internal budgets and economic policies reduced the space that national governments had for acting and being responsive and accountable toward their citizens. After the start of the sovereign debt crisis, the introduction of the New Economic Governance, and the launch in some countries of the austerity policies for debt reduction and financial stabilisation, the impact of monetary integration appeared particularly intrusive. It transformed European democracies, driving them away from the welfare state model that had arisen after World War II. This process inspired scepticism about the desirability of further integration and the legitimacy of the EU.

The transformation of the European democratic model cannot be entirely due to monetary integration. Worldwide phenomena contributed to moving away from the post-war model of democracy. Since the 1980s, globalisation and financialisation made obsolete the socio-economic structure that arose after World War II. The ineffectiveness of post-Keynesian national economic policies became evident in many European countries, and international constraints and conditionings undermined the welfare state and European government responsiveness. European democracies were already in crisis before the EMU.

On the contrary, at least in its early phase, monetary integration was an attempt to regain effective sovereignty and reinforce national democracies in Europe. This attempt failed, and "the European rescue of national democracy" from globalisation resulted in an impossible mission. What was the role of monetary integration in this transformation? Did it determine the transition or just facilitated it? In other words, did monetary integration undermine democracy in Europe as suggested by many scholars?

The identity crisis of the EU and the doubts about its democratic nature result mainly in the strident contrast between "real" and "perceived" Europe, i.e., the way in which Europeans understand the logic, philosophy, objectives, and values of European integration. The prevalence of the economic and monetary side of integration magnified this contrast and put in doubt the veracity of the fundamental values proposed as European. This doubt delegitimised the EU and fed doubts about its democratic nature. However, the "perceived Europe" was the picture of Europe created by European propaganda and Euro-idealism. European citizens and many politicians and EU officers believed in that "European mythology" created since the 1950s to justify and legitimise European integration. This mythology was based on universal values of peace, solidarity, shared interests, and values, as well as an unrealistic goal: the uniting of Europe. This purpose and the implications of the shared values adoption remained ambiguous and poorly defined in official European debate and treaties.[5] Therefore, EU supporters, academics included, continued to believe in an ephemeral picture built upon their perception of European integration.

This picture worked well until 2001 and the introduction of the euro. It permitted the building of a consensus for European integration referring to universal values and avoiding technicalities. Unfortunately, avoiding technicalities was no more possible after EMU completion. Hence, today, analysing the relationship between democracy and monetary integration in Europe is essential to understanding the real political impact of integration and its democratic or undemocratic nature, or the evolution of European democracy.

The European project has probably been substantially undemocratic since its early days. It was the need and ambition of national governments to gain more independence from national electors that induced them to turn to supranational governance. Integration was an opportunity to empower national governments by outflanking electoral accountability and adopting blame-shift tactics to charge "Europe" for unpopular choices. However, the non-democratic and technocratic nature of "Eu-

[5] The famous statement in the 1957 Rome Treaty in which the main ambition of the signing countries was a badly defined "ever closer union" testifies to how full integration was not the main aim of the process just started.

rope" was a pragmatic solution to the limits of European national democracies and an arrangement that was coherent with the "European rescue of the nation-state" identified by Milward (1992) as the core strategy to save European nation-states after World War II. Thus, the crisis and decline of national democracy in Europe is a long-term process accelerated by monetary integration, not generated by it.

Nevertheless, the undemocratic nature of European integration as perceived by many European citizens became one of the most powerful arguments of anti-Europeanists. Is democratising the EU, or at least the EMU, a solution for re-legitimising European institutions and advancing in EU reforms and integration? This is another question posed by the impact of the EMU on EU politics I will try to answer in the next chapters.

5– Book outline

This book tells the story of the process and explains the mechanisms that transformed monetary Europe from a "Europe apart" to the problematic core of integrated Europe. In this introduction, I depicted the main topics to be discussed in the rest of the book. The real nature of European monetary integration will be explained in Chapter 1. We will analyse the origins of the European monetary problems and the way in which their solution converged with political and economic integration. In Chapter 2, we will focus on the creation of the single currency and the fragility of the political consensus that inspired its construction and governance. Chapter 3 is devoted to methodological problems in using history for policy analysis. The approach adopted in this book to connect historical and political analysis will be introduced here. Both academic criticisms of common currency sustainability and the political problem of divergent national interests will be discussed in Chapter 4, while in Chapter 5, we will try to understand what went wrong in

European monetary unification and why the euro was close to collapse in the early 2010s. In chapters 6 and 7, we will analyse how the euro crisis and the rise of the New Economic Governance that followed the sovereign debt crisis influenced the reshaping of institutional structure and power distribution among EU institutions.

The remaining chapters will be devoted to understanding the political impact of the euro crisis. Chapter 8 will analyse the impact of monetary integration on democracy in member countries through studying the theoretical debate on democracy and integration. In Chapter 9, we will study how opposition to the EMU fostered populism and the rise of anti-European parties and movements.

The conclusion of this book deals with a crucial problem for the discussion on the relationship between monetary and political integration. Today, it seems that the activation of neo-functionalist mechanisms and pressures for further integration can arise mainly from the need to improve EU economic governance. Therefore, the future of European integration depends on the survival of the euro and the possibility of managing it without further political integration. The fundamental question remains the old one: is it possible to have a euro without Europe? In other words: can monetary Europe survive and work without a European state? This is a crucial question that has been posed since the 1990s. Today, after that twenty years of monetary union and enormous sacrifices paid for adapting member states' economies and political systems to the EMU made it the essential step in the whole history of European integration, an alternative question is just as important: Can the EU survive the failure of the EMU?

PART I

THE RISE OF THE EMU

Chapter 1

The Origins of the European Currency Problem

The adoption of the euro in 1999 by all the leading EU member states except the UK indicated the start of a new era for European monetary and currency policy and the end of decades of precarious arrangements and ephemeral attempts to coordinate European currencies within an international payment system. European monetary integration was the last, and apparently the most successful, of these arrangements. Plans and debates about monetary integration in the EEC emerged from the early 1960s. The possibility of creating a common currency for the EEC member states was examined and resulted in a viable solution, albeit there were many problems to solve.[1] However, it was only in the late 1970s that monetary integration became a workable and autonomous solution to currency instability in the European Economic Community. Before, almost all the agreements and arrangements adopted included both EEC and non-EEC countries. So these attempts were European because they involved many European countries instead of only EEC ones. This is also true for the Werner Plan and the effort to create a single European

[1] From the early 1960s, the European Commission organised various committees to study the problems of economic and monetary integration. These committees joined politicians and economists from various countries, and their suggestions influenced the final design of the monetary unification plan. See Barre Plan 1963; Werner Report 1970; Marjolin Report 1975; Optica Report 1976; MacDougall Report 1976; Delors Report 1989; Delors Report papers 1989.

currency in the early 1970s.[2] In fact, central bankers considered the inclusion of the pound sterling in the project to be crucial even though the UK was not an EEC member yet. Also, the Werner Plan treated monetary integration in Europe as part of a worldwide reorganisation of monetary relations on the eve of the fall of Bretton Woods. So it was not a European solution only, like the EMS ten years later.

In the mid-1970s, European integration was close to failing. The international economic crisis and the oil shock fragmented the EEC commercial space, and the end of the international monetary system created at Bretton Woods made European currencies exchange rates floating. So the framework that granted economic integration and monetary stability in the EEC from the 1950s disappeared. These events endangered the cohesion of the Common Market and the arrangements that regulated the Common Agricultural Policy.[3] Moreover, the most critical effect of currency instability was not just the matter of European integration. In losing control of the external value of their currency, governments lost control of domestic economic policy. Today, many opponents of the EMU claim that monetary integration has paid the price of surrendering national sovereignty and the people's right to decide on the economic policies their governments have to implement. They forget that most of the economic policy choices adopted by European countries before the EMU, particularly in the 1970s, did not originate from the will of the people. Instead, those choices were expedients, often unsustainable in the long

[2] The Werner Plan was a project for monetary integration in the EEC (incoming members included) proposed in 1970 by a working group chaired by Pierre Werner following a request from the European Summit at The Hague in 1969. See Magnusson and Stråth (2001); Werner Report (1970).

[3] The Common Agricultural Policy was launched in 1962 with the aim of supporting rural development, sustaining farmers' income and stabilising agricultural products' prices. It worked with a complicated system of subsidies and compensation seriously endangered by monetary instability.

term, which had been adopted because there was no better solution.[4] Thus, the problems solved in the late 1950s through European economic integration and convertibility in the Bretton Woods system reappeared. They were the fragmentation and crisis of the international economic and monetary system and the isolation of EEC economies that led once again to European integration as a "one-size-fits-all" solution and the insertion of the currency problem in the European box.

Integration continued to be the European solution for a multiplicity of challenges. However, economic matters gained prevalence, and political integration retreated from a front-line position into the background, becoming an ideal that was useful for justifying the empowerment of European institutions and their "technical" governance functions. So, in the late 1970s, there was a "second European rescue of the nation state".[5] Then, a 50-year-old process of currency management and coordination merged with the political and economic integration started in the early 1950s.

The long and detailed analysis of European currency history that follows permits us to stress the temporal dimension of the problem supporting the theory of European integration as a result of the long-term process of converging integrations. European integration historiography usually adopts as a starting point the early second post-war period or the initial steps of integration in the 1950s. However, matters like tariffs, trade, communication and currencies required international cooper-

---

[4] Fuel rationing and limits to cars' circulation introduced in Italy after the 1973 oil shock are examples of the economic policy choices "undemocratically" imposed by external constraints.

[5] Milward (1992) proposed the thesis of European rescue of the nation state to explain the start of European integration. He suggests that the early steps toward European integration derived from an attempt to support the recovery of European nation states by means of supranational coordination. This interpretation clashes with the traditional view of the uniting of Europe as the main aim of integration.

ation and created tension in Europe decades before the launch of the European Coal and Steel Community. Only later did these problems find a working solution in European integration. So, focusing on the 1950s as the starting point of the story distorts the perception of the many and different processes that finally converged to create "Europe" as we know it today. Seeing the real influence of these processes requires us to dismiss the traditional approach toward European integration history and to consider European integration as a phase of a secular process of convergence, conflict and cooperation. In this process, creating supranational institutions serves for coordinating cooperation and granting the application of common rules, not for creating "Europe".

In this chapter, we will adopt this long-term approach to analysing the rise of the European currency problem and the solutions taken before the choice for European monetary integration. In particular, we will depict how the collapse of the international monetary system in the 1930s influenced the path of European currency coordination toward regional integration.

1 – A paradise lost? European currencies before World War I

The whole international monetary history of the 20th century was heavily influenced by the consequences of the Gold Standard collapse in 1931. The end of the Gold Standard and the attempts to find alternative arrangements generated a situation in which a worldwide system (Gold Standard) was substituted by regional or continental systems (currency areas) because some links among countries survived the dissolution of the global system of which they were part. This meant that the possibility of creating currency areas was inscribed in the internal structure of the Gold Standard. We need to understand this structure to explain the rise and consolidation of currency areas, particularly the European one.

The classical Gold Standard is the most widely studied international monetary system. For many authors, it represents a "lost paradise" in which economic growth and financial stability coexisted thanks to the automatism of this system.

Theoretically, under Gold Standard rules, countries with a balance of payments deficit lost gold paying their creditors. So deflation pressures reduced prices and wages in deficit countries. This made their export more competitive, and the deficit disappeared. Conversely, the gold influx in the creditor countries created inflation and reduced or reversed the balance of payments surplus. Consequently, a new equilibrium was reached.

In practice, however, the classical Gold Standard worked in a more complicated way (Williams 1968; De Cecco 1984). Until 1914, the role of Great Britain as an exporter of long-term capital was crucial. Moreover, the role of the London financial market in financing world trade and permitting the clearing of international debts transformed London into the centre of the global economy and the UK into the leading country of the international monetary system.

The centrality of the British Empire in the Gold Standard derived from the worldwide expansion of the British banking system that caused the rise of an international banking network centred in London (Baster 1929 and 1935; Williams 1968; Jones 2000). This banking network connected raw materials producers in the British Empire with Continental Europe and the United States using the facilities and the money markets existing in London (capital market, discount market, markets of particular raw materials) (Powell 1915; Lavington 1929; Madden and Nadler 1935; King 1936). During the 19th century, new banks appeared in the British colonies and other peripheral countries (Latin America, Eastern Asia). These banks had main branches in London and offices in many other nations as they were able to finance the international trade of specific countries using the opportunities offered in London by a consolidated financial structure (Baster 1929 and 1935). Many bank transactions, debits and credits were in sterling, making it the leading international currency. As a result, sterling was "as good as gold", becoming the key currency in an international monetary system that Williams calls "the sterling system". In other words, sterling, not gold, was the real means of payment used for international transactions (Williams 1968, 268–70).

London was also the principal capital market for European and Latin American countries and the Dominions. World trade was financed in London, and part of the investments that supported economic growth in both developed and underdeveloped countries arrived from there. In the meantime, London became the ideal place for keeping short-term funds because its financial market also allowed profitable investments for funds to be recalled soon for international payments. This advantage enabled the Bank of England to regulate the inflow and outflow of money in London and to stabilise the sterling value using the interest rate.

No complex negotiations were required to enter the classical Gold Standard. All those countries that declared their national currencies convertible into gold at a fixed rate and that respected this commitment to paying gold on demand for their local currency were under a Gold Standard regime. The suspension of convertibility excluded the country from the system. Thus, the value of government bonds fell, and obtaining foreign credits became more expensive or impossible. Exiting from the Gold Standard was not an irreversible choice. There were various cases of countries that suspended convertibility in particular moments of difficulty, rejoining the system later when the problems had been solved. So the chief peculiarity of the classical Gold Standard until the early 1900s was that it did not need international cooperation to work. This almost automatic way of working was its strength in the light of the enormous problems of coordination experienced since the 1920s.

The classical Gold Standard vanished at the outbreak of the World War I. Then, Great Britain and all the other nations at war suspended effective convertibility. During the war, other problems appeared to make a return to convertibility impossible for years after the end of the conflict. Gold reserves and foreign assets were liquidated to pay for war imports. Moreover, war expenditures caused inflation in the fighting countries that issued paper currency and new governmental debts to satisfy the financial needs created by the war. So, at the end of the war, the remaining gold reserves were insufficient to guarantee convertibility at pre-war value for the paper money circulating.

The coincidence of war and convertibility suspension induced many scholars to consider war as the cause of the Gold Standard crisis and return to currency convertibility as the best solution to the problems caused by post-war economic instability. Instead, the classical Gold Standard showed structural limits years before the war (De Cecco 1984).

The pre-war Gold Standard stability derived from the continuous growth in international commerce that characterised the second part of the 19th century until the war. That growth allowed high levels of investments in the underdeveloped countries that provided industrialised nations with raw materials and acquired capital goods from them (Williams 1968, p. 280–83). So rebuilding it in the 1920s was not sufficient to rebuild a stable international economy (De Cecco 1984).

London was at the centre of the network of multilateral trade and gained from its work as a financial intermediary as much as from investments placed overseas. Other Gold Standard countries obtained different but equally essential advantages from their participation in this monetary system. For example, industrial countries were able to achieve raw materials and foodstuff from the British Empire and remote regions. Moreover, the Continental Europe industrialised nations benefited from the facilities offered by the London financial market. These facilities allowed them to accelerate their industrial growth, filling the gaps in their national financial systems using the financial instruments developed in London over the previous centuries. In other words, Continental Europe countries borrowed in London not only capital but also financial structures. This aspect of the growth of the so-called "latecomer industrialised nations" became crucial when the system went into crisis.

Another advantage for both Great Britain and the Continental European countries derived from the leadership of the Bank of England as the central bank of the sterling system. The Bank of England was able to manage the gold reserves of the other Gold Standard countries, attracting gold towards London or redistributing it in the continental central banks' reserves. In this way, the Bank of England increased its ability to stabilise the value of sterling, thanks to its influence over a more significant amount of gold than the Bank of England reserves only. At the same time, continental central banks increased their effectiveness in stabilising their currencies as a result of the international monetary policy planned and pursued by the Bank of England (De Cecco 1984, p.103–110).

Obviously, there were significant advantages for raw materials and foodstuff producer countries from selling their products and attracting investments from the London capital market. These benefits allowed the development of national economies and infrastructures, enabling these countries to stay connected with the international economy.

The Gold Standard also involved costs and problems. One problem was external shock transmission to national economies. The Gold Standard mechanism, based on the inflow and outflow of funds, and the resulting inflation or deflation, created internal economic instability. It was the price to pay for external stability. Internal instability affected the level of economic activity and other variables (employment, wages and domestic prices), and this had significant socio-political repercussions. Before 1914, these consequences had a relatively small political impact because of the elitist electoral systems that did not allow political opposition to transform into electoral discontent. This situation changed after the war, due to the transition to mass democracy and universal male suffrage. So the problem of combining monetary politics and internal politics became complicated to face, and fed bitter political tensions that sometimes resulted in destabilisation of political regimes. Thus, difficulty in combining national democracy and international economic relations was a severe problem decades before the rise of the European Monetary Union, and in various cases, this problem was faced with curbing democracy or just hindering its rise and consolidation.

Other problems arose for the British Dominions and Latin American countries, both induced to hyper-specialise in production and external trade. Their hyper-specialisation created dependence on a single product or a small group of products and led to internal economic instability caused by the international price fluctuation of these commodities. Furthermore, some British Empire countries were forced to accept the burden of a policy of international stabilisation. This was the case in India, which was the largest buyer of silver, thereby acting as a stabiliser of its price (Keynes 1913; De Cecco 1984, p. 62–75).

3 – Rebuilding the Gold Standard in the 1920s

During the ten years from 1914 to 1924, among the leading industrial countries, only the United States maintained real convertibility. Instead, in the rest of the world, the Gold Standard system was gradually restored only in the second half of the 1920s. In 1925, Great Britain returned to convertibility, fixing the gold price of sterling at the pre-war price (Moggridge 1972). This choice was a crucial component of the

British strategy to regain world financial leadership. In fact, returning to pre-war parity reassessed the idea that sterling was as good as gold.

Other countries pegged their national currency in gold with some degree of depreciation in comparison with the pre-war value. Their wartime inflation, much higher than the British one, and the limited remaining gold reserves made it almost impossible to return to the pre-war parity. So the continental winning countries decided to fix their currency parity in gold considering the effect of the new parity on their commercial competitiveness. In some cases (e.g. Belgium), the exchange rate adopted by the leading commercial partners was an essential element that addressed the choice of the new gold parity. In the Italian case, another and purely political element contributed to the gold parity choice. Mussolini aimed to sustain the prestige of the Italian fascist regime and his role in re-establishing order in the country. So he insisted on fixing the Italian lira parity at the same level (the so-called "quota 90") he found when he came to power in 1922. Also, the Italian lira exchange rate was fixed in terms of liras for dollar instead of liras for sterling due to the intention of Italian firms and municipalities to borrow money on the American financial market massively (Falco and Storaci 1977; Di Quirico 1998, p. 61–70; Di Quirico 1999, p. 77–78).

The return to currency convertibility in Western Europe caused social tensions that anticipated the contrast between democracy and economic governance discussed today. Defining a new currency convertibility rate meant changing economic relationships at home, redistributing the advantages and the costs of currency stabilisation among different social groups. Revaluing currency imposed wage reductions and other cuts that hurt mainly the working class and favoured rentiers and the financial sector. Industrialists could face the loss of competitivity and gain from the access to international financial markets, but they needed salaries to be cut to keep production costs low. So the return to convertibility and a stable currency became a point of friction between the needs of the economic system and the interests of the working class. While in Italy the return to convertibility was carried out by a dictatorial regime that imposed the new exchange rate on all social classes and stakeholders (compensating some of them and repressing the others), in democratic countries tensions resulted in general strikes and parliamentarian contrasts. So the final convertibility rate adopted in different countries also depended on the strength of the different political components and indirectly on the prevalence of economic government or democratic responsiveness.[6]

The return to gold parity in the successor states of the defeated empires resulted in the establishment of new currencies to substitute the irremediably hyperinflated currency of the early post-war period. Some of these countries were just part of the fallen empires and did not have either a state structure or an administration. This was the case in Austria, Hungary and Poland (League of Nations 1926a, *idem* 1926b). Instead, other countries inherited new lands due to the dissolution of the Central European Empires and had to reorganise their administration as in the cases of Romania and the Kingdom of Yugoslavia. In both groups of countries, the lack of external funding, the difficulty in collecting taxes, and the need to rebuild public administration and economic infrastructures made the recourse to the printing press the only viable solution for the government, at least during the early post-war period. It was only in the mid-1920s that the financial stabilisation policies and the return of external funds permitted the

[6] The relevance of social struggle in the economic policy field as a relevant component in the currency stabilisation policy of Italy, France and Belgium in the post-World War I period is stressed by Falco and Storaci and linked to the wider issue of the reconstruction of the "bourgeoise order" studied by Charles S. Maier (1975). The British case has been studied by Moggridge (1972).

creation of gold and hard currency reserves to make the domestic currencies convertible (League of Nations 1944).

Germany followed a different path toward currency stabilisation. The post-war economic collapse was followed by the political consequences of the Ruhr occupation by the French army and the German government's attempt to fund passive resistance by printing money. This caused the most famous case of hyperinflation in history and the need to introduce a new currency to replace the unmanageable one. Solving the political and economic stalemate was only possible with external support, mainly American, and the arrival of funds to financially stabilise the country and start paying the reparations decided at the Versailles Conference (Aldcroft 1977).

Nevertheless, the Gold Standard reconstruction remained incomplete because of the changes in the international economy induced by the war. The economic conditions in Continental Europe had worsened dramatically, while the multilateral trade pattern on which the classical Gold Standard had been based became obsolete. Also, in the 1920s, various European countries needed financing to keep their industrial systems efficient and to consolidate the government budget. This was the case in Germany and the successor states of the former European Empires. To some extent, it was also the case in some other European countries, which underwent radical developments in their industrial structure during the war and which needed to sustain this process of industrial growth.

Another obstacle to the full restoration of the Gold Standard in the 1920s was the scarcity of gold. The enlargement of monetary circulation and the use of gold reserves for war and post-war payments made the existing reserves insufficient to cover paper money in circulation. In addition, the influx of gold in the USA as a consequence of war and post-war payments modified the international distribution of reserves. Finally, the maintenance of such a large gold reserve was costly because it meant immobilising a considerable sum that did not pay interest. So various central banks preferred to keep reserves in hard currencies (mainly sterling and dollars). Part of these reserves was assets in London or New York financial markets. However, this evolution of the way in which central banks keep reserves made the international monetary system utterly dependent on the stability of just two currencies, one of which was no longer affordable as it was in the past.

In this situation, the pre-war scheme of multilateral trade disappeared because the leading importers of raw materials and foodstuff in Continental Europe were unable to pay for these imports without receiving funds from London or New York. In the meantime, London was no longer able to grant massive long-term loans to finance infrastructure building, but only short-term funds for trade finance. The United States alone was able to allow long-term funding to debtor countries, in particular in Europe and Latin America. However, the USA was still unable to assume the role of the primary international financial market (Parrini 1969). So the working of the international economy became more complicated than in the pre-war period and required a more sophisticated monetary system than the almost automatic Gold Standard. The new system was required to have the capability to coordinate a multilateral and multicentric payment system in which many national currencies were linked to each other more by financial markets than just by gold parities.

This was an epochal transformation that changed completely the way in which monetary matters influenced international relations and domestic economic policies. While in the pre-war period gold reserves guaranteed a "neutral" payment instrument to each country, the new international payments system depended on a few key currencies and the capability of international financial markets to collect and redistribute them to face the needs of both international trade and country economies. So the financial market became crucial for domestic economic policy in many countries, mostly the European industrialised ones. Dollar gaps in the early 1920s and late 1940s, the scarcity of hard currencies in the 1930s and 1970s, dollar floods in other periods and finally the rise of petrodollars determined the national economic policy choices until today. In the meantime, the rise of new international financial centres and globalisation of finance made the financial markets the real alternative to gold and the only one capable of coordinating the financial and monetary needs of such a complex and interconnected international economic system as the existing one.

The world trade and finance structure that emerged after the war period required a significant shift in the international financial system leadership. After the war, the United States balance of payments was in surplus with most of the countries of the world. This situation increased the need for the USA to act like Great Britain during the pre-war period when it transformed its balance of payment surplus into investments permitting debtor countries to pay for their imports. However, the United States could act as a world leader only if the borrowers returned to convertibility. This condition would preserve credits from devaluation and guarantee the mobility of investments. So the United States and Great Britain, which aimed to maintain, at least in part, its role as international financial centre, brought intense pressure on debtor countries, inducing them to stabilise their currency by rejoining the Gold Standard.

In contrast with the pre-war period, in the 1920s many countries were almost compelled to join the Gold Standard because convertibility became a *sine qua non* condition for obtaining credits. These loans were essential for government budget consolidation, industrial plant enlargements and reconversion to peacetime production. So governments in need of credit had no margins in their decision to join the Gold Standard because their national economies or the governments itself risked bankruptcy.

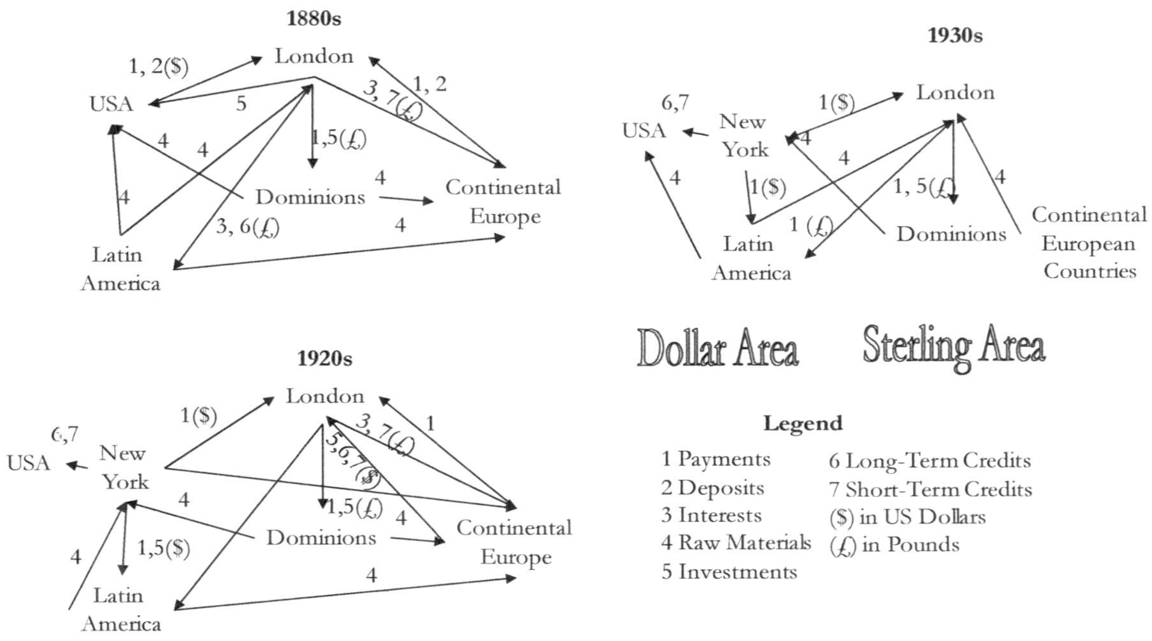

Fig. 1.1 – The evolution of the international payment system.

Furthermore, the exit option became more problematic. During the 1920s, Continental European economies were more heavily dependent on external credits than before the war for various reasons. The first was that hyperinflation and the crisis of both the Vienna financial market and the German banks made it almost impossible to find local capital for governments and firms, at least in the successor states.

Moreover, the import needs of the early post-war years created a considerable balance of payments deficit to be financed with external credits. Finally, the United States' new position in world trade made the dollar scarce, creating a "dollar gap". As a consequence, importers and banks found it difficult to gain dollars, and they had to find new channels for hard currency collection. This attempt led to the use of all possible sources of finance, particularly short-term credits (bank acceptances, call deposits), to finance the importation of national economies. As a result, relations between the countries of Continental Europe and international financial markets became more fragile and unstable, and subject to a crisis in the case of capital outflows, because of the increased importance of short-term funds.

European firms, banks and municipalities returned to issuing bonds and shares on the New York financial market after the signing of agreements for war debt repayment and the gradual restoration of the Gold Standard. In the meantime, New York had become the largest capital market in the world. This opportunity helped to solve the dollar gap problem but created a new unstable linkage between Continental Europe's economies and an external financial market. European firms and banks were in search of capital for financing long-term projects of industrial development or reconversion, not just trade. So they needed not only temporary access to the New York capital market but stable access for an extended period to this market because a sudden interruption of money flow before new plants have generated returns could endanger the whole economic structures involved. This break happened when Wall Street crashed in 1929. That crash made it impossible to issue new bonds on the New York financial market. Consequently, one of the crucial reasons for debtor countries to remain in the poorly restored Gold Standard regime disappeared.

4 – The fall of the Gold Standard

The causes of the crisis in the 1930s and its effects on the world economy are more complicated than those listed above. However, due to the analytical approach adopted here, what matters is the impact on the European countries, and the way in which inability to coordinate efforts among these countries made the crisis devastating. This is an element particularly important in comparing the crisis of the 1930s and that of the 2000s in Europe. Today, many authors just see the euro zone crisis as it is and forget to consider it as it could be in the absence of coordination structures such as the EU and the ECB.

Central European countries were affected first by the mounting international financial crisis. Their economies were heavily dependent on foreign credits and primary product exports (Basch 1944; Hertz 1947; Ránky 1983; Schubert 1990). Moreover, some countries experienced continuous turmoil as a consequence of the war and failures in their attempts to reorganise the internal economy. Austria was the most important of these countries. After the early post-war years' hyperinflation, the Austrian government tried to attract foreign capital and favoured mergers between banks. This policy was not sufficient to solve the structural problems of the Austrian economy. So the mergers of many banks in crisis only created a few more giant banks with more massive problems (League of Nations 1926a; Rothschild 1947; März 1984). Thus, it is not surprising that the financial collapse of Central Europe started in Austria. The fall of the Austrian banking system caused a sudden outflow of short-term funds from Central Europe that spread the Austrian financial crisis to the other Central European countries, Hungary and Germany in particular. In summer 1931, these countries introduced exchange controls to avoid capital outflows like those experienced in Austria. In doing so, they infringed the Gold Standard rules and exited from the system (Ellis 1941).

This was the only choice they had because remaining loyal to Gold Standard rules would have led to the collapse of their internal economy. In fact, without capital controls, Austria, Germany and Hungary risked having to repay almost all their foreign debts. It was the essential duty that debtors assumed on entering the Gold Standard and the necessary assurance for creditors. In reality, the problem did not regard the rules, but the considerable involvement of Central European countries in international borrowing. External funding of national economies and the financialisation of the international economy required stability in the long term for the financial market and monetary system. All those countries that based their post-war recovery and growth on the financial market used an attractive perspective but assumed an enormous risk they probably did not perceive at that time.

The crucial role of foreign loans (in particular short-term loans) in satisfying Continental Europe's needs for funds made the capital outflow consequences dramatic. Without funds, the economy risked collapsing, causing economic losses and political instability that were unacceptable for the Austrian, Hungarian and German governments (Arndt 1944). It was to avoid these costs that the same countries accepted the Gold Standard rules and duties. The risk of having to face them in all cases led these countries to search for new solutions outside the Gold Standard. Unfortunately, it was too late to block the ascendency of fascist movements that gained broader consensus from the collapsing economy. In fact, in those countries more touched by the financial crisis, fascist parties adopted national populist policies and political programmes aimed at protecting national producers and workers by dismissing the international obligations derived by financial links. For example, in Hungary, the government prohibited land requisition for those debtors, mainly farmers, incapable of repaying their debts. In these cases, the government supported domestic banks that could not recover their money, while foreign banks had to suffer the full consequences of the new rules. On the other hand, credit frozen in these countries made international banks weaker and needing to call back more funds from those countries not yet in trouble.

The fall of the post-war Gold Standard became irreversible when Great Britain abandoned convertibility, condemning the system to die. Various factors caused the breakdown of the "sterling standard". One of them was the economic instability in Continental Europe. Many authors have stressed the role of Continental European central banks in supporting the Bank of England action as an international lender in the pre-war period (Williams 1963, p. 514; De Cecco 1984). After the war, internal economic problems, the scarcity of gold and political tensions reduced the potentialities of some central banks and left the Bank of England almost alone in the attempt to stabilise the continental economies.

Other problems arose from the global agricultural crisis, which reduced the working balances kept in London by foreign traders. These troubles resulted in cuts of funds available for short-term credits. Moreover, in the late 1920s, funds moved from London to Wall Street or were repatriated in France after the *de jure* stabilisation of the French franc. Finally, the London money market became increasingly involved in government and home industry finance, reducing the proportion of funds available for external borrowers (Williams 1963, p. 520–21).

In summer 1931, the Central European banks' crisis drastically reduced liquidity on the London money market. Simultaneously, the commercial banks of other European countries (Italy, Belgium, Netherlands, Switzerland, Sweden) withdrew funds from London or required new funds because of their liquidity problems due to the Central European crisis (Kindleberger 1973). The growing outflow of money from London induced

British authorities to devalue the pound and to suspend convertibility. Therefore, it was mainly the collapse of the system centred on the London financial market that persuaded Great Britain to exit from the Gold Standard. During the whole 1925–1931 period, governments' intervention almost wholly focused on the domestic consequences of the war and the new post-war economic order. When that order collapsed, almost nothing was done to coordinate the countries' reactions to this event.

Great Britain probably did not use all the options at its disposal to save the system. As Williams shows, one of the main changes in the London money market after the pre-war period regards its increased involvement with the home industry. Moreover, the London capital market was an essential instrument for safeguarding the solidity of the British Empire. Financial flows from London to countries with close political ties with Great Britain allowed the so-called "Proto-sterling area" to be supported (Williams 1963, p. 521). These aspects explain the Bank of England's reluctance to raise interest rates during the last years of the Gold Standard, notwithstanding higher interests could attract funds from abroad to face the crisis in the system. London's increased role in home industry and Proto-sterling area countries' financing reduced the flexibility of the London market. So Britain's decision to exit from the Gold Standard partially depended on the contrast between international commitments and internal (to the British Empire) priorities.

Central European countries' dependence on external credit explains why they decided to exit from the Gold Standard for first. Other countries were not heavily indebted in the short term and were capable of paying for capital outflows or attracting gold. So they remained in the Gold Standard. In the perspective adopted in this study, the most exciting aspect of their experience regards the reasons why these countries stayed in the Gold Standard regime for such an extended period notwithstanding the defection of other members, the leader country included.

In the case of France, a strange situation arose. The *de jure* stabilisation of the French franc in 1928 induced French capitalists to repatriate capital exported during the years of financial instability. This inflow reinforced the French gold reserves. Furthermore, the exchange rate adopted for the franc led to undervaluation of the French currency and favoured exportations and tourism. As a result, the French balance of payments led to a surplus and the franc gave the impression of being a strong currency (Wolfe 1951). Finally, France had a decreasing population that appealed heavily to foreigners because of its workforce needs. This permitted French authorities to regulate the unemployment level just by varying the number of working permits awarded to immigrants.

This particular situation profoundly influenced the course of events and French politicians' perception of the internal and international situation. In reality, in the early years of the depression, the French position was not under threat. The unemployment rate was low and the state budget balanced, while the gold influx increased as a consequence of the London crisis, which transformed Paris into an ideal market for refuge-seeking capital (Wolfe 1951, p. 92). This idyllic situation induced French politicians to misinterpret the position of France in that period, ascribing the merits of this elusive success in combatting depression to their deflationist policy. Initially, this conviction led the French government to maintain its budget-balancing policy based on budgetary curtailment, high taxes, and price and wage deflation (Wolfe 1951, p. 105). When depression arrived in France, the damages of the French budgetary policy became evident, but French political instability and the limited economic knowledge of political leaders made it difficult to fight the economic slump.[7] The rise in

[7] For example, the communists opposed fiercely the devaluation of the French franc, considering this eventuality disadvantageous for workers. Moreover, many people misinterpreted the relationship existing between devaluation, budget disequilibrium, inflation and financial instability.

power of the Popular Front and the economic policy adopted were unable to solve the problem of the French economy. After the situation deteriorated, the French franc was finally devalued. France was the last European country to be affected by, and the last to recover from, the depression. It seems this delay was the main reason for France remaining in the Gold Standard until the second half of the 1930s.

Italy was a debtor country that tried to maintain a good reputation. It rejected the introduction of exchange controls and remained loyal to Gold Standard rules. Thus, Italy suffered from both fund outflows and short-term credits frozen in Central Europe. Also, being one of the few debtor countries that maintained convertibility, external creditors recalled funds from Italy to regain the liquidity they lost because of the default of Central European debtors. Finally, mainly in 1930, Italian firms bought back their bonds issued on the New York market during the 1920s. These depreciated massively due to the Wall Street crash. So Italian companies found it very convenient to repurchase their bonds because they were able to reduce their debts at a lower cost (Storaci and Tattara 2001, p. 68–9). Capital outflow and bond repurchase reduced the Bank of Italy's reserves. They were also debilitated from the overvaluation of the Italian lira, mainly after the devaluation of the pound in September 1931.

Consequently, the Italian economy underwent a profound crisis in 1932–33. The recall of short-term loans and foreign bank deposits, together with the fall in industrial production and the crisis in exports, caused a banking crisis that led the Italian government to direct involvement in the national economic management. Thus, the state became the owner of a large part of the industrial and banking system, rescuing the larger Italian banks and many Italian industries from bankruptcy. Despite all these problems, the Italian government decided to maintain the convertibility of the lira, and in 1933 joined the so-called "Gold Bloc" together with France, Belgium and Poland. Italy officially devalued the lira only in 1936, at the end of the League of Nations' sanction against Italy for the invasion of Ethiopia (Storaci 1993, p. 441–486).

The reasons for the Italian government's choice can be found mainly in the dictatorial nature of the Italian government at that time. On the one hand, Mussolini's fascist regime was not obliged to resolve the widespread dissatisfaction with the mounting economic crisis, as in democratic nations. On the other hand, the economic elite, which was in need of financial support from the government, was unable to bring pressure in the field of economic policy. The Italian government lacked a realistic perception of the consequences of the crisis for the Italian position in the international economy. Mussolini gave significant political value to the stability of the lira. In his view, it represented the premium paid to the middle class for supporting fascism. Also, the Italian lira's convertibility abroad acted as an element of prestige for the fascist government (Falco and Storaci 1977).

Moreover, monetary stability was the primary requirement for obtaining foreign credits. In all likelihood, Mussolini and his advisors did not realise (at least until the late 1930s) what the Gold Standard breakdown meant. So they tried to maintain international confidence in Italian financial soundness, hoping to attract new capital as soon as the crisis was over.

The United States kept dollar convertibility until 1933 when the dollar was devalued and gold exportation prohibited (Kindleberger 1973, p. 200). This was mainly a political choice. The USA had the most significant gold reserve in the world and no capital outflow problems. Its balance of payments surplus resisted for almost all the 1930s. So there was no significant reason for the USA to exit from the Gold Standard; the choice to devalue was a reaction to the inconvertibility of other currencies (sterling in particular).

In contrast with the European countries, the financial crisis in the USA did not cause a currency crisis. The stock market crash and the fall of industrial production, prices and the level of employment were the most relevant aspect of the American crisis. In fact, in the USA the crisis mainly affected the internal economic activity. The Roosevelt government, in particular, devoted a substantial part of its action to sustaining the domestic market and tried to increase prices to stimulate industrial production and agriculture and to reduce unemployment. In this context, the decision to devalue was instrumental in creating the condition to improve the internal situation. The devaluation of sterling reduced the competitiveness of American goods in the overseas countries of the British Empire that were linked to Great Britain by the imperial preference system. So the decision to devalue was a new step toward isolation, as in the case of the adoption of the Smoot-Hawley tariff in 1930. In that case, the American government tried to sustain the internal market with protectionist measures. Instead, with devaluation, the Roosevelt administration attempted to regain external markets for American goods and in the meantime to raise domestic prices, as became evident with the adoption in February 1934 of the new gold price of 35 dollars per ounce. In both cases, the Americans mainly addressed their internal problems without giving sufficient consideration to the international consequences of their policy. So domestic priorities prevailed in orientating the USA foreign economic policy as well as in the cases of Central European countries, the UK, France and Italy. Almost the same happened in Great Britain. However, in the British case, they were the Empire's priorities that prevailed, not just the British ones.

Cooperation revealed itself to be not an option. The contemporary lack of international institutions in charge of coordinating cooperation, international lenders of last resort and effective intergovernmental decision-making, as well as the absence of previous experience in managing such a massive international financial crisis, made coordination almost impossible during the early phase of the turmoil. Later, the rise in power or the consolidation of fascist regimes in Europe rendered impossible any agreement to recreate an international monetary system. Instead, new aggressive and domestic-oriented economic policies carried out by both fascist and democratic governments destroyed the remaining opportunities to recreate a working international payment system rapidly.

5 – The sterling area and the origins of British marginality in European monetary integration

The abandonment of the Gold Standard in 1931 fragmented the international economic system. Different blocs of countries characterised by particular currency arrangements appeared. One was the so-called "Gold Bloc", which included France, Italy, Belgium, Switzerland and Poland. These countries decided to reject devaluation and to maintain their gold parity. Based on the old Latin Monetary Union created in the late 19th century by France, Italy and Belgium (Einaudi 2001), this bloc was enlarged to include Switzerland and Poland. Switzerland maintained gold convertibility because of its role as an international capital refuge. On the other hand, Poland's political ties with France induced it to join the bloc. Unfortunately, the bloc had no internal coherence, and its existence derived mainly from the individual countries' choice to maintain gold convertibility for some time after the sterling abandoned the gold parity. At the end of 1936, the Gold Bloc was practically dissolved. The French and Belgian francs were devalued as well as the Italian lira, and exchange controls were introduced in former Gold Bloc countries (Wolfe 1951, p. 114; Kindleberger 1973, p. 246–60; Storaci 1993).

Another currency bloc, the so-called "Reichsmark Bloc", emerged in Central Europe. Historians discussed the real nature of the Reichsmark Bloc because of the relevance of this case for Hirschman's theory of economic dependence

(Hirschman 1945; Milward 1981, p. 377–411; Ritschl 2001). The system of trade agreements and clearings created during the 1930s by Nazi Germany with other Central and Eastern European countries was mainly a trade bloc based on the German mark as the primary account unit. It aimed to create the conditions for regional trade in the absence of hard currency assets. However, the predominant role of Germany in the system gave it enormous power over poor agricultural countries in Central-Eastern Europe incapable of selling their products on the dissolved international markets. Germany used this power to build a system of political alliances into which Italy finally fell when the international sanctions suffered in response to the Ethiopia invasion isolated the Italian economy from its traditional commercial partners, except for Germany.

Of course, the Reichsmark Bloc dissolved at the end of the war. In contrast, the remaining two currency areas that emerged following the dissolution of the Gold Standard, the dollar area and the sterling bloc, survived for a long time. After the war, the former became the core of the international monetary system rebuilt at Bretton Woods. The latter played a crucial role in the global economic relations of the early post-war period. It later declined as it lost its importance.

The relevance of the sterling area experience for the study of European integration is twofold. First, its rise generated both a structural divergence between Continental Europe and the British economy and a never composed fracture of the Anglo-European financial system. This fracture caused the financial isolation of Continental Europe in the 1930s that facilitated the consolidation of fascist regimes. So British entrenchment in the sterling area had significant political consequences for Continental Europe and the whole world. Second, the choice of the sterling area explains in part the choice to stay out of the EMU. It could seem strange proposing a strict connection between two events so distant in time. Instead, we will demonstrate in what follows in this book that the connection exists.

After the 1931 crises, the British Empire, except for Canada, remained linked to sterling. Dominions and other countries like Portugal decided to peg their currencies to sterling rather than gold. Then the economic connection of most of these countries with Great Britain was reinforced by the Ottawa Agreement, which created the imperial preference system.[8] As a result, sterling became the core currency for the international trade of these countries and the group of countries appeared as a currency bloc, the so-called "sterling bloc". Later, other countries like Iran, Latvia and the Scandinavian countries joined the bloc. Finally, a group of countries that included Argentina and Japan decided to link their currency to sterling, but these countries were not considered members of the sterling bloc (League of Nations 1944, p. 47).

The close economic and political connections between Great Britain and the other countries of the sterling bloc appeared to be the fundamental reason for the rise of the sterling bloc. Its member countries oriented their international trade towards Great Britain and its Empire. The imperial preference system further reinforced the attractiveness of the British economic area. In the meantime, Great Britain signed trade agreements with the Scandinavian countries and Argentina. These agreements attracted those countries towards the sterling bloc. However, they preferred just pegging their currencies to sterling to minimise exchange rate fluctuations against their most important trading partner currency (Aliber 1982, p. 151).

Financial ties were equally important. Accessing the London financial market was an excellent opportunity to satisfy the financial needs of less developed countries. Finally, the system of currency boards adopted in various countries of the British Empire automatically linked the local currency to

[8] In July 1932 at the Ottawa Conference a system of preferential tariffs was set up to favour the trade inside the British Empire. This system disadvantaged trade with non-imperial countries and represented a kind of protectionist barrier. See Drummond (1972, p. 96–104).

sterling. In fact, local currency boards granted full coverage of local currency in sterling. So before 1931, these countries were linked to gold by sterling. After the abandonment of the sterling convertibility, their currencies just remained tied to sterling (Williams 1968, p. 273–74).

The sterling bloc became the sterling area with the outbreak of World War II. In September 1939, the countries that accepted keeping their currency reserves in London managed by the Treasury established a unified exchange control system. Most of the countries external to the British Empire renounced pegging their currencies to sterling, and the sterling bloc (now the sterling area) became virtually equivalent to the British Commonwealth without Canada (League of Nations 1944, p. 47).

The history of the sterling area can be divided into three parts: the war period, the early post-war period (1945–49) and the 1950s. The return to convertibility of sterling in 1958 is commonly considered to be the end of the period in which the sterling area played an important international role (Schenk 1994, p. 16 and 132).

During the war period, the role of the sterling area was that of supporting the war economy and supplying food and goods for the war. In this regard, the role of sterling as an international currency was crucial. The sterling area enabled Britain to obtain food and raw materials while avoiding payment in dollars. It simply paid in sterling, which soon became a sort of "blocked currency" because it was almost impossible to obtain goods from Great Britain during the war. As a consequence, sterling balances had to be accumulated by central banks of creditor countries waiting to use them in the post-war period.

Moreover, trust in sterling and the relative share of international trade controlled by the sterling area led countries not included in the sterling area to accept accumulating sterling balances in payment of their export to Great Britain. This was the case with Argentina and Brazil (Fodor 1986; Paiva Abreu 1990, p. 450–469). Thus, Britain gathered a significant amount of outstanding sterling balances (approximately 2,900 million) used for paying its war and immediate post-war imports (Meyer 1952, 46; Bell 1956, p. 22).

The management of these assets became one of the most significant problems during the post-war period. After 1945, the UK signed agreements with sterling balance owner countries to regulate the use of sterling assets. A sort of payment hierarchy rose in which the sterling area countries were favoured (Meyer 1952, p. 9). So countries with large amounts of sterling balances like India became reluctant to leave the sterling area, fearing they would lose their privileged position due to the use of these assets.

Fear was a powerful instrument in the hands of the British government and helped to maintain cohesion in the sterling area. In the early post-war period, the UK permitted the use, or the transfer of, sterling balances within a well-defined limit, inducing countries to maintain a minimum level of these assets. The risk of expulsion from the sterling area and the consequent blockage of sterling balances was suggested for nations that refused to reach a reasonable agreement (Fforde 1992, p. 89–93). In other words, the sterling area allowed British influence to be maintained over a disintegrating empire because of massive debts in sterling balances. Newly independent countries in the sterling area feared losing these balances, and Great Britain was willing to pay to keep the now sovereign states in its sphere of influence, shifting sterling balances from the independent nations (in particular from India) to British colonies still under strict control. In other words, Britain redistributed the burden of keeping sterling balances favourably for independent countries and especially for the newly independent ones like India where the British Empire was no longer capable of maintaining military control (Krozewski 1993, p. 239–65).

Table 1.1 – Sterling balances in non-sterling countries

	1945	1946	1947	1948	1949
Sterling area countries					
United Kingdom colonies	411	461	470	519	546
Other sterling area countries	1,986	1,906	1,780	1,636	1,612
Total	2,397	2,367	2,250	2,155	2,158
Non-sterling area countries					
Dollar area	34	33	18	19	31
Other western hemisphere	163	212	235	135	80
OEEC countries	351	363	419	309	356
Other non-sterling countries	622	635	576	534	518
Total	1,170	1,243	1,248	997	985
Non-territorial organisations	0	26	388	398	576
Total	3,567	3,636	3,886	3,550	3,719

	1950	1951	1952	1953	1954
Sterling area countries					
United Kingdom colonies	719	919	1,024	1,093	1,221
Other sterling area countries	1,830	1,717	1,518	1,705	1,703
Total	2,549	2,636	2,542	2,798	2,924
Non-sterling area countries					
Dollar area	79	38	34	62	97
Other western hemisphere	45	57	6	40	8
OEEC countries	314	328	239	223	244
Other non-sterling countries	496	518	398	370	430
Total	934	941	677	695	779
Non-territorial organisations	577	566	567	511	476
Total	4,060	4,143	3,786	4,004	4,179

	1955	1956	1957
Sterling area countries			
United Kingdom colonies	1,280	1,281	1,269
Other sterling area countries	1,599	1,575	1,430
Total	2,879	2,856	2,699
Non-sterling area countries			
Dollar area	58	37	35
Other western hemisphere	9	32	31
OEEC countries	213	193	258
Other non-sterling countries	417	303	244
Total	697	565	568
Non-territorial organisations	469	669	645
Total	4,045	4,090	3,912

Notes: [1] Bell estimates the total of sterling balances in the sterling area was 760 million in 1938. [2] Other aggregate and disaggregate estimations of the same data had been proposed by Bell and by Schenk. Their estimations are slightly different from those proposed by Conan.

Sources: Conan 1961, 55; Bell 1956, 22; Schenk 1994.

Great Britain also made the sterling area an instrument of international economic policy used to safeguard, at least in part, its role as a world power. Thus, the maintenance of the sterling area reduced dependence on the USA and the need for dollars. A dollar shortage during the war was partially avoided thanks to the sterling area and the imposition of restrictions usually associated with a war economy. However, with the end of the war, the dollar gap became strident. In the early post-war period, the sterling area maintained its role as a collector of dollars and allowed the effects of the dollar shortage on its members to be softened.

Nevertheless, gold and hard currency pooling was ineffective at satisfying the dollar's need for the sterling area. After the war, those sterling area countries traditionally in surplus with the dollar area showed a deficit and became dollar consumers. Thus, managing the gold and dollar pool of the sterling area in the late 1940s was only possible thanks to the dollar area loans and the rise in South Africa's gold production (Henshaw 1996, p. 197–223).

On the other hand, the sterling area supported the price competitiveness of British goods in the area. The scarcity of dollars, the non-convertibility of sterling and the lack of an accounting system that regulated the use of sterling assets meant that the sterling area countries were not free to buy in the dollar area. Thus, they were compelled to use their sterling assets for "unrequired imports" from Great Britain (Meyer 1952, p. 51; Bell 1956, p. 20). It was the system Britain used to pay for the war. However, it was probably one of the most important causes of the 1949 balance of payments crisis. Great Britain had to pay for the imports of raw materials it needed to produce goods for exporting to sterling balance owners, and it was impossible to obtain all these imports in the sterling area. This resulted in a reduction of the hard currency reserve because of payments outside the sterling area (Meyer 1952, p. 53; Bell 1956, p. 20–21).

The perseverance of Great Britain in the 1950s in following its path toward solving the currency problem that arose in the 1930s explains in part British marginality and isolation in European monetary integration. When the British Empire and the sterling area started to fragment and induced the economic and financial decline of Great Britain, integration with Western European allies was the only possible way for the UK to recover. However, it was too late, and the UK appeared to the EEC members to be a problem rather than a resource. An enormous amount of sterling balances remained unpaid, and the political weight of the UK put French predominance in the EEC in danger. These problems led to a double and humiliating rejection of the UK's application for membership. The UK joined the EEC only in 1973, too late to save it from the IMF's conditionality.[9] Then, British membership of the EEC became instrumental to access to the Western European market. However, political and monetary integration never attracted the British government seriously. Instead, Great Britain resisted decisive steps toward deeper political integration and lost interest in monetary integration when the City in the 1980s partially regained its centrality in the international financial market.

6 – The Bretton Woods Agreement and the American plans for multilateralism

When the war turned in favour of the Allies and the defeat of the Axis armies became just a matter of time, the problem of rebuilding the world economic order entered the agenda of the winning powers. However, the interests of the leading

[9] In September 1975, the mounting sterling crisis induced the British government to ask the IMF for support. An agreement with the IMF was signed in January 1976 and domestic measures for reducing payment imbalances were adopted (Needham 2014, p. 97–100; Hirowatari 2015, p. 151–153).

powers diverged significantly. Obviously, the Soviet interest in a worldwide capitalist financial system was non-existent. The USA instead aimed to dismiss the "ancient" economic regime based on colonial empires and nationalist economic policies respectively considered instruments of protectionism and empowerment of authoritarian regimes. Also, colonialism was historically the enemy the USA defeated in gaining freedom, and this gave an idealistic aura to the American anti-colonial instances. Conversely, Great Britain aimed to recreate an international economic order on the same basis as the pre-war one, notwithstanding it was clear to the British government that innovative solutions were required to correct the problems of the system that were felt in the 1930s and to face the other issues that arose as a consequence of the war effort like the blocked sterling balances.

It was undoubtedly a shock for the British negotiators in Bretton Woods to discover that while they were winning the war, they were surely losing the peace. They imagined having to sustain their enormous war efforts before the USA entry into the war was acknowledged by the allies and the economic condition for the post-war period would allow their sacrifices to be monetised. Instead, before the end of the war, it had already become clear that what truly mattered was the new balance of power between the USA and the British Empire, and that the Americans were the strongest. US priorities were sustained by the economic and financial strength of the US economy and the contemporary weakness of the British economy that, instead, was close to bankruptcy and incapable of resisting without American support.

When delegates from 44 countries met at Bretton Woods in 1944, the diverging views of the British and the Americans emerged. The US delegation, led by Henry Dexter White, aimed to create a new economic order based on free trade and the Gold Standard. This was coherent with the US ambition to gain worldwide economic leadership, penetrating markets previously denied to US trade by tariffs, imperial preferences, and other barriers. Also, with the USA being the owner of the most abundant gold reserves in the world, a Gold Standard system was the best solution to maximise the advantages granted by their position.

The British delegation, led by John Maynard Keynes, supported the creation of an ambitious, complex multilateral clearing system based on an international currency called "bancor". In Keynes's view, this system could guarantee the management of trade imbalances and the international liquidity needed to keep the system working. The British solution was compatible with the survival of colonial empires, the sterling area and the preferential system, and allowed the blocked sterling balances that endangered the international financial credibility of Great Britain to be sterilised (Steil 2013).

The sterling area represented a point of sharp contrasts during the Anglo-American negotiations after Bretton Woods. The Americans considered the sterling area and the imperial preference system to be connected topics and the main obstacle to multilateral trade. In the post-war period, the Americans' most essential objective was to dismantle trade barriers. The return to multilateral trade also passed through the re-establishment of sterling convertibility. This was a means for destroying the sterling area and the imperial preference system. In fact, American negotiators considered sterling inconvertibility the critical tool in the British hands for discriminating against imports from the USA in the sterling area.

The Americans prevailed at Bretton Woods, and the final agreement created a system of international institutions (the International Trade Organisation, the International Monetary Fund and the World Bank) and a new Gold Standard system named the "Gold Exchange Standard" based on the gold convertibility of the US dollar and the British pound. However, the new system as conceived at Bretton Woods never came into force. The American Congress denied the approval of the International Trade Organisation while sterling returns to convertibility failed miserably.

The return to a convertible sterling failed mainly because of the existence of significant sterling balances in the hands of owners mostly interested in having dollars. In 1946–7, Britain obtained a large loan from the USA, agreeing in return to reintroduce the convertibility of sterling by 1947. In the Anglo-American loan agreement signed in 1946, Article VII established that sterling would have to return to being convertible for current account transactions one year after the signature of the agreement. During the short period of sterling convertibility (15 July – 20 August 1947), sterling became a sort of intermediary currency to obtain dollars. Sterling balance owners converted sterling massively into the dollars they needed for imports from the USA, and the dollar reserves of the United Kingdom decreased rapidly, leading to the suspension of convertibility (Gardner 1980).[10]

During the last years of the 1940s, it became evident that the dollar gap and the international trade system fragmentation were structural problems that were impossible to solve immediately and with limited funds. Also, the Americans realised they were unable to impose their preferred international economic order because of both structural problems and the influence Great Britain still had as the centre of the sterling area. The understanding by the American government of these challenges favoured the adoption of a different approach to reconstructing an international economic order. The American strategy included structural interventions such as the European Recovery Program (ERP), also known as the "Marshall Plan". Also, they supported intra-European coop-

[10] Newton suggests that the failure of the sterling convertibility attempt was also due to the drain of dollars from capital transactions and that the sterling area countries and Britain's creditors within the transferable account area were responsible for these drains (Newton 1984, p. 400).

eration in various forms, including the OEEC and the European Payments Union. In this way, they sustained the economic recovery of a region (Western Europe) that was crucial for rebuilding a multilateral system centred on areas rather than on single countries.

In the 1950s, the sterling area continued to function. However, relations between Great Britain and the rest of the sterling area lost importance. The outbreak of the Korean War and the increase of USA expenditure on imports eliminated the dollar gap. So the importance of the sterling area in saving dollars decreased. This induced sterling area countries to ask for a certain amount of their receipts to be kept in gold and dollars to create their currency reserves (Wright 1954, p. 566). Furthermore, some British products became obsolete and showed low quality. This reduced the level of competitiveness of British exports in the rest of the sterling area (Schenk 1994, . 85–7). As a result, sterling balance owners preferred to convert them and to import from the dollar area. Finally, the economic relationship between Great Britain and the OEEC countries in Continental Europe became much more important and led Great Britain to participate in the European Payments Union. In 1958, sterling became convertible once more, and the importance of the sterling area as a discriminatory block ended.

7 – The origins of the European currency area

The end of the war did not mean the end of the economic isolation affecting Continental Europe during the 1930s.

After the failure of sterling's return to convertibility in 1947, it became even harder to reintegrate European economies into the international trade system. That failure deprived Western European countries of the possibility of exporting to the UK and gaining sterling convertible into dollars to use for paying for essential importation. So, with the return to inconvertible sterling, the opportunity to rebuild an international payment system similar to that dismantled in the early 1930s vanished.

The problems that arose in the 1930s and were still unsolved at the end of the 1940s needed innovative and efficient solutions for various reasons. One was the constant American pressure for European integration that would lead to economies of scale similar to the American model, seen as the reason for the American superiority. Another reason was the fear of Soviet invasion. Changes in the economic relations with extra-European areas also mattered. In fact, the reconstruction needs rendered Western Europe unable to export, collect hard currencies and buy products on international markets. Also, the post-war dollar shortage made it even more difficult to import the raw materials and industrial commodities required to keep plants at work.

What followed was both continuity and change. Insuperable obstacles and political choices led Western European countries to avoid the path they took after World War I. This time, the solution for reinserting Western European countries into the international monetary system was to resume and reshape previous practices of exchange rate controls and intra-European trade arrangements. The clearing system developed during the 1930s was changed to a multilateral clearing system backed by a clearing fund, namely the European Payments Union. The following figure helps to explain how the EPU worked.

We can assume, approximately, that the black area in Figure 1.2 represents the trade that could be possible in a unilateral clearing system, while the white area represents the advantage derived by multilateral compensation of previous surpluses and deficits accumulated in the previous years. Finally, the grey area is a good proxy for the increase of trade permitted by credits and loans granted respectively by other EPU members and the EPU central administration. Compared with the 1930s clearings, the EPU system granted a dramatic increase in intra-EPU trade. Political tensions and trade barriers in that period made the complex mechanism required for balancing clearings surpluses and deficits in a multi-annual period using unilateral clearings impossible. Finally, the entire grey area is obtainable only in a multilateral clearing system endowed with lending and borrowing instruments.

Figure 1.2 shows a rough approximation (just for explicative purposes) of the potential trade that could be created in different clearing systems. The advantages of the EPU multilateral clearing system are evident, notwithstanding further financial instruments existent in monetary unions can grant a further increase in intra-area trade.

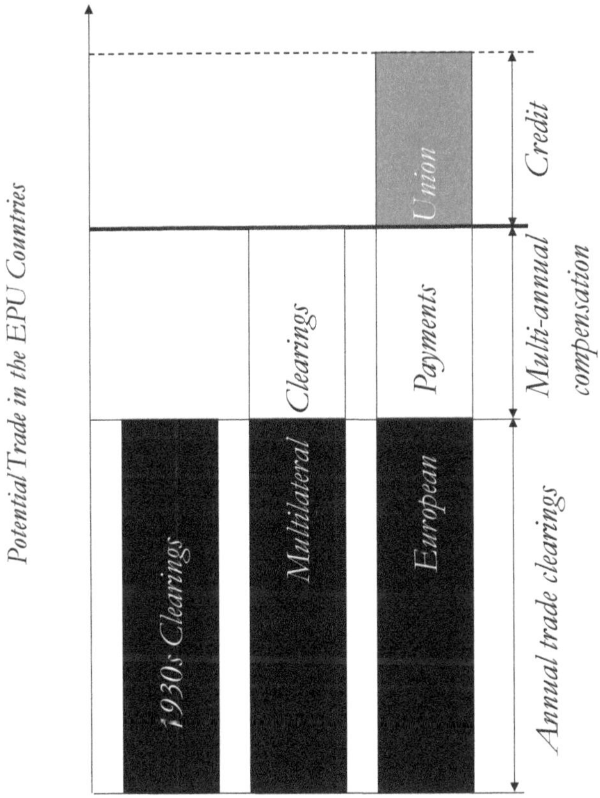

Fig. 1.2 – Comparison of potential trade under different clearing systems

From 1950 to 1958 the EPU fostered the recovery and development of intra-European trade and thus the gradual return to convertibility of the OCSE countries. The credit fund allowed the commercial credit to be increased for those countries in temporary balance of payments disequilibrium, which was a severe obstacle to the recovery and growth of intra-European trade. However, data about credits and balances in the EPU reveal the re-emergence of German economic predominance in European trade as early as in the early 1950s as well as the rise of a German-centred block of creditors that demonstrates a structural tendency to economic dualism in Europe after the early steps of European integration. Also, the following tables suggest that in the EPU, Germany and some small countries hauled up the economic recovery and growth in many other countries, France and the UK included.[11] Finally, by the end of the existence of the EPU, Germany had accumulated an enormous, and probably not immediately eligible, credit towards the EPU, a similar situation to today's accumulation of TARGET2 balances, which we will discuss in Chapter 5.

In contrast to the inter-war clearing system that facilitated the political predominance of the economically stronger countries, the EPU supported integration and hindered political predominance by the wealthiest members. Conversely, the EPU hindered the British ambition to regain influence in Continental Europe using its traditional financial tools. This made the UK the least supportive member of the EPU.[12]

The EPU worked well and favoured the start of European integration, and in particular, economic integration. For eight years, the EPU remained cohesive, even when faced with awkward moments such as the German crisis of the early 1950s.

[11] They were mainly the smaller colonial countries like Belgium, the Netherlands and Portugal that gained hard currencies selling raw material from their colonial empires to the other EPU members.

[12] For the various reasons for British opposition to the EPU, see Kaplan and Schleiminger (1989, p. 44–82).

Table 1.2 – Net deficits and surpluses in the European Payments Union (US million $)

	Quota[1]	1950–51	1951–52	1952–53	1953–54	1954–55	1955–56	1956–57	1957–58	Final semester[2]	Cumulative net position[3]
Austria	70	-104	-38	42	106	-103	-6	23	-4	24	-60
Belgium/ Lux.	360	236	509	-33	-55	80	222	14	153	66	1,192
Denmark	195	-68	46	-17	-92	-94	4	-43	10	-1	-255
France	520	194	-602	-417	-149	115	-180	-969	-576	-317	-2,901
Germany	320	-281	584	260	518	296	584	1,336	826	350	4,473
Greece	45	-140	-83	-28	-40	-27	40	5	7	-49	-315
Iceland	15	-7	-6	-4	-5	-2	-4	-3	-3	-9	-43
Italy	205	-30	194	-223	-210	-225	-125	-94	219	73	-421
Netherlands	330	-270	477	139	-42	84	-62	-36	86	181	557
Norway	200	-80	21	-59	-61	-70	-27	41	-78	-30	-343
Portugal	70	59	28	-23	-19	-59	-33	-38	-54	-37	-176
Sweden	260	-59	284	-44	-37	-104	6	111	-30	11	138
Switzerland	250	11	158	85	73	10	-66	-83	-189	20	19
Turkey	50	-64	-96	-50	-94	-38	-27	-36	-50	-14	-469
Sterling area	1,060	604	-1,476	371	107	136	-327	-225	-317	-267	-1,394
Total (+/-)[4]	3,950	1,104	2,301	898	804	722	857	1,529	1,301	725	6,378

Sources: Rees 1963, p. 116; Kaplan and Schleiminger 1989, p. 350.

Table 1.3 – Credits granted to the European Payments Union by member countries (US million $)

	1950–51	1951–52	1952–53	1953–54	1954–55	1955–56	1956–57	1957–58	Final semester[2]	Cumulative net position[3]
Austria	80	0	0	19	58	1	0	5	2	7
France	0	150	0	0	0	0	0	0	0	0
Germany	0	0	206	339	463	534	598	879	1,030	1,127
Greece	115	0	0	0	0	0	0	0	0	0
Iceland	4	0	0	0	0	0	0	0	0	0
Italy	0	12	125	0	0	0	0	0	3	12
Netherlands	30	0	153	225	164	183	125	94	87	121
Norway	50	0	1	0	0	0	0	0	0	0
Portugal	0	37	51	39	20	0	0	0	0	0
Sweden	0	0	142	121	73	9	2	21	3	1
Switzerland	0	11	110	154	140	124	79	41	3	6
United Kingdom	0	292	0	0	0	0	0	0	0	0
Belg./Lux.	0	147	294	276	179	182	192	154	156	159
Total	279	649	1,081	1,172	1,098	1,032	997	1,193	1,284	1,433

Sources: Rees 1963. *Notes for tables 1.2 and 1.3:* [1]. Million US $; [2]. From 1 July to 27 December 1958; [3]. At 27 December 1958; [4]. This is the sum of all the amounts of the same sign and represents the compensation of deficits and surpluses in the year, apart from small adjustments. This total and the data in the table do not include payments for interest and returns of credit as well as 75 million US $ for France and the UK (50 and 25 million, respectively) due to adjustments in 1952.

The UK's repeated pressures to dissolve the EPU created the tensest moments, but in the end, the UK remained in the EPU. The difference between the UK and other members' attitudes toward this system can be explained mainly by the different alternatives available. The UK had a currency still widely used internationally, and especially a free trading area (the sterling area) for importing raw materials and exporting finished goods. In contrast, the other countries did not have any alternative because of the smaller size of their colonial empires (such as for Belgium and Portugal) or their fragility (such as for France) and the severe shortage of hard currencies with which to pay outside the EPU.

Within the EPU area, it was possible to pay in local currency using the centralised clearing system. In this perspective, the EPU seems an example of European rescue of the nation state as it offered a supranational solution to problems impossible to solve at the national level, reinforcing national states instead of dismantling them.

The EPU permitted the creation and development of a continental currency area in Europe. This new area appeared initially as the European Payments Union and survived in different forms (the European Monetary Agreement,[13] the European Monetary System and finally the European Monetary Union) until today. So we can consider the whole European currency experience in the 20th century as a continuous process of currency coordination to face the consequences of the end of the Gold Standard. In other words, the 20th century could be divided into four parts. While until 1931 European countries were internationally integrated thanks to the Gold Standard, from 1931 until 1958 Continental European countries became isolated (or deintegrated) by the rest of the world as a

[13] The European Monetary Agreement took the place of the EPU after its folding. It aimed to coordinate support activities among members to face currency turmoils capable of endangering the stability of Western European exchange rates. See Kaplan and Schleiminger (1989, p. 205–228).

consequence of the Gold Standard fall. This situation induced them to search for a solution at local level initially using clearing and bilateral agreements and, after the war and under American pressures, creating supranational structures and arrangements as the European Payments Union to manage in a coordinated way the currency problems of the whole area. The third period almost coincided with the Bretton Woods period and lasted until the complete abandonment of international monetary cooperation in the mid-1970s. Finally, the last phase of European currency history started in 1978 with the initial steps toward European monetary union.

Chapter 2

The Choice for Euro

In the previous chapter, we analysed the reaction of the USA and the leading European countries to the Gold Standard collapse in the 1930s. Those responses were different and mainly oriented toward satisfying domestic interests. Sometimes, cooperation among states became ephemeral, as in the case of the Gold Bloc. In other cases, such as the Reichsmark Bloc and the sterling area, cooperation worked only because an asymmetrical balance of power granted a dominant position to a hegemonic country. Nevertheless, the fragmented world economic system generated by the collapse of the inter-war Gold Standard was a suboptimal system in which it was impossible to resuscitate the capital flows and the short-term credits that supported growth before 1931.

The restoration of the Gold Standard after World War II appeared to be the solution to the European currency problem and an efficient way to reconnect Continental Europe to the world economic and financial system. Soon, this appearance proved illusory. The collapse of the Gold Exchange Standard in the early-1970s created a situation of European monetary isolation similar to that of the 1930s. Once again the leading European currencies became not convertible into gold, but this time they could remain in contact with the leading financial markets fluctuating against the dollar and each other. Also, as happened with Great Britain after 1931, the American attitude toward international monetary cooperation was weak, and the USA did not help assuming the burden of stabilising the system.

However, in the 1970s, there were no obstacles such as Nazi Germany that made European cooperation and policy coordination impossible in the 1930s. Instead, there existed a consolidated framework of collaboration based on the EEC institutions and treaties. When international cooperation and monetary policy coordination proved impossible, and the impact of exchange rate fluctuations on the domestic policies of European member states became problematic, the most obvious solution was to use the EEC framework to coordinate monetary policy too.

It was at the end of the 1970s that European integration and monetary coordination definitively converged and merged into the communitarian box. At that time, monetary integration, which was one possible solution to the European currency problems since the late 1940s,[1] became the only cooperative option on the table. However, the outcome of this choice was shaped by many other processes at work at that time and in the following 20 years. Many elements profoundly influenced the path toward monetary unification in Europe and the forms it assumed in the early 2000s. Among these elements, there was financial globalisation and the rise of new relevant actors in the international economy such as Arab countries and, later, Asian industrial countries. Finally, the abandonment of Keynesian economic policies, the diffusion of neo-liberal approaches, and the collapse of the communist world played a significant role in accelerating monetary integration in Europe. So the idea proposed by many European integration theorists, mainly neo-functionalists, that monetary integration was inscribed in the logic of integration and granted by spillover mechanisms seems questionable. Instead, many exogenous and unpredictable events attracted the EEC member countries toward an "in-house solution" previously considered a second-best choice, namely European monetary integration.

[1] In 1948–49 there was the first concrete proposal to create a European common currency named the "ecu" or the "europa" (Milward 1987, p. 295–296).

In this chapter, we will analyse the impact of these processes and that of American economic and monetary policy on European monetary integration. We will explain the rise of monetary Europe as a "second European rescue of the nation states", adopting the traditional theoretical framework proposed by Alan Milward and initially applied to the first phase of European integration (Milward 1992). In addition, we will suggest that the final shape of the EMU did not result from a deliberate attempt to create a neo-liberal Europe and to destroy the European welfare state democracies, as suggested by many critics of the EMU and European integration. Conversely, the nature assumed by the European Union as a consequence of monetary integration derived from the way in which EU member states joined the international economic system and accepted long-term processes activated by the collapse of Bretton Woods without governing them, mainly because they were incapable of doing so.

1 – The end of Bretton Woods and the 1970s crisis

The Bretton Woods system was not the stable and efficient system that its apologists describe today. Instead, it was an international arrangement that fell into crisis just a few years after it became fully operative. Planned and agreed at the conference of Bretton Woods in 1944 and mutilated a few years later by the 1947 British failure to return to convertibility and the rejection by the USA Congress of the International Trade Organisation (Eichengreen 2008, p. 99), it became fully operative only in the late 1950s when the leading European countries returned to convertibility.

In the early 1960s, the growing deficit of the US balance of trade and the increasing outflow of gold reserves suggested that the fixed exchange rates could not resist forever. Instead, the growing commercial surplus of Germany and Japan, as well as the rising price of gold on the free market and the "provocative" conversion of dollars into gold by France, created disequilibria in the international monetary system (Eichengreen 2008, p. 99). This problem could be solved in three ways: adjusting US domestic economic policy, negotiating expansionary economic policies in surplus countries to increase American export, or changing the Bretton Woods parities. Coordinating national economic policies was an unwelcome choice for the US government because it imposed a restrictive monetary policy and the reduction of domestic economic activities. On the other hand, European countries (Germany in particular) demonstrated a negative attitude toward expansionary monetary policies and inflation as an instrument for international trade balancing. Moreover, they had interest in maintaining the competitive advantages derived from the undervaluation of their currencies at the parity agreed at Bretton Woods, now obsolete because of the recovery and growth of European economies. This attitude also made the devaluation of the dollar or the revaluation of European currencies (at least the Deutsche mark) and the yen a solution very hard to pursue because US allies were unwilling to revalue their currencies, making their export less competitive. On the other hand, Americans disliked dollar devaluation because this endangered its role as a reserve currency and the image of the US dollar as the fulcrum of international monetary architecture (Helleiner 1994; Solomon 1999).

The crisis of the Bretton Woods system worsened as a consequence of the Vietnam War and the increase of the US trade deficit. Gold outflow due to reserve conversion and its rising price on the free market eroded the US gold reserves and made the Gold Exchange Standard fragile and indefensible if challenged by massive dollar conversion. The USA and its allies tried to face the crisis with financial arrangements and cooperative efforts such as the gold pool, Roosa bonds and swap agreements (Coombs 1976; Eichengreen 2008, p. 127–128). However, the limited effectiveness of these endeavours and the unwillingness of the USA and Western countries to submit their domestic economic policies to the constraints of the Gold Exchange Standard made the USA gold reserves' drain unstoppable. Faced with the choice between radical internal restrictive policies and the exhaustion of reserves, in August 1971, President Nixon declared the end of dollar convertibility (Bergsten 1975; Block 1977; Gowa 1983).

The Bretton Woods system's structural imbalance was not its only problem. The system defined in Bretton Woods was a form of "embedded liberalism" (Ruggie 1982), which means an economic system limited in its operations by rigid controls, in particular on capital flows. This characteristic was essential to keep exchange rates stable and internal economic policies autonomous. On the other hand, these limits kerbed the potentiality of the system to finance world trade and the expansion abroad of multinationals (Helleiner 1994, p. 3). Also, limits to capital flow reduced the opportunities for foreign investments in growing economies because of the risk of having funds frozen in the country. When worldwide economic growth and the need for the financial sector to find new business opportunities collided with controls and other barriers to capital circulation, the limits of embedded liberalism agreed at Bretton Woods emerged.

The rise of the eurodollar market in London helped to outflank the problem. Since the late 1950s, American firms had deposited a growing amount of dollars in the London banks that used these dollars for short-term credits similar to the pre-war acceptances, no longer denominated in sterling but in dollars (Helleiner 1994, p. 84). The American government also accepted these practices for mitigating American multinational and bankers' opposition to exchange controls introduced by the government to kerb dollar outflow (Helleiner 1994, p. 90). So the London money market resurrected and regained part of the relevance it had during the inter-war period. However, the rise of the eurodollar market demonstrated the inefficiency of the Gold Exchange Standard and its excessive rigidity for the growing international economy. Also, the contradictory position of the US government, which imposed capital flow controls but tolerated the offshore operations of US multinationals and banks, was a sign of the increasing incompatibility between the USA's role as the core of the Bretton Woods system and the opportunities that arose from the relevance of New York as a financial centre.

Another element that played a crucial role in eroding the pillars of the Bretton Woods system was the mutated relationship between gold, key currencies and world liquidity. In the classical Gold Standard, convertibility and the liquidity of the international financial system were assured by a balanced mix of national gold reserves, financial arrangements and tools mainly guaranteed by London. So the relation between gold and liquidity was almost rigid, apart from a certain level of elasticity granted by the London financial market facilities. Also, each country had its own gold reserve, and it was easier to regulate domestic liquidity by sterilising funds influx just by accumulating gold or investing funds on the London money market. After 1947, the relationship between reserves and international liquidity became complicated because rigid proportions disappeared and currency accumulation became a problem capable of endangering the stability and sustainability of the whole system. Great Britain and, later, the USA had the problem of keeping frozen in "friendly portfolios" their currencies circulating abroad. This was the case for the sterling balances we discussed in the previous chapter, but the rising "dollar flood" and its role in granting convertibility into gold of the other currencies made "dollar keepers" essential for keeping the system operative. This need became dramatic after the end of convertibility and the abandonment of the Bretton Woods System when vast amounts of US dollars circulated outside the US without gold coverage. The need to sterilise

US dollars abroad induced the USA to accept the rise of external financial markets based on the American currency like the eurodollar market in London. It allowed US dollars to be kept operational and reduced the risks of conversion into gold and the consequent gold outflow from the US reserves (Helleiner 1994, p. 84–91). However, tolerating loopholes from the capital flux controls required by the Bretton Woods system meant weakening the system itself.

At the end of the 1960s, all these incongruences became evident. US economic leadership was vanishing as trade deficit became recurrent. Moreover, the political costs of sustaining the Gold Exchange Standard by adapting internal economic and monetary policy to the needs of the system became unacceptable for the US government. Also, international cooperation and collective management of the system with Western allies and Japan became ineffective. In fact, what happened in the 1960s completely reversed the economic balance of power that emerged from World War II, and that orientated the US strategy at Bretton Woods. The USA conceived the Gold Exchange Standard as a system where the cost of adjustments falls on debtor countries, but in 1960 the USA became one of them. Then, the original architecture of the system became uncomfortable for its chief promoter. We will see that the problem of who has to pay for adjustments (creditors vs debtors) is a critical problem in managing every kind of payments system at every moment of international monetary history, the EMU included. Gold outflows and the decline of USA reserves continued inexorably. Finally, restrictions on capital flow endangered the opportunity for the USA to substitute the lost leadership in international trade with leadership in international finance, a chance that American bankers did not want to miss (Helleiner 1994, p. 14).

So the USA interest in keeping alive the Bretton Woods system decreased. When reserves became dangerously scarce and negotiation with Western allies and Japan inconclusive, the Nixon administration had to choose between policy autonomy and international coordination. In August 1971, Nixon opted for autonomy and "closed the gold window" (Gowa 1983), practically dismissing the Bretton Woods system.

The USA exit from the Gold Exchange Standard left Western European countries disorientated. Dollar devaluation and the introduction of a 10% tariff on imports in the USA eroded their commercial competitiveness and destabilised exchange rates between ECC partners (Eichengreen 2008, p. 131). This situation endangered both the communitarian agricultural policy based on subventions and the internal balance of trade between members.[2]

ECC member states developed a twofold strategy to face the crisis and collapse of the Bretton Woods system. Since the end of the 1960s, they had perceived the risk of the collapse. So they planned to create a single European currency, establishing a monetary union among the EEC countries. That union had to also include the UK and sterling as soon as the negotiation for UK membership ended. This union had been designed with the Werner Plan in 1970, and a three-step timeline for full monetary integration agreed. When the Bretton Woods system collapsed, ECC countries developed a parallel strategy. They continued to pursue monetary unification, while, in the meantime, they searched for an agreement with the USA to restore international currency stability. In December 1971, the so-called "Smithsonian Agreement" defined a new system of pegged exchange rates in which currencies fluctuated against the dollar within restricted bands. EEC member states agreed to maintain narrower fluctuation bands between communitarian currencies to avoid excessive revaluation and devaluation that

[2] Howarth (2000, p. 16) contests the relevance of the currency floating impact on the Common Agricultural Policy aid system.

could endanger internal stability. Thus, they created the so-called "Monetary Snake".[3]

Both European strategies proved ruinous. The Werner Plan was an untimely attempt at monetary integration, and the financial turmoil in the early 1970s undermined its realisation. On the other hand, the dollar fluctuations after 1971 and the weak American commitment to stabilising its currency made the Smithsonian Agreement useless. So the Monetary Snake had to be changed and unlocked from the dollar. It became a regional monetary system to stabilise EEC currency reciprocal exchange rates and to keep them within a limited fluctuation band.

Unfortunately, the diverging impact of dollar devaluation on EEC member states' economies and the first oil shock in 1973 made the Snake unsustainable for many countries and, as a consequence, the Werner Plan for monetary unification unachievable. The dramatic rise in oil price led to a balance of payments deterioration in many countries and only those countries with a considerable surplus were able to face the consequent crisis. The others had their currency devalued, and they were unable to stabilise their exchange rates and remain in the fluctuation bands of the Snake. By

---

[3] The Monetary Snake in its first version (named "Snake in the Tunnel") emerged from an agreement signed in April 1972 by the EEC members and joined by the UK and Denmark in May 1972. Norway also agreed to be associated with the Snake to keep its currency exchange rate toward the EEC currencies stable. The agreement established fluctuation margins for the agreement subscribers' currencies that were stricter than those established by the Smithsonian Agreement and referred to the dollar. This allowed fluctuations between European currencies to be reduced. When the Smithsonian Agreement was abandoned and fluctuations were no longer referred to the dollar, a new version of the Snake (now named simply "the Snake" or "the Snake without the tunnel") remained operative for a few years in an attempt to maintain stability between the Snake members' currencies (Apel 1998, p. 36–41; Eichengreen 2008, p. 149–157; Marsh 2009, p. 66–71).

1974 the Snake had almost dissolved and only Germany and a few other minor countries remained members.[4]

The 1973 oil crisis was a turning point for another reason. In fact, it drew the evolution of the international financial system toward a path that was incompatible with the reconstruction of the Bretton Woods system. The dramatic rise in the oil price diverted a considerable amount of funds toward the Arab countries. However, these countries did not have a banking structure and financial markets capable of using such an amount of money. So they searched for a safe place to keep their money and found it in Western Europe (mainly in London) and the USA. In London, the eurodollar market became crucial to recycling the so-called "petrodollars", which means dollars paid to Arab countries for their oil. Banks used petrodollars to finance the trade deficits of industrialised nations as well as the most promising developing countries (Solomon 1999, p. 34–35). Also, Arabs used petrodollars to buy US bonds and agreed with the USA to quote and sell oil only for dollars. This agreement revitalised the US dollar's role as the leading international currency. In other words, the oil crisis and the agreement with the Arabs restored the role of the US dollar as the main reserve currency, creating a sort of "oil exchange standard" in which the "black gold" took the place of the real gold (Spiro 1999). However, petrodollars recycle and the new international monetary system required excellent capital mobility, financial market liberalisation and sophisticated financial instruments to manage investments. These needs and the interest of the USA and the UK in using their competitive advantage in financial activity fuelled the rise of financialisation of the international economy. This process explains USA and UK pressures for free circulation of capital since the early

[4] The UK and Denmark withdrew from the Snake in June 1972. Italy and France left in February 1973 and January 1974, respectively. France rejoined the Snake in June 1975 but left again in March 1976 (Eichengreen 2008, p. 153).

1980s and the indifference of the USA toward rebuilding a fixed exchange rate system like the Bretton Woods one.

On the other hand, sterilisation of dollar balances became crucial to stabilising the dollar exchange rate and granting its role as the primary international currency. The USA needed commercial partners disposed to collecting and keeping a significant amount of dollars, thereby avoiding massive and sudden sales of the American currency on the international markets. So a situation similar to the blocked sterling balances of the 1940s and 1950s emerged. However, the role of dollars collector gave the collector an advantage in negotiating with the USA and increased the relevance of these countries in international politics.

2 – The rise of the communitarian solution

The Jamaica Conference in 1975 indicated the official end of the Bretton Woods system and the passage to an international monetary system of fluctuating currencies (Haberler 1977, p. 1–30). In the meantime, the collapse of the Monetary Snake in Europe induced EEC countries to search for arrangements other than the fixed or pegged exchange rates. However, attempts to cooperate with the USA on dollar stabilisation proved unsuccessful.

The 1978 dollar crisis was the turning point for both the USA and EEC member states. In the USA, the dramatic fall of the US dollar induced President Carter to change his economic policy, supporting the rise of Paul Volker as Chairman of the Federal Reserve System. Volker made inflation reduction his primary target and increased dramatically the discount rate, initiating a period of restrictive economic policy (Helleiner 1994, p. 131–135; Solomon 1999, p. 7). In Europe, the French President Giscard d'Estaing and the German Chancellor Schmidt agreed to create the European Monetary System. One of the main reasons for this choice, probably the most important one, was their ambition to contrast the impact of dollar fluctuations on EEC member states' domestic economy (Henning 1998, p. 557; Dyson and Featherstone 1999, p. 2; Howarth 2000, p. 1; Eichengreen 2008, p. 145; Mourlon-Druol 2012, p. 279). So, as happened in the late 1960s, monetary integration was not a deliberate strategy to change the European faith and reshape the economic and political structure of the ECC member states. Instead, it was a third-best solution adopted because of the lack of a broader range of solutions and the inability of national politics to face the impact of exogenous shocks.

The new American monetary policy implemented by Volker and the almost simultaneous rise in power of Margaret Thatcher in the UK and Ronald Reagan in the USA shaped the future of the world economy and made EEC monetary coordination still more problematic. This situation strengthened EEC member states' interest in monetary integration. In the meantime, the dramatic rise in US interest rates undermined the stability of Latin American economies, increasing the cost of their public and private debt. This increase triggered a general debt crisis initiated by the Mexican crisis and ended only in the early 1990s (Solomon 1999, p. 34–37).

The second oil shock derived from the Iranian revolution and the rise in power of the Khomeini regime hit Western countries and generated inflation. The oil shock, combined with the American monetary policy impact, also boosted interest rates outside the USA. So industrialised nations went into recession in 1982 (Solomon 1999, p. 37).

The election of Ronald Reagan as President of the USA and the launching of the so-called "Reaganomics" magnified the impact of American economic policy on EEC domestic economies and contributed to destabilising the currency balance between EEC members further. In fact, during the first years of the Reagan administration, high-interest rates attracted funds in the USA and sustained the US dollar revaluation. A rising deficit in the US balance of trade appeared, mainly financed by the incoming funds. The other pillar of Reaganomics, tax cuts inspired by the supply-side approach, boosted the US budget deficit. So a "double deficit" appeared in the trade balance and US budget (Solomon 1999, p. 8). Both of these deficits were sustainable only in the short term. Capital inflow and demand for US bonds as interest-bearing reserves in dollars covered the twin deficits for a while. However, this situation could not last forever.

In the mid-1980s the US government felt the need to reverse its economic and monetary policy, searching for a devaluation of the US dollar against the German mark and the yen, i.e. the USA's strongest commercial competitors. The problem was that of coordination with Western partners to avoid undermining the dollar's position as a reserve currency. In fact, it was the role of the US dollar as the main international currency to grant funds to cover the twin deficits and the independence of USA domestic economic policy from external constraints.

The relationship between domestic economic policy and external constraints is the crucial element in explaining the government's attitudes toward currency matters. Electoral dynamics and the stay in power of governments heavily depend on the ability to manage the national economy and welfare. So an unmanageable domestic economy destabilised by the influence of exogenous decisions and the structural constraints of the international economic system is the worst scenario for national governments. This statement was especially true in 1980s Europe where state intervention in the economy and welfare state was the essential tool in gaining and maintaining consensus. So the problem America tried to avoid in the mid-1980s with international monetary cooperation was particularly significant for the European nation states too. They did not have the power and the influence to insulate their domestic economies from international disturbances the USA had thanks to the dollar. The need to face the impact of American monetary policy, the convenience of coordinating EEC currencies before agreeing on coordination with the USA, the power asymmetry that favoured the USA and the rising influence of international finance made EEC currency coordination unavoidable. This does not mean that European monetary integration was inevitable too. However, the need for EEC currency coordination made monetary integration and monetary union a potential outcome.

The relevance of external constraints in limiting domestic economic policies became evident in France during the early years of the Mitterrand presidency. When the socialist party gained the French presidency, the new President François Mitterrand tried to implement a left-inspired economic policy centred on state support for the industrial sector and employment, and the reduction of the working week. However, this economic policy resulted in inconsistency with the international position of the French economy. Capital outflows, French Franc devaluation and inflation followed, and France lost economic competitiveness, particularly if compared with Germany. This induced Mitterrand to make a so-called "U-turn" in economic policy and the search for currency stability (Helleiner 1994, p. 140). The Mitterrand economic plan is a reminder of many of the proposals of today's critics of monetary integration. It is astonishing that the lesson of mid-1980s France and the evidence of the impossibility of developing an autonomous economic policy merely by ignoring the international context and exogenous constraints have been forgotten by modern opponents of the EMU.

The new French economic policy defined during the 1980s was based on two essential elements: the *franc fort* and the *désinflation compétitive*,[5] both oriented toward creating a sta-

[5] The *désinflation compétitive* was the strategy adopted by France from the mid-1980s to regain competitivity toward German production. Instead of devaluing the franc as happened in the past, the French government tried to reduce inflation to a lower rate than the German one. This would progressively make French goods cheaper or just not more expensive than the German

ble link between the French and the German economy. The *franc fort* policy aimed to avoid French franc devaluation against the German mark while *désinflation compétitive* was the only strategy France found to recover competitiveness against low-inflation countries such as Germany without devaluing the French franc.

So in the 1980s there was a twofold cooperation problem. EEC countries had to cooperate with the USA for international monetary stability, and in the meantime, they had to work together to preserve EEC internal monetary stability and to maintain reciprocal positions in the balance of trade gained by EEC members. Keeping intra-European trade balanced also meant keeping internal levels of employment stable and having the possibility of developing midterm strategies and policies without undermining electoral consensus; this means respecting the primary constraint that links economics and politics.

The increasing financialisation of the international economy made European and international monetary cooperation more complicated to achieve. In fact, increasing capital mobility and pressures from banks and the financial sector against capital controls as well as the technological evolution in telecommunication emphasised the destabilising potential of capital flows and speculation. Also, the growing British and American advantage in the financial sector attracted EEC countries toward capital liberalisation. In the meantime, European firms oriented toward mass production needed a broader internal market to expand their production and keep costs low to compete with American and Japanese concurrences. Both of these requirements (financial liberalisation and internal market enlargement) derived mainly from the evolution of the international economy. This development resulted in a reduced level of international coordination and a

ones. In the meantime, the stability of the French franc (the *franc fort*) should avoid the capital outflow experienced in the early 1980s (Malinvaud et al. 1992; Aeschimann and Riché 1996; Howarth 2000, p. 102–106).

prevalence of specific national policies that imposed on other countries an adapt-or-perish logic. However, the globalisation of finance was not only the consequence of the shift from embedded liberalism to deregulation induced by the prevalence of the neo-liberal economic paradigm. Diverging interests and economic paths made it almost impossible to rebuild an international financial system using international agreements.

EEC countries in the late 1970s and early 1980s faced these external challenges using the integration strategy and the existing set of institutions, rules and tools. The creation of the European Monetary System and the relaunch of European integration using the Single European Act followed.[6] These events marked the full entry of the European monetary problem into the communitarian box. However, there is no proof that this was a long-term strategy defined from the start of European integration. Instead, European integration at that time seems to have been a garbage-can-style policy by which a solution successfully applied before, intergovernmental management of a shared problem using supranational institutions, was rekindled to face new collective problems that the single member states proved unable to solve alone. Again, as happened in the 1950s, further European integration "saved" European nation states, or rather the economies of member states and the ability of national governments to continue to manage them.

3 – The road to Hannover. National interests, supranational challenges and European economic governance before the euro

The history of monetary integration in the 1970s and 1980s reveals two fundamental characteristics of that process. First,

[6] The Single European Act was signed in 1986 and enforced from July 1987. It reformed the decisional procedures and other elements of EEC political cooperation. However, its main innovation regarded the launch of the single market and the cohesion policy. For the negotiation of the Single European Act see Moravcsik (1999, p. 314–378).

monetary coordination and its insertion in the communitarian context, as well as some other fundamental steps in European economic integration, was a reaction to external challenges that single member states were unable to face by themselves. However, national solutions and international cooperation remained the first and preferred strategies to address these challenges. So, as suggested by Mourlon-Druol (2012, p. 6), European monetary integration during that period can be understood only by adopting a combined approach of supranational, transnational and intergovernmental perspectives. When both national and international arrangements failed, European integration became the only game in town, at least the only that could work. This meant that European integration in some instances (and monetary integration was one of them) resulted from the need of solutions to remain connected to an international monetary and economic system that ECC countries (Germany and France in particular) were unable to influence and shape to their needs.

Second, the domestic needs of national governments were the main criteria that inspired monetary integration. The U-turn in French economic policy under Mitterrand, as well as the German agreement to monetary coordination by the EMS and later the desperate efforts of Italy, Spain and Greece to join the EMU, did not indicate a deliberate deviation from national political traditions. On the contrary, these choices derived from the attempts of national governments to regain autonomy in their domestic policies and, consequently, to continue governing their countries without changing the structure of power that granted the electoral consensus to the governing elites. This logic explains why today some of the EMU member states (e.g. Italy) that see EMU governance and rules as a threat to their internal structure of power have moved toward contesting the EU and its regulations. On the other hand, this explanation challenges both the neo-functionalist and, partially, the intergovernmental theories of European integration. Notwithstanding national governments appear to be the leading actors of European integration, it is not their agreement that explains the advancement of integration. Rather, it is their conflicting domestic interests and the power asymmetries that determined the choices and the forms of integration. These resulted in the prevalence of the domestic interests of some member states over those of the others. More specifically, it was the combined and balanced interests and strategies of the French-German axis that prevailed in many cases. Monetary integration was one of them.

The case of the European Monetary System and its evolution from its rise to its crisis support these conclusions. Probably the EMS, as organised in the early 1980s, was the best working solution for European economic integration. Instead, monetary unification was not an unavoidable need for an efficient European single market as suggested by the neo-functionalist approach (Connolly 1997). If we consider something more than simple market integration, including convergence, monetary policy and asymmetrical shock management in member countries, probably the pegged but adjustable exchange rates in the EMS of the early 1980s were the better compromises. The EMS, as organised at that time, allowed agreement on the central parity of each EEC country collectively and enabled it to be adjusted to the real performance of its economy keeping its value close to the market value. This agreement made adjustments and declared parities credible and avoided the rise of structural imbalances as happened during the early years of the EMU.

The main problem with the EMS was a political one. In fact, it did not mirror the political balance of power in continental Europe, namely the French leadership. Instead, the EMS reinforced the German economic predominance and made the Bundesbank monetary policy the leading policy that oriented the economy in all the other member states. German predominance was acceptable for many EEC countries, both those considered German satellites like the Netherlands and those that could rely on realignments of their parities such as Italy. France, on the other hand, could not accept having its domestic economic policy subordinated either to German or American monetary policies. The adoption of the *franc fort* and the *désinflation compétitive* strategies made German influence more annoying for the French government. Both strategies were oriented to keep France "as affordable as Germany" and "as competitive as Germany". Unfortunately, this meant that Germany led the game, because of the strength of the mark. It remains unclear whether France perceived the risk of favouring German monetary predominance when it supported the establishment of the EMS and, later, the progressive dismissal of exchange rate adjustment due to the passage to the "hard EMS".[7] Probably, what French negotiators undervalued was that the EMS rules gave Germany excessive discretion in interventions in the monetary market to keep the Deutsche mark stable. Germany profited from this opportunity by discharging on weaker countries the cost of realignment and maintaining broad autonomy in domestic economic policy.

As a consequence, the EMS became the battlefield for gaining economic predominance in Europe. The alteration of the central parity of member states' exchange rates could change the balance of competitiveness of EEC national economies. This change was not a significant problem for Germany because its low inflation allowed it to regain the competitiveness lost as a consequence of the devaluation of high-inflation countries' currencies. Moreover, in the 1980s the German and the Southern European economies were complementary, and devaluation of these currencies did not pe-

[7] During the period 1987–1992 there were no more realignments of EMS member countries' currencies, except for the Italian lira (slightly devalued in 1990). That period is sometimes referred to as "hard EMS" and considered a sort of preparatory phase for complete monetary integration. See Höpner and Spielau (2018).

nalise excessively German producers. Instead, France had to keep inflation low to implement the *franc fort* and the *désinflation compétitive* strategies and could not follow its main European competitors in devaluing. So freezing exchange rates and avoiding the German mark predominance in the system (the so-called "EMS asymmetry") became the primary aim of the French government.

The attempt to pursue this strategy caused the stiffening and the subsequent collapse of the EMS. In fact, after 1987 and the Basle-Nyborg Agreement, parity adjustments were tacitly eliminated, and the EMS became unofficially an almost fixed exchange rate system. France probably saw the new EMS as a prototype of an incoming monetary union (Connolly 1997, p. 80 and 110). Again, the accusation by anti-euro activists against the EMU, which they saw as a German creation, of imposing its predominance is denied by history.

The EMS did not survive long enough to move to a monetary union. In the early 1990s, a deadly mix of problems undermined the EMS's stability and made fixed exchange rates almost unsustainable for many EEC member states. Capital flow liberalisation, international recession, a reduction in competitiveness in high-inflation countries and the impact of German reunification destabilised the EMS. The high-interest rate policy adopted by the Bundesbank to attract funds for reconstruction in the East caused capital outflows from the peripheral countries that were compelled to raise their interest rates. Capital outflows and interest rate escalation had deadly consequences for member states' economies, particularly in those hit hard by years of an overvalued currency. When speculative market pressures became unsustainable, the weaker countries started to leave the EMS. France too had to face speculative attacks that it rejected thanks to German support. By the end of 1993, the EMS had become an almost fluctuating monetary system where oscillation bands had been enlarged to ±15% of the central parity.

The lesson of the EMS is crucial in anticipating the EMU problems. Many difficulties emerged during the EMS period that did not disappear after the crisis with the system. They remained in the shadows until a new monetary system, more rigid and inescapable than the EMS, was built. Then, most of the problems and misfunctioning of the EMS reappeared to endanger the suitability of EMU and the euro. This means that these problems were structural problems magnified by rigid monetary systems that cannot be ignored while rebuilding a new and definitive European currency.

Notwithstanding their economic nature, most of these problems had predominantly political origins. The political nature of monetary integration is evident in the case of France. Since the early years of the Mitterrand presidency, binding German monetary policy to the French one was a strategy to contrast the German economic predominance in Europe and reduce French dependency on German economic policy. On the other hand, other countries like Italy saw monetary integration as a tool for imposing internal stability and reforms as well as attracting cheap money for funding the public debt. So both France and Italy (and other countries) considered the EMS and monetary coordination primarily for domestic policies and as a means to stabilise European economic relations and to reduce their impact on domestic policy. Germany accepted monetary coordination and the EMS in the same internal policy light, notwithstanding a different perspective. In fact, what Germany needed to do was to protect the internal economy from both dollar fluctuation and devaluation of other EEC members' currencies. So stable exchange rates were an advantage for the German economy, and the French pressures for monetary coordination were acceptable, but the other EMS members had to adapt their economic policies to the German ones while Germany continued to adopt its economic policy model. Unfortunately, the German model of *Stabilitatghemeinshaft* and the "Latin" model of *Gouvernement Economique* are politically incompatible (Dyson and Featherstone 1999, p. 31–32). In fact, the government's consensus and the fate of political elites in those countries with a tradition of governmental intervention in economic management depended on the results of this action. So adapting these economic systems to the principle and the policies required by the German model had enormous political and economic costs. Consequently, the capability and the willingness of some countries to accept the consequences of German economic policy and respect the obligations derived from the EMS agreements were limited. Germany accepted the EMS as a different and more favourable context in which continuing to work in the same way Germany was usual to work.

On the other hand, Southern European countries were politically and economically weaker than France and Germany and their ability to resist adaptive shocks induced by the EMS working rules was low. So after the 1980s these countries demonstrated their limits in following rules, keeping exchange rate parities and reforming their economic systems to make them compatible with the EMS, particularly when the hard EMS was adopted. Thus, devaluation was avoided, and peripheral countries lost competitivity progressively while their governments had to face the effects of capital mobility liberalisation on their public debts. So funds' volatility and interest rates became the fundamental international economic problem they had to face.

The EMS crisis in 1992–93 and the events that generated it revealed the limits of the EMS and the whole European monetary construction. When Germany had to choose between funding reconstruction in the Eastern regions regaining consensus lost because of the effects of reunification, and avoiding spreading that impact to the other EMS member states generating a constant rise in international interest rates, Germany opted for domestic interest. On the other hand, when the economic impact of German policy in the most affected countries became economically and politically unsustainable, these countries exited the EMS (Solomon 1999, p. 59–61; Höpner and Spielau 2018, p. 165).

Asymmetric economic models and policies, the predominance of domestic interests, and the limited affordability of Southern countries' governments in accepting the consequences and costs of membership in a fixed exchange rate system were the main lessons derived from the EMS experience. However, two other elements emerged in the early 1990s as a consequence of the EMS and its crisis. First, the inability of governments and central banks in a regime of capital mobility freedom to keep international speculation and financial markets under control became evident. The collapse of the EMS was also a defeat for the nation states and a demonstration of the power of new actors no longer constrained by political will. Second, the EMS crisis and fall demonstrated how the economic crisis in the de-ideologised post-cold war Europe could activate political mechanisms of consensus collapse and political structure reshaping as happened in Italy in the first half of the 1990s where tensions generated by the EMS constraints fed the collapse of a political system based on clientelist relationships supported by the government budget.

5 – Building the European Monetary Union

The lessons described above poorly influenced the following steps toward EMU. They were probably not only forgotten but voluntarily undervalued by the EMU architects. The latter considered the choice for monetary integration a predominantly political decision and they saw at the "momentum" as a unique and unmissable opportunity for such a final jump toward integration.

The collapse of the EMS was almost concomitant with the signature of the Maastricht Treaty, which defined a three-stage road to monetary unification. So the central dilemma for European monetary integration during the 1990s was deciding who to admit into the EMU, while also considering the situation of each country after the EMS collapse. But inadequate attention was paid to the structural obstacles to monetary integration that emerged with the EMS crisis. The need for effective governance of the EMU as well as for clear rules and coercive instruments to enforce these rules was undervalued or almost ignored.

Paradoxically, failing to stay in the EMS made some countries better candidates for the EMU. These countries (e.g. Italy) profited from currency devaluation and gained competitiveness toward French and German competitors. So leaving these countries outside the EMU meant leaving them free to gain from their "bad behaviour" in the early 1990s and to devalue further to remain competitive. In fact, one of the main problems of building the EMU was that it did not reform the existing status of the ECC/EU member countries, it just integrated it. So being excluded from the EMU did not mean exclusion from the single market as happens today for those countries that could legally leave the EMU only leaving the EU.

These considerations inspired by the national interests of the leading EC countries opened the door to the admission of almost all applicants for EMU membership, notwithstanding many of them did not fulfil the requirements to be admitted. It was a political choice in which economic reasoning was poorly considered. It was evident that some countries that were economically weak like Greece and Portugal or overburdened by high public debt and limited administrative capacity like Italy were not suitable for respecting the admission criteria or converging quickly toward the most advanced European economies. In the same way and for the same reason, the original EMU governance was inadequate, inefficient and unable to compel member states to respect both the stability criteria and the logic of monetary integration. Nevertheless, the primary objective of the French-German axis was to create a full monetary union that would force their leading European trade partners to adapt their own economic policies to theirs. These countries agreed to join this "monetary prison" because in the short term they had a lot to gain and almost nothing to lose. The so-called "satellites" of France and Germany had already adapted their economic and monetary policy to those of their more powerful partners. However, peripheral countries saw the opportunity to gain from EMU admission in terms of reduced interest rates and political capital to invest in structural reforms justified by the entry prize.

Another political reason induced the adoption of flexible criteria for admission in the EMU. While the Germans worried about Italy's instability and poor ability to stay in a monetary union, France saw Italy as a potential ally in counterbalancing the German predominance in the EMU (Dyson and Featherstone 1999, p. 8–9). When Lionel Jospin became the French Prime Minister, he called for a less technocratic and ordoliberal vision of the EMU and more attention given to social aspects of integration. Here, there was a broad convergence with the Italian government. So admitting Italy into the EMU became a political objective and the relaxation of the admission criteria an operative need. Again, political considerations prevailed in terms of economic logic and the EMU became larger than expected and weaker than required.

Chapter 3

History and Political Choices in European Monetary Integration

In the previous chapters, we analysed the historical process that shaped monetary relations in Europe from the ending of the classical Gold Standard to the introduction of the euro. These chapters are not merely a lengthy introduction to the current situation and the problems the EMU is facing today. Neither are they an independent part of this book devoted to one of many perspectives for analysing monetary integration. Rather, the aim of the first part of this book is to use the history of monetary integration to identify those processes that define the politics of the EMU today. This is what we will try to do in this chapter.

Studying politics through history is a widespread and widely tested method. Some scholars refer to history for demonstrating their theories or drawing lessons for policy-making. Others study the past believing that what happened necessarily explains what happens today. Unfortunately, these approaches to the "use of history" are too simplistic and handicapped by poor methodological assumptions as well as limited mastery of the additional disciplines needed to understand history. So many non-historians draw from history only those elements that support their theories, dismissing other aspects they undervalue, while many historians apply to today's problems obsolete explanations and lose many contextual and structural influences they never observed in the past.

The Latins called history *Magistra vitae* (teacher of life), suggesting that what happened in the past gives us lessons we can apply in ordinary life. Notwithstanding this concept was abandoned by professional historians decades ago, reminiscences of this ancient view have survived in many other students from different disciplines who try to use history for building their theories or explaining long-term processes. Unfortunately, there are structural reasons that made history a confused teacher in an empty classroom. So "using history" for theory building and policymaking requires a robust methodological approach that draws abundantly from many different disciplines and scientific methods. This is particularly true for economic history, which in the case of the EMU connects three cultures: history, economics and political science.

In the European integration case, history is crucial for two sectors: policy design and theory building. While policies previously adopted in history help in designing better policies or anticipating risks, history is crucial for defining how the rise and consolidation of the European Union was determined. So history as output helps policy design and history as a process supports theory building, at least in those cases in which European integration theory aims to explain the whole process of European integration.

This chapter will analyse the difficulties of using history for policymaking and theory building, identifying some methodological problems, drawing some lessons and applying them to the case of monetary integration. It will be demonstrated that many historical lessons are not applicable to policymaking due to the specific mechanisms of the decisional process and the retroactivity of historical experiences, the inconceivability among different historical perspectives and the instrumental use of history in politics. In addition, the use of history in European integration theory when applied to monetary integration will be criticised mainly because of certain biases deeply rooted in the historical approaches to European integration.

1 – Many histories and multiple truths

History is a discipline fragmented into many different sectors. In the case of European integration, economic history, political history, diplomatic history, cultural history and the history of institutions propose different approaches to the same process, emphasise the relevance of different elements, and identify different and sometimes conflicting explanations for the same outcomes. These differences are partially explained by the different methodological approaches adopted and the different importance assigned to the components of the processes analysed. Economic history derives from the historical materialist approach and evolved from a socio-economic analysis of economic activities to structural analysis of economic interactions. So political decisions are often interpreted as the consequence of structural constraints imposed by the economic system, particularly the international one.

Conversely, diplomatic history pays much more attention to the interaction between politicians and between institutions' representatives (e.g. central bankers, officers, delegates). So the key explanatory roles are reserved for personal and attitudinal elements in negotiations and policymaking while structural constraints are widely undervalued. Political history and the history of institutions' focus mainly on political actors, national politics, the evolution of domestic and international institutions, and the political processes that shape the national and European context, sometimes adopting a comparative approach. Finally, under the label "cultural history", many specific approaches to European integration can be regrouped, mainly centred on the influence of different ideas, theories and ideologies in shaping the process. Recently, the rise of the feminist approach to international relations also increased the relevance of gender history and new elements to explain the whole process of integration will probably gain relevance in the future.

What is important now is to understand that so many approaches to the same historical process support many conflicting explanations of the process. Consequently, it is difficult for decision-makers and theoreticians to draw pragmatic elements from history.

The fragmentation of history described above becomes particularly complex when history interacts with other disciplines. If we consider just one case (economic history), we note that it evolved in at least two different directions with different objectives, methodologies and focuses. Since Adam Smith, elements of what we call today economic history have been used in economic theory. Marxist theory emphasised economic history as an analytical perspective for politics, economics and sociology. Later, many other economists like Keynes, Schumpeter and Friedman used economic history in support of their theories. However, economic history remained mainly history and used the traditional methodologies of that discipline. Later, quantitative and econometric instruments were applied to economic history and part of the discipline was included in economics while the focus became testing economic theories and discovering long-term trends. So economic historians were split between those with a historical background and a specific interest in social and political fields and those with an economic education mainly interested in economic variables. In this book, we have adopted the first approach we call the political science approach to economic history to stress that it aims to support a political science analysis of the intended. More specifically, our aim in using economic history is to support both policy analysis and European integration theory building.

European integration has been studied mainly by economic, political and diplomatic historians. This influenced deeply the way in which European integration has been interpreted and represented, and how it influenced theories of European integration and, less incisively, political decisions. None of these approaches is exhaustive, and none is comfortably merged with the others. So the prevalence of one of these perspectives and its contamination of other scientific disciplines created more distortions than knowledge.

Another essential element of fragmentation in historical analysis is the time perspective, in particular, the dichotomy of the long-term vs the mid- and short-term perspective. This dichotomy depends on a different view of history flow and historical processes. While some scholars see history as a continuum and consider historical processes as a chain of cause-effect relationships, others reject this view, representing history as a segmented line interrupted or deviated by epochal events, critical junctures, turning points, external shocks and crises. While the continuity approach works better in the short-term analysis, the segmented approach fits much better for long-term processes. Also, different historical perspectives fit differently with short-term or long-term perspectives. Diplomatic and political history capture better the "spirit of the moment", while international economic history and the history of institutions allow more in-depth analysis of mid-term and long-term processes as well as the correct evaluation of external influences notwithstanding many elements, sometimes crucial in determining a crisis or a turning point, are lost.

Before starting to analyse how history shapes policy analysis and theory building it is crucial to distinguish between "scientific history" and "narrative history". Policymaking results from actors' interaction in policy arenas. Each actor has specific interests, aims and strategies it carries out using a partisan approach and negotiating some common solutions with other actors. So historical experiences appear to be relevant for policymakers only if these experiences support their view. This means that history can help policymakers during the policy planning phase, especially in technical environments, but its impact on final policy choices depends more on the predominant policymakers and less on the relevance of the historical experience. Also, when history plays a role in addressing policymaking, it will be the specific perspective accepted by policymakers that plays that role instead of history in general. In the case of theory building, different and simplified analysis of history addresses theory toward diverging results and reduce the theories' soundness in a comparable way to the level of history simplification preferred by theorists.

Lessons drawn from history are different and contradictory depending on the analytical approach adopted. Both neo-liberals and Keynesians refer to history for their policymaking prescriptions. Liberals and Marxists did the same thing in the 19th century. However, their interpretations of history diverge consistently, and policy proposals contrast, notwithstanding history unicity. Sometimes, retroactivity of historical experiences shapes policy design, often in a negative way. Policy choices that had been depicted for decades as characteristic of political adversaries or associated with abhorred regimes will be discharged almost automatically notwithstanding their effectiveness or the possibility of adapting them to new political regimes. Finally, history has been used almost continuously as a policy tool to legitimise policy choices or to make political communication more convincing. In this case, scientificity has lost all its relevance and the history used is an "imagined history" misunderstood and misleadingly interpreted, and sometimes it never happened. This kind of history is the one preferred by extreme and populist parties and movements and it is crucial in the public and media debate on the EMU.

In terms of policy analysis, time perspectives and decisional styles are crucial. Long-term analysis is problematic when interests are under consideration. Voters, entrepreneurs and politicians think from a short/mid-term perspective. On the other hand, political cultures, institutions, ideologies and practices change over more extended periods, and sometimes for an extended period only. Decisions also depend on different elements that have had an impact on decisional styles. In individual and collective choices, psychological, psychiatric and neurological components have a different weight. They could be relevant in personal decisions, making them more erratic, while collective choices respond to more regular decisional models widely studied.

2 – History and policy analysis: the case of the EMU

As explained above, the connection between the historical process of monetary integration discussed in the previous chapters and the politics of monetary integration discussed in the chapters that follow depends on the analytical perspective adopted. In this case, we decided to take a policy analysis perspective in which history is instrumental in defining three elements: processes, strategies and policies. Processes have been depicted in the previous chapters of this book. Their analysis permits the identification and discussion of some policy dilemmas that are still crucial for monetary integration today in defining strategies and policies that have addressed monetary integration as well as the different options at the disposal of policymakers for consolidating, reforming or dismantling the EMU.

What remains unclear to many opponents and apologists of the euro is that many of the crucial dilemmas that national and European policymakers faced in the 1990s still remain unsolved today. Also, some of these dilemmas have fed scientific and political debate since the 1930s, and the crisis of the late 2000s just revamped debates instead of solving them. Answering these dilemmas is an unavoidable step toward long-term policy choices such as those proposed today about consolidating or dismissing the euro, the relevance of European integration for the survival of nation states in Europe and the best economic policies for overcoming the crisis. However, these dilemmas remain unsolved and could stay unsolved virtually for decades. So, as usual, policymakers cannot rely on certainty and need to adopt other criteria than undefined optimality for deciding strategies and policies. Moreover, they have to define a mix of policies to catch a mix of targets they consider relevant and sufficient to solve the problems to be faced. Finally, they have to do all this by drawing on suggestions from different disciplines with different and sometimes divergent perspectives that propose conflicting and difficult-to-integrate solutions. We will see later in this book that policymakers' opponents have to do the same in proposing their alternative policy programmes. So the result is "policy ideologies" that take elements from different theories and disciplines and merge them into a seemingly coherent framework that inspires their choices or, better, that justifies them.

This policy planning method suggests that what matters in history for policy analyses are the solutions proposed in the past for problems still unsolved today as well as the constrictions for today's policy choices imposed by the past. Debates, solutions and results obtained in the past are the main contribution that history offers for policymakers as well as for policy theorists. In the meantime, understanding the historical context in which these results were obtained is crucial in understanding the reasons for success, failure and applicability to actual problems. Finally, history helps in identifying the long-term impact of past public policies, allowing continuity and coherence to be given to overlapping policies and making it possible to check whether successful choices made in the past still work or need to be dismantled to solve or face better the old problems in a new context or should be applied to new problems. So unsolved policy dilemmas are pivotal in defining the operative link between history and policy planning. These dilemmas are still unsolved on the table and add to new policy dilemmas in creating the challenges policymakers have to face today. However, solutions to unsolved dilemmas have been tested in the past. This means history offers explanations and data about past failures that can help to exclude ineffective solutions or to improve their effectiveness when applied to today's policy dilemmas. This is the path from history to policy we follow in this book.

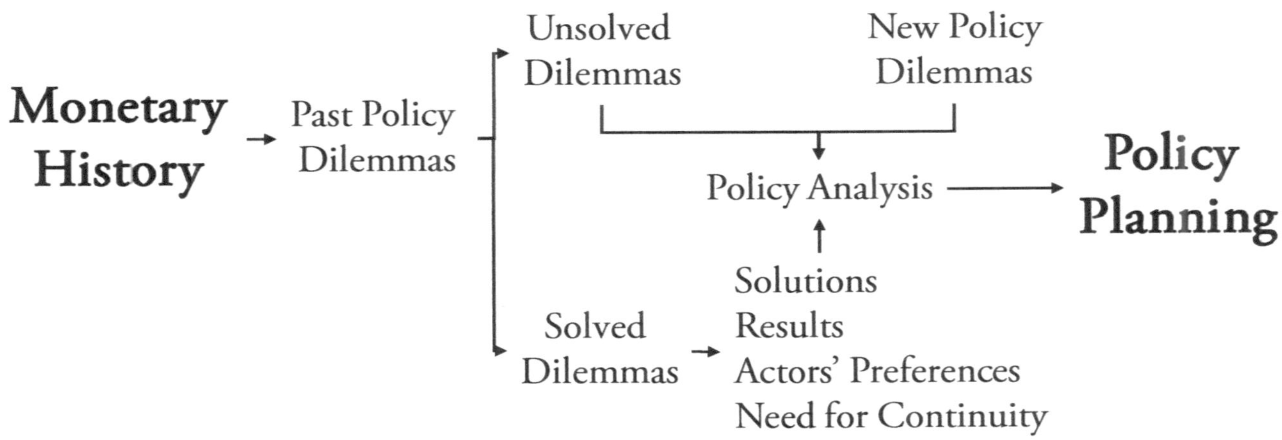

Fig. 3.1 – History analytic flow for policy planning.

There are at least four unsolved dilemmas that are crucial for contemporary European monetary policy planning as well as for understanding the choices that led to the euro. The first deals with the structure of international monetary relations and the dichotomy of "fixed vs floating" exchange rates. It emerged after World War I and remained on the table for the whole period examined in this book, becoming crucial between the late 1960s and the late 1970s. Today, in Europe, this dilemma is the core of the debate on staying in or leaving the EMU.

The second dilemma regards the level of government that best fits the international monetary problems, particularly those of European countries. In this case, there are three options: international cooperation, supranational agreements (European integration included) and independent national policies. This policy dilemma is particularly relevant in debates on the EMU's economic governance and on sovereignism supported by anti-EU parties (*see* Chapter 9). All these options were tried and tested during the historical period under examination in this book, and all of them showed some advantages and some problems that reverberated in the European integration process. This happened in particular for the EMU, connecting the second dilemma to the third one.

The third dilemma regards the troubled relation between economic governance and democracy. This dichotomy emerged almost at the same time as the instauration of democracy in industrialised countries and persists today as the engine of the most significant political contradiction of the European Union. Today, the conflicting priorities of EMU governance and democracy in the member states feed anti-Europeanism and make the euro one of the preferred targets for criticising European integration by both Eurosceptic parties and groups of academics.

Finally, the EMU faces today a fourth policy dilemma, which deals with the never exhausted debate about state intervention in the economic sphere. This debate, started by Adam Smith, found in the dichotomy of Keynesianism vs neo/ordoliberalism the way in which this dichotomy is debated today. Still today, the debates about the policy to face the international and the eurozone crisis as well as the economic convergence and the financial stabilisation policies depend on this dichotomy. Many academic critics of the EMU show Keynesians' attitudes (mainly neo-Keynesians) and see in the EMU rules and governance the main obstacles that hinder recovery and growth in the EU.

The four unsolved dilemmas profoundly influence both policy design and political debate in the EU member countries today. Academic debate, electoral programmes, political choices and many other elements in EU member states' politics turn around these four questions and shape proposals, interpretations, attitudes and political communication. So these dichotomies represent cleavages that characterise opponents in the EMU political arena. Governments and European institutions selected a set of answers to these dilemmas: fixed exchange rates, European-level agreements, economic governance priorities and liberalism. Opponents adopted the discharged options to build alternative scenarios to set against the "Europeanist front": floating exchange rates (including exiting the euro), the national level of government, the democracy priority and Keynesian-style economic policies.

The following classification of policy actors involved in EMU policy shaped by historical and unsolved debates on policy issues emerges from the economic history approach adopted in this book. In the table below, the systemic actors are all those policymakers, institutions, political parties, governments, academics, opinion makers and groups that support or at least accept the policy mix that prevailed in the EMU. On the other hand, anti-system actors are those who reject this policy mix and are almost compelled to focus on the alternative set of policy choices because of the coherence between policy solutions and the need to support their opposition with widely diffused and popular ideas and policy solutions. This mechanical convergence toward the alternative set depends on the complementarity of its elements. In fact, prioritising one element made the acceptance of the other elements of the same set almost compulsory both in policy design and in political communication. Past debates and academic literature connect these options and make it easier to justify these policy proposals furnishing a scientific background. So interdependencies between choices create "alternative coherences".

Table 3.1 – Policy preferences of contemporary actors

Policy dilemmas	*Systemic actors*	*Anti-systemic actors*
Exchange rates	Fixed	Floating
Level of government	Supranational	National
Political priority	Economic governance	Democratic responsiveness
Economic policy	Neo-/ordoliberal	Keynesian

Each couple of preferences depicted in Table 3.1 represents an unsolved policy dilemma for monetary integration, which we will discuss in what follows in this chapter, while also referring to the examples depicted in Table 3.2 and drawing from the historical evidence proposed in Chapters 1 and 2 of this book.

3 – International monetary systems and levels of governments

The first couple of interlinked dilemmas regard the structure of the international monetary system. Historically, we observed three kinds of monetary systems. The first was a worldwide monetary system based on fixed gold parities. This was the case with both the Classical Gold Standard and the Bretton Woods system. The second kind was a floating exchange rate system in which exchange rates depend on market transactions and single countries' balance of payments. This was the case in the early post-

World War I period and the post-Bretton Woods period (1970s–1980s). The third kind of monetary system is a regional system (instead of international) of fixed or pegged exchange rates. This was the case with the European Monetary System (pegged and adjustable and later almost fixed) and the EMU (fixed, non-adjustable). This third kind is a hybrid that usually coexists with an international floating system.

Table 3.2 – Monetary systems governance

Governance level	Exchange rate system	
	Fixed	*Floating*
International	Gold Exchange Standard	Jamaica System
European	EMU	Monetary Snake
National	1930s Bilateral clearings	Post-crisis systems
	Strong	*Weak*
	Governance strength	

The three kinds of systems were historically based on agreements at different levels of governments: international for fixed rates, national for floating rates and supranational (European in the case cited) for regional systems. This correspondence is a structural one; this means that these systems can be created and kept operative only if managed at their corresponding levels of government. So the choice for one of these exchange rate systems imposes agreements at the correspondent level and, as a consequence, the choice of a system determines the choice of the level of government that will implement that choice. The reverse is not necessarily true; this means that sometimes national governments can decide independently to peg their currencies to other states' currencies or an international standard. Similarly, the supranational level of government can arrange or coordinate monetary agreements at the international level representing a group of countries as in the sterling area case.

The debate on the best international exchange system (fixed vs floating exchange rates) gained relevance mainly in the 1960s when the limits of the Bretton Woods system became evident and the risk of its collapse concrete. Before, specifically in both the early post-war periods, few doubts existed about the preference for an international monetary system based on fixed exchange rates. After World War I, the restoration of the Gold Standard was a shared goal for all the leading countries, while in 1944 the two main alternatives were the restoration of the Gold Standard on a US dollar base (White Plan) or the establishment of an international clearing system based on an international currency (Keynes Plan). The latter was a kind of fixed exchange rate system that was more flexible regarding international liquidity management and balance of payments adjustments than the Gold Exchange Standard. However, it was substantially a fixed exchange rate system agreed and to be managed at the international level.

Doubts about the sustainability of an international monetary system of fixed exchange rates emerged in the early 1960s when both academic research and policy experience dismantled the certainties about the superiority and the sustainability of the fixed exchange system. From the academic side, the formulation of the optimal currency areas theory demonstrated that the world is not the ideal geographical dimension for a working monetary system based on fixed exchange rates. On the policy side, increasing difficulties in managing dollar convertibility and international monetary cooperation demonstrated that system governance was the main problem with this kind of system and that, if cooperation is lacking, managing convertibility is almost impossible. So the governance gap, determined by conflicting national interests and the inability to distribute the costs of adjustment in a balanced way, made both the post-war Gold Standard systems unmanageable and unstable, causing their collapse.

The historical analysis carried out in the previous chapters shows that the same problems that emerged for the international system undermined the regional systems. The collapse of the EMS and the problems of the EMU we will analyse in the following chapter emphasise the relevance of poor governance in making the system unstable. However, regional systems have at least two advantages if compared with the international fixed rate monetary systems. The first is a smaller number of members than a worldwide system. So making and managing agreements is easier than keeping a worldwide system operable. Second, regional partners, in particular in the case of the EMS and the EMU, share more common interests than the whole international system. This makes cooperation more convenient because members can distribute the costs of system adjustments in more sectors than just in the monetary one and side payments can compensate for the costs charged to some members when corresponding advantages emerge for other members.

The alternative to international or regional systems of fixed exchange rates is a floating currency system in which each country manages its currency following its national interests and, most importantly, exogenous and structural constraints. History demonstrates that this solution grants more flexibility than fixed exchange rates in national economic policies. In the meantime, the result is an anarchic international system with a massive imbalance in national power and international economic relations. While national governments have more room for independent economic policies, weaker countries are often victims of stronger countries and limited in their policy choices by unmanageable external constraints. On the other hand, in internationally managed systems of fixed or pegged rates, power imbalances are mitigated by the needs of the predominant members to keep the system operative and the members respecting the agreements. So another element to consider in defining preferences for a fixed or a floating exchange rate system is the economic and political relevance of each country.

Finally, historical evidence demonstrates that both the architecture and working of an international or supranational system depend on the interests of participants and the balance of power among its members. The White and the Keynes plans in Bretton Woods were "partisan" proposals inspired by the national interests of the USA and the British Empire, respectively. The international monetary systems proposed in Bretton Woods were shaped on the USA or British priorities and their current situation instead of the system workability and the general interests of its members. This made the system unstable when the relative interests of members and the leadership changed. The White Plan was the expression of a creditor country, as the USA was in 1944 and expected to remain for a long time after the end of the war. So the Americans proposed a system in which the debtors have to support the costs of the adjustments. When the American balance of payments changed and the USA became net debtors, that architecture was no longer comfortable for the system's leading country. In the meantime, those other members now advantaged by the new balance of power resisted the USA pressures for adjustments. Something similar happened in the European Monetary System where the distribution of the costs for keeping the system operative became unbalanced and some countries adopted domestic economic policies that were irrespective of the other members' interests and needs. So it has been historically demonstrated that international or supranational systems are structurally unstable and require flexible architecture and adaptability as well as members that pay due attention to the common interest and the system workability in the long term. Unfortunately, it seems very difficult to adopt these attitudes for a long time. Many factors change in the mid term (economic structures, exogenous variables, leaders, short-term national interests) and make divergence and systemic crisis almost assured. If applied to the EMU, this conclusion suggests that the euro as it is today cannot last forever and the architecture of the EU and the EMU governance needs to be updated and reinforced continuously to fit with an evolving context. This need is pivotal in the absence of a European political union.

4 – Economic governance and political regimes

Another crucial question that remains unsolved and is still crucial for defining today's policy choices regards the balance between economic governance and democratic responsiveness. It is widely demonstrated that authoritarian and oligarchic regimes have fewer problems to impose unpopular economic policies than democracies. However, the unstoppable diffusion and consolidation of democratic regimes in Europe since the 1920s made the friction between economic governance needs and voters' political requests the main point of friction for European governments. Also, the success of socialist and communist parties enhanced both the relevance of economic matters in a political fight and the awareness of the impact of these economic factors on everyday life by less educated people who were previously kept quiet by nationalist propaganda or religious paternalism.

The problem of respecting economic constraints, those derived from international agreements in particular, notwithstanding widespread domestic opposition was solved in the 1920s with repression by authoritarian regimes and democracy-outflanking measures by democratic governments. However, the rise of Nazi and filo-Nazi regimes in 1930s Central Europe led to the refusal to accept external economic constraints and the rejection of external obligation in favour of "the people's will".

After World War II, the contrast between the economic governance of internationally negotiated constraints and the democratic choice of economic policies was contained mainly by three arrangements. The first was the so-called "embedded liberalism" that inspired the Bretton Woods system (Ruggie 1982). State controls on capital flows, public investments for reconstruction, international trade expansion and international liquidity in dollars limited the domestic impact of the system constraints. However, it was the polarisation of Western European party systems that made the Bretton Woods system fitting with the "manipulated" democracy of the 1950s and 1960s. The ideological cleavage and the marginalisation of neo-fascist, communist and Marxist-Leninist parties as enemies of democracy induced the USA to friendly economic policies in favour of its allies and to the assumption by the Americans of the costs derived by this policies. Also, economic growth helped in relaxing of social conflicts.

The second arrangement that allowed economic governance and democracy to be combined was the welfare state. It was the pivotal compromise that reconciled capitalism, globalisation and democracy in Europe and acted as a side payment to popular classes for accepting capitalism and its duties. Also, it was the link that connected right and left parties (extreme left parties too, at least in some cases) and a crucial anchor for democracy. The welfare state was a "long-term promise" the governments made to the working class and the state employees for a progressive transfer of resources and benefits guaranteed by a state that had to survive and prosper to keep its promise. This legitimated governments in their economic governance and economic policies, particularly when the economic trend favoured further concessions.

The third arrangement that allowed economic governance and democracy to be combined was the adoption of Keynesian-style policies based on public investments and the promotion of full employment. It is widely accepted that a growing economy fuels support for the government in charge and makes unpopular choices more acceptable. Also, when an economy grows it becomes difficult to distinguish between the costs of external constraints and the impact of economic governance. So the opposition is low, and the government action legitimised.

Unfortunately, all these arrangements were interconnected, precarious and depended on variables that were out of the national government's control. In the previous chapters, we saw how the "embedded liberalism" created by the Bretton Woods system was unsustainable in the long term. The collapse of that system did not eliminate the national government's ability to keep their countries "embedded". However, the costs of embedding and losing opportunities increased. Also, the economic crises that followed the Bretton Woods system dismissal delegitimated governments in charge and reduced the resources for further welfare state enhancement and budget-spending economic policies.

Moreover, the mix of economic crisis and dismissal of convertibility resurrected something similar to the currency gap problems of the 1930s and early 1950s, at least for the weaker countries. Western European countries that did not have a universally accepted currency needed not just funds but hard currencies to keep their domestic economies operative. Thus, external constraints that resulted from the Bretton Woods agreement were replaced by external structural constraints that were more challenging to manage than the previous ones. This problem is a structural one, and it still exists today, notwithstanding many supporters of the EMU dismission widely undervalued it.

The welfare state in Europe has been gradually reduced because of high costs, budget constraints and the unsustainability in the long term of expensive systems conceived in a time of demographic expansion. The enrichment of workers in Western Europe and the possibility of letting them pay more for welfare as well as the attempt to keep national economies competitive through wage cuts or containment made welfare reduction sustainable in the mid term. However, welfare reforms made the "promise" of increasing and irrevocable well-being and social security ephemeral and no longer credible. Also, welfare reorganisation coexisted with a reduction of the workers' rights conceived to increase profits using the precariousness of jobs and the wider exploitation of workers. It is important to distinguish between the two processes (welfare reorganisation and the reduction of workers' rights) because they are two different outcomes of the interaction between globalisation and neo-liberalism. Budget constraints and the demographic trends were unavoidable while the reduction of workers' rights resulted in a simplistic and partially ideological reaction to the reorganisation of the world economy and trade after the fall of the Bretton Woods system. Financialisation, the inclusion of low-wage countries in advanced economic areas like the American and the European ones, and the rise of the Chinese economy created insurmountable pressures for a "beggar-your-workers" rush, state retreat from the economy, and fiscal cuts to keep or regain competitivity and market shares.

The contrast between economic governance and democratic responsiveness has been magnified by the nature of economic policy associated with each option. While the financial crisis of the 2000s revealed the limits and real costs of the neo-liberal economic approach, Keynesian-style policies and their effectiveness remain an unsolved question. Proposed in the 1930s and applied extensively (but in ambiguous ways) after World War II, the Keynesian approach was abandoned after the 1970s crisis and progressively substituted by its neo-liberal nemesis. When the 2008 crisis burst, Keynesian-style policies regained ground in the economists' and politicians' view. Proponents of countercyclical policies to face the crisis and avoid its worsening draw from the inter-war experience and rely on the widely accepted view of Keynesianism as a working "general theory" for a period of crisis. However, after the early years of crisis, European governments dismissed Keynesianism as a working solution for the European problems and chose financial stabilisation policies and the resulting austerity. Today, neo-Keynesian economists and political scientists, as well as politicians, particularly Eurosceptics, see Keynesian-type policies as the correct economic policies to overcome the crisis and fuel recovery and economic growth in Europe. Almost automatically, they criticise the EMU and the whole EU economic governance architecture and objectives. On the other hand, governments in charge and some economists defend the financial stabilisation policies and dismiss Keynesianism as a solution for European economic problems. These economists are probably more sincerely convinced of this than many politicians in the governments because the latter have to respect European treaties and rules and cannot delegitimate their governmental action.

In the EMU case, the contraposition between neo-liberal and Keynesian economic policies has been made more complicated by the working mechanism of the EMU. The choice between the economic policy approaches is not independent of the EMU structural needs. In other words, unavoidable needs to keep the EMU operational impose a neo-liberal style management of the euro. The euro area's lack of a government makes convergence in fiscal, budgetary and economic policies an inescapable constraint for EMU governance. On the other hand, the main characteristics of Keynesian policies, if applied at the national level, are irreconcilable with the EMU governance. So, paradoxically, only concentrating the powers of nation states at the European level can make Keynesian policies a working solution for EMU economic governance. However, this requires the creation of a European government for a European state; this is the reverse of what anti-EMU activists aim for.

5 – The limits of the unsolved dilemmas approach

The unsolved dilemmas discussed in the previous section are particularly relevant for today's debate on the European crisis as well as the policy choices. We have already seen (Table 3.1) that there is a strict relationship between political proposals by anti-system actors and their answers to the unsolved dilemmas discussed here. Also, the diachronic comparison between present and past conditions is a crucial tool for political communication and legitimisation of their proposals. As a consequence, history applied to politics gained relevance in the EU political arena, notwithstanding the naivetés of many historical analyses used as rhetorical and communication tools.

The methodological limitations of the political use of history in today's debate is an essential element to consider before agreeing to discuss European monetary integration and, more generally, the whole integration process following the rhetorical schemes adopted by pro- and anti-EMU sides. Joining this discussion is not the aim of this book, but in the following chapters, the rationale of some political proposals will be explained, taking into consideration the impact of these limitations as a determining factor in policy proposal formulation. Instead, this section will show that the main reason why some dilemmas remained unsolved is their context sensitivity and interdependence. This means that the better policy options cannot be selected uncritically and ideologically. Instead, the context in which the policy has to be applied determines its suitability. In other words, the different policy options cannot be applied universally, and their workability depends on variables that change frequently.

Neither fixed nor floating exchange rate systems worked for a long time. The former proved to be very rigid and was difficult to adapt to a changing context, while the latter was too flexible and difficult to manage for many countries and in the case of exogenous shocks and constraints. If applied to the EMU case, this conclusion suggests that the only working solution in the long term is monetary unification associated with a central government and EMU area common economic policies. However, there are no certainties that the EMU will be capable of changing in this way. Also, this doesn't mean that the EMU cannot survive for a long time without political union in Europe.

Welfare state sustainability depends on many economic and social variables and cannot be confused with workers' rights. The idea that welfare is a right to be granted notwithstanding economic and budgetary constraints is irrational and historical comparisons used to support this idea misleading. Supporters of welfare state restoration forget that the most generous (and expensive) welfare state systems delayed and passed on a relevant part of their costs to subsequent generations and favoured the "voting generations" at the time of welfare enhancement. The welfare systems of the past worked for decades, but this does not mean they could work forever. At best, they require drastic reforms because of the mutation of many variables. Also, economic growth in those times in which the welfare system grew and became a critical sector of state activity was a determining variable in supporting the welfare state. The period 1950–1970 was a period of economic growth and limited state indebtedness. Later, growth declined and public debt increased, making generous welfare systems unsustainable for the state budget. Also, the demographic trend reduced the contribution base and made the original promise unsustainable in the long term.

Many critics of the EMU saw the Bretton Woods period as an optimal solution to regain prosperity. Maybe the Bretton Woods system and the embedded liberalism (or the constrained capitalism that resulted from it) guaranteed the bases for economic growth and domestic economic policy independence. However, the Gold Exchange Standard collapsed, and it seems very difficult to recreate it today. Also, rebuilding an international currency system to create a condition for domestic economic freedom and welfare state reinforcement is utterly incoherent with the proposals to dismantle the EMU usually carried out by those Eurocritics that see welfare state reduction as an undemocratic outcome of European integration. This does not apply to welfare state supporters that ask for EU and EMU reform to strengthen the social dimension of European integration.

Our historical analysis suggests that working Keynesian-style policies require a managed international payments system and barriers to capital flows, a small public debt at the start of the policy cycle and preconditions capable of supporting economic growth. In other words, single countries were able to strictly control their domestic economy and decide on internal policies because an international system enabled instability induced by external fluctuations to be avoided. When the system disappeared, external instability led to the domestic economy being poorly managed and prone to emergency measures to face exogenous shocks. So the national economic policy independence of the pre-EMU period recalled by anti-Euro activists is just a myth. External constraints to domestic economic policies existed with or without fixed exchange rate systems, before and after the introduction of the euro, when Keynesian-style policies were implemented and when neo-liberal policies took their place. So dismissing dependence on external constraints was never an option for European countries. The only and relevant option was choosing the kind of external constraints to accept and being coherent with the system that imposed the selected constraints.

Both Keynesian-style and neo-liberal-style economic policies have significant political consequences. The adoption of each of them changes the political arena in which policy choices happen. This results in empowering or weakening each actor, changing electoral strategies, transforming policies' relevance and government priorities, and changing the interaction mechanisms that shape political behaviours and government effectiveness.

The political impact of neo-liberal-style policies has been widely debated, and the literature on the 2000s (in particular after the world crisis burst) stressed how neo-liberal policies dilated the gap in wealth distribution and fed inequalities in advanced countries. Also, deregulation and financialisation created the conditions for the international economy fragility that culminated in the world crisis. Finally, neo-liberal-style policies induced the states to take a step back from economic management and workers' rights protection. However, the evidence of the fault of neo-liberalism does not solve the limits of the Keynesian approach.

Keynesian-style policies had been vehemently criticised in the past. Today, these criticisms seem forgotten, probably because they were formulated many years ago before the abandonment of Keynesian-style policies.

The most incisive criticisms of the impact of Keynesian-style policies on politics came from Buchanan, who stressed how deficit spending policies emphasised the contrast between short-term and long-term objectives and demonstrated that those kinds of policies are detrimental to democracy through the distortion of those democratic decisions he called the "public choice" (Buchanan and Tullock 1962; Buchanan 1967; Buchanan and Wagner 1977). Buchanan suggested that governments with a positive attitude to deficit spending policies and a pervasive role in the domestic economy systematically tend to use the opportunities offered by their role as an economic actor to feed clientelist relationships and consolidate consensus without caring about the long-term consequences of their choices. In fact, politicians have a limited time horizon due to their electoral mandate and have a reduced interest in the distant future of the country's economy after their dismissal from power. So the long-term impact of economic policies (indeed all policies) becomes irrelevant in policy planning, particularly when voters do not perceive this impact. In their view, the advantages of expansionary economic policies are reserved for the current generations and costs are in part discharged on the following ones (Buchanan and Wagner 1977, p. 12). Finally, Buchanan believes that Keynesian-style policies distort the market functioning and move financial resources from productive investments to less productive ones, making the economy less competitive and charging to entrepreneurs and taxpayers the costs of poorly managed state intervention (Buchanan and Wagner 1977, p. 69).

So both Keynesian-style and neo-liberal-style policies have relevant social costs, distorting the effects on policymaking and the market economy, and are detrimental for democracy. This suggests that neither of them can solve the contrast between economic government and democracy. If neo-liberalism insurgence curbs the quality of democracy on the freedom and equality side, Keynesianism reduces the quality of democracy in terms of accountability, democratic legitimacy and sometimes the rule of law.

One final aspect to consider deals with the difference between Keynesian, post-Keynesian and neo-Keynesian economic policies. The attribute "Keynesian" has been applied indiscriminately to different economic policies just joined by deficit spending attitudes. However, there are substantial differences between the economic policies proposed by Keynes, the application of Keynes's ideas in the second post-war period and the recovery of Keynesianism proposed today. When we refer to Keynesian policies we are talking about policies strictly coherent with the Keynes theory as exposed in the general theory. On the other hand, we call post-Keynesian policies the application of Keynes's ideas after World War II, in particular in the United States and Western Europe until the 1970s. Those applications were sometimes in contrast with the Keynes theory or use some elements of Keynes's thought to design expansive policies influenced by theories and concepts proposed years after Keynes passed away.

Distinguishing between different kinds of Keynesian-style policies is crucial to understand the political dimension of the contemporary debate on anti-crisis economic policies. Many Keynesians today, in particular those non-economists involved in political debates, ignore or misunderstand the distinction described above. More specifically, it happens that they refer to neo-Keynesian economists, look at post-Keynesian policies and legitimise both of them using Keynes's prestige as a genial economist. Thus, they ascribe to Keynes's policy suggestions in contrast to his theory, see in the application of these non-Keynesian ideas the reason for the post-war economic recovery and growth, and propose uncritically reapplying today those policies as a solution for the crisis.

Two serious misunderstandings undermine this pseudo-Keynesian approach. First, Keynesian policies did not succeed in solving the 1930s crisis. In those countries where the Keynes theory influenced policymakers, his theories gained ground in the few years before World War II but did not have the time to demonstrate their effectiveness. It was the war that changed the level of economic activity. Also, economic activity recovered just in the production sector while the financial sector simply shifted to war financing. Also, the international payment system that supported post-war recovery was not adequately based on Keynesian ideas. Keynes himself proposed his view of post-war reconstruction at Bretton Woods, and it was dismissed in favour of the American one. Some crucial elements of today's neo-liberal order have been created at Bretton Woods, notwithstanding the Bretton Woods system permitted many countries to adopt Keynesian-style economic policies at home. So Keynes's theories did not solve the 1930s crisis because strictly Keynesian policies were almost unapplied before the war.

As a consequence, the effectiveness of strictly Keynesian policies had been inferred, not tested. Moreover, evidence of their effectiveness mainly derived from the application of post-Keynesian policies, which proved to be inadequate when the international framework where they rose disappeared. So the trust shown today by Keynes fans in Keynesian economic policies' effectiveness in overcoming the European crisis is poorly legitimated by historical experience, particularly when applied in a decontextualized perspective.

Second, neo-Keynesian economists today are not purely Keynesian. Their theory is influenced by neo-classic economic theory and some Keynesian ideas are just a re-elaboration adapted to a liberal theoretic framework (Skidelsky 2009). So they share only some beliefs with "political Keynesians" while they diverge from them on other themes such as globalisation and free trade. Moreover, some economists who criticise bitterly the neo-liberal austerity policies supported by the EU propose the application of the Keynesian and post-Keynesian concept, sometimes based on a very peculiar interpretation of Keynes's statements poorly accepted by neo-Keynesian economists. So the real nature of the Keynesian alternative to neo-liberal economic policies remains ambiguous.

6 – History and European integration theories

The second field in which the use of history has a relevant role is theory building. Since the early days of European integration, explaining the reasons for the process and theorising its evolution has attracted the interest of those scholars who saw in European integration a worldwide important event. However, the flow of time changed the approaches, perspectives and aims of European integration theory as well as the relevance of history as an analytical tool.

The first theorists had a minimal historical background to rely on for explaining European integration and anticipating its future, notwithstanding their ambition was to depict a long-term process that they supposed was probably destined to conclude with the rise of a united Europe. Haas published a seminal book in concomitance with the launch of the European Economic Community, i.e. a few years after the official initiation of the integration process (Haas 1958). Other crucial contributions to the neo-functionalist literature appeared in the 1960s and early 1970s (Lindberg 1963; Haas 1964; Schmitter 1971), i.e. when it was too early to infer relevant suggestions from European integration history. Historiography on European integration at that time was almost inconsistent and limited to the mere knowledge of some events and decisions that led to the first steps of the process. Instead, crucial documents were still buried in undisclosed archives. So European integration did not have a history and scholars focused mainly on its future. This created a "time bias" for integration theory, i.e. an attempt to explain a phenomenon still in process and badly defined. In the meantime, the scientific approach that inspired this literature derives from international relations and the main topics of the discipline (Wiener and Diez 2009). So the reasons for building international institutions, their interaction with nation states, the actors that support integration and the preference formation process became the main topics that shaped both the neo-functionalist literature and the criticisms of this approach formulated by its opponents. In particular, it was the debate about the obsolescence or consolidation of the nation state that became the main divide in the early phase of European integration theory building (Hoffman 1966).

In the 1970s, the crisis of the integration process influenced the theoretical debate about its reasons and future while the interest in the topic decreased. The perspective of a sudden stop or failure of the integration process reverberated in the theoretical literature and imposed a rethinking of the whole process, its perspectives and the expectation for the future (Haas 1975). The relevance of the "time bias" in theory building emerged again. It became evident that theorists, having witnessed just a small fraction of a process they anticipated as being a long-term one, had few elements to elaborate a historically sound analysis of European integration capable of explaining the origins and the structural mechanism at work in determining the process evolution. So rhetorical elements widely used by politicians in speeches and public documents shaped the early phase of European integration theory building. This addressed the rise and consolidation of a "European mythology" that still influences the EU propaganda and many academics today (Della Sala 2010; Kølvraa 2016; Karagiannis 2016).

The relaunch of integration in the 1980s revitalised the debate on the topic and pushed scholars to re-engage with theory building. However, new theories suffered for the previous limitations that shaped theory building at its early stage and for the distorted vision of European integration that emerged from historiography at that time. Historical analysis mainly focused on the political side of integration and saw economic integration as a "technical" dimension of a process interpreted as a mainly political process. Also, official sources emphasised the political ambitions of the "founding fathers of Europe" and the idealistic view of "an ever closer union" of European member states as a preliminary phase toward continental unification. This reinforced the political predominance approach that has characterised the European integration theories since the 1990s, and that is still rooted in many minds today.

On the other hand, new approaches to European integration theory emerged with the rise of new theoretical questions. While early theories aimed to explain how integration started and how integration will evolve, new theories focused on how European integration was at the moment proposing two new questions: how integrated Europe works, and how it evolves. So mid-range theories dismissed the long-term perspective of the so-called "Grand Theories" and focused on the present and the evolving relationship between the national and supranational level of government and the connected problems of European governance. The evolution of European institutions remained a core topic for these theories and granted their insertion in the theoretical debate on integration. However, the inadequate attention devoted to the evolving nature of integration caused their obsolescence within a few decades. History remained in the background both because of the incompleteness of historiography and the short-term perspective of new theories.

It was in the 1990s that history (economic history in particular) became a crucial element in theory building and its use changed dramatically the analytic perspective adopted by theorists. The seminal work of Alan Steel Milward demonstrated the predominance of economic factors in explaining the origins of European integration and the strategies adopted in the early decades of the process (Milward 1992). Also, Milward depicted the whole process of European integration as a "rescue of the nation states" by the European supranational level, i.e. the reverse of the path toward European unification claimed by a large number of theorists and historians of previous decades. The impact of Milward's work was twofold. First, he offered the historiographic base for revamping the Grand Theories debate empowering the opponents of neo-functionalism and facilitating the rise of a new and specifically Europe-centred version of intergovernmentalism named "liberal intergovernmentalism". This theory recovered from intergovernmentalism the centrality of the national level for the formation of preferences, identified bargaining as the crucial process to agree on common preferences and explained the creation of supranational institutions as a way to grant the implementation of common decisions as previously explained by traditional neo-realist and intergovernmentalism literature (Morawcsik and Schimmelfennig in Wiener and Diez 2009). Second, the nation state rescue theory proposed by Milward and the centrality of economic elements in shaping that rescue undermined the political prevalence approach and, more generally, the belief that European unification was the main aim and the logical outcome of the integration process.

The emergence of liberal intergovernmentalism and the new historical perspectives proposed by Milward revamped the Grand Theories debate and the attempts to explain the whole process of European integration and to estimate its possible outcomes. In particular, it was the historical institutionalism approach to European integration to gain more from the recovery of history as an analytic tool (Pollack in Wiener and Diez 2009). Scholars who adopted this theoretical approach depicted European integration as a continuous process addressed by an internal coherence mainly due to "path dependence" mechanisms capable of constraining actors' choices. So decisions taken in the past, sometimes at historical junctures (Capoccia and Kelemen 2007), influence future choices and also feed the process of integration because of unexpected consequences of the Commission and the Court decisions (Burley and Mattli 1993; Pierson 1996).

Historical institutionalism recovered some elements already advanced by neo-functionalism like process continuity and unicity, and compelling mechanisms capable of favouring, if not imposing, further integration. So new opportunities arose to rethink neo-functionalism and oppose liberal intergovernmentalism and, more generally, those approaches that rejected continuity and unicity as essential elements in European integration.

Meanwhile, other mid-range theories emerged in which history is applied just in a mid-term perspective and the consequences of deeper integration for nation states and societies assume a central role. The most important among these theories are post-functionalism and new intergovernmentalism. Both of these theories saw the Maastricht period as the watershed for integration. Post-funtionalism saw the acceleration in integration caused by the Maastricht Treaty and the more profound politicisation of the integration process at national level as the reasons for the shift from a "permissive consensus" that left elites and interest groups to decide on the route of integration and the transfer of sovereignty from national to supranational level, to a "constraining dissensus" that limits that possibility (Hooge and Marx 2009). In the meantime, post-functionalism abandons the economic and elitist approach of both neo-functionalism and liberal intergovernmentalism to focus on more abstract elements like identity. So it moves away from the political predominance approach, at least in its traditional interpretation that focuses on European institutions and the politicisation of the integration process.

New intergovernmentalism, on the other hand, has recovered many elements of traditional intergovernmentalism and focused on EU institutional evolution since Maastricht. This theory stresses the dynamic of integration in the mid term and shows that integration proceeded mainly on a route toward enlargement of the number of institutions rather than enlargement of institutions' powers. In other words, there were more institutions and agencies but not increased empowerment of the supranational level (Bikerton, Hodson and Puetter 2015b, p. 704–5).

In this book perspective, what matters is the relationship between these theories and history. None of them pay much attention to history for theory building, apart from the events of the last 30 years. However, they stress the existence of "breaking points" to set against the "critical junctures" that inspire the neo-institutionalist view of history. So they support the idea of discontinuity in the historical process while other theories mainly see European integration as a continuous and internally coherent process characterised by clear origins, internal mechanisms and predictable evolution.

7 – European integration theories, EMU and the lessons of monetary history

The previous section depicts the evolution of European integration theory and shows common elements and some limits (sometimes called "bias") of the different theories. The primary limits identified are the time bias, the pro-integration bias, the theoretical bias and a diffused attitude to accepting European mythology. The time bias and the European mythology have already been introduced. Instead, pro-integration and theoretical bias need to be explained better. Pro-integration bias refers to the idea that more integration equates to problem-solving (Ritterberger and Blauberger 2017; Borzel 2018, p. 477). This bias intrinsically pollutes some theories (mainly inspired by functionalism). The same is true for those mid-range theories that concentrate on recent periods (in particular the euro age) or the attempts to draw lessons from the eurozone crisis in favour or against the main integration theories.

Theoretical bias refers to the attitude of theorists in centring their theories on few elements and discharging many others that may be influencial and crucial in explaining the process under scrutiny. Oversimplification of history is one of the most relevant examples of theoretical bias. All these biases also influenced the relationship between monetary history and the theory of integration, in particular the monetary integration issue.

The EMU and its growing impact on European integration emphasised the relevance of monetary history in the field of integration theories in two ways. First, some scholars started to apply integration theories to monetary integration to explain the rise of the EMU. Second, theorists referred to monetary history and specific events in the monetary field to integrate theory or to support or dismiss the main theories of European integration.

Some intergovernmentalists saw geopolitical elements as the main reason to explain the choice of EMU, in particular, the end of the Soviet Union and the reunification of Germany. This book demonstrates that these elements explain (only in part) the timing of that choice, not the choice itself. On the other hand, neo-functionalists saw monetary integration as the obvious spillover of market integration. However, this approach could explain the success of negotiations for the EMU, but lacks an explanation of the reasons for previous attempts at monetary integration as well as the monetary integration restart in 1979, years before the launch of the single market. Also, historiography has shown that France pushed ahead with monetary integration for other reasons than structural needs of the single market. The original flexible structure of the EMS was a more efficient solution for the single market than the single currency. So the only thing that can explain the EMU in a neo-functionalist perspective is a distorted perception of structural links on the part of policymakers, not a structural need of the single market. This makes more convincing the constructivist approach to monetary integration in which (neo-liberal) ideas shape the road to Maastricht and the subsequent process of monetary integration (McNamara 1998). Unfortunately, constructivism barely explains the EMU architecture, and certainly not the reasons for its creation. In fact, supranational governance of economics fits poorly with neo-liberal ideology. Besides, some elements of EMU architecture, like convergence and limited inflation rates, had been identified as unavoidable decades before neo-liberalism and monetarism diffusion as leading ideas for economic governance in the EU. Liberal intergovernmentalism still fails to explain in full monetary integration. Its emphasis on bargaining, national preferences and commercial interests marginalises the relevance of other elements like the attempts of EMU countries to regain control of monetary affairs in international economic relations, as well as of non-commercial interests of countries with embarrassing problems on the fiscal and budgetary side. Moreover, feedback on the monetary integration of member states' politics and preferences identified by post-functionalists was almost ignored in liberal intergovernmentalism, at least in its early formulation.

Historical institutionalism seems capable of using history more efficiently in theory building. However, historical institutionalist explanations suffer for many history biases that distort the perception of the flow of events, causality and process unity as well as the relevance of actors. In fact, institutions remain the crucial actors in these theories as well as in neo-functionalism. Also, almost all automatic mechanisms activated by path dependence have a relevant role in explaining the evolution of a unitary process in which external elements and the national-level impact of integration are marginal elements. Finally, the unicity of the process suggests that it is a continuous one (shaped but not interrupted by critical junctures) and that all the elements involved in this process are inexorably destined to be part of it from the start. The way in which monetary affairs joined the integration process conflicts with this vision of the European integration process. So historical institutionalism, as well as many of the other theories, sacrifices complexity to parsimony and theory elegance selecting limited periods and few apparently prevalent issues, dismissing an exhaustive historical analysis and a long-term perspective.

Recently, some theorists referred to monetary events to integrate theory or to support or dismiss the main theories of European integration. It was the eurozone crisis that attracted attention as a case study to rethink and improve the debate on European integration. A questionable interpretation of the evolution of EMU governance has been proposed to demonstrate the solidity and predictive capability of neo-functionalist argumentation (Vilpišauskas 2013; Niemann and Ioannou 2015). It was claimed that liberal intergovernmentalism was confirmed by the eurozone crisis case (Schimmelfennig 2015a). The remaining chapters of this book will raise some doubts about the real meaning of the eurozone crisis and the more recent evolution of European integration for the debate on European integration theories.

PART II

THE WORKING OF THE EMU

Chapter 4

The Original Sins of the Common Currency

The choice to create the European Monetary System was the turning point for both European integration and currency coordination in Europe. At that time, a common strategy was adopted to solve two problems that had been faced separately for decades. Within a few years, the same approach had been taken for other issues such as safeguarding the environment, economic backwardness in Southern Europe, technological obsolescence and the decline in competitiveness of European products. Thus, European integration, supranational governance and coordination became a standard solution to multiple problems of the growing European Community.

Merging European integration and currency coordination did not eliminate the obstacles and challenges faced by both until the late 1970s. Conversely, the merged problems and coordination of so many "integrations" also became problematic. However, the communitarian structure with common institutions and common rules supported the efforts of member states to pursue the convergent integration strategy, creating synergies and increasing the possibility of compensations and side payments. On the other hand, convergent integration magnified the impact of common choices and supranational policies on member states and made national policies more and more dependent on communitarian decisions. This dependence created stronger structural connections between member countries' economies and emphasised tensions. Thus, contrasts arose through divergent national interests.

The way in which the EMU was decided upon and realised was an incremental and poorly planned process based on distorting political compromises. Also, monetary union was a political choice that paid inadequate attention to economics and emphasised "the spirit of the moment", i.e. the opportunity arose with the redefinition of European geopolitics after the fall of the Soviet Union. So the EMU was born with many "original sins" that shaped its future and undermined its functioning.

The associative nature of the EMU was its worst original sin. In fact, the constitutive logic of the eurozone was an attempt to balance national priorities and to adapt this solution to the constraints imposed by the communitarian framework. So Italy, which had access to the EU market granted by its membership in the EU, cannot be let outside the EMU by Germany or France (its main commercial competitors) to avoid allowing Italy to have a relevant competitive advantage (Dornbusch 1996). Italy had a debt that put it largely out of the convergence criteria, but the same was true for French "satellites" like Belgium, which is inextricably linked to Luxembourg. So the main argument for keeping Italy out of the EMU was not usable to avoid it being applied to Belgium, with consequences on Luxembourg and (probably) the Netherlands (Marsh 2009, p. 199). Also, France saw Italy and Spain as allies to politically counterbalance the German predominance (Dyson and Featherstone 1999, p. 8–9) Today, the aggregative origin of the EMU remains one of the most significant problems for EU governance, because the EMU rose on the back of fragile arrangements and unsolved contrasts that made the management of the single currency weak and ineffective, at least during the 2000s.

Another original sin of the EMU deals with its economic sustainability. Many economists drew attention to the structural weakness of the EU's area, arguing that it lacked the characteristics to be an optimal currency area (Jonung and Drea 2009). Others focused on the difficulty for weaker economies of competing with Germany renouncing independent monetary policy and competitive devaluations (Krugman 1998). These problems were perceived from the 1960s when the first studies on monetary integration appeared. However, many workable solutions had been proposed to face the adverse impact of monetary integration. Unfortunately, few of them were implemented at the right time.

The third original sin of the EMU was its poor political legitimacy. The pervasive nature of monetary integration had been evident since the signature of the Maastricht Treaty and critics arrived from both left and right parties against the rising "Europe of bankers" and the menace for national sovereignty, workers' rights and the welfare state, i.e. the essence of the post-war European model of democracy. On the other hand, the chronic and unsolved problem of coordinating democracy and currency management re-emerged when EMU rules started to conflict with national and electoral priorities. This problem was the same faced and unsolved since the 1920s. However, today democracy is a consolidated, overriding and vital set of values. So currency management needs legitimisation in a democratic framework because doubts about its legitimacy offered Eurosceptic and anti-European parties a powerful rhetorical tool with which to oppose integration.

In summary, at least three original sins of the rising EMU emerged before the introduction of the euro: the confrontational nature of member states' coordination, the uncertain economic sustainability of the single currency and the legitimacy gap of monetary union.

After the introduction of the common currency, a new problem emerged, i.e. the reduced effectiveness of the governance tools provided by the treaties. This issue was another of the EMU's original sins, but, unlike the previous three, it was not fully perceived before the introduction of the euro. It was only with the euro crisis in the early 2010s and the introduction of the New Economic Governance that some "old" solutions were recovered and implemented. So a governance gap undermined EMU sustainability during the first ten years of its existence and enabled the rise and consolidation of disequilibria, which added to the impact of the international crisis. At the end of the day, this "governance gap" resulted in the most dangerous gap in the creation of the EMU and the one that put more seriously at risk its survival. However, it was also the only one of the four that was possible to face quickly and effectively.

In this chapter, these original sins and the obstacles they create to a broader and more efficient monetary and financial integration will be discussed. Furthermore, the chapter will try to demonstrate that these barriers were not insurmountable and their existence did not make monetary union unsustainable and predestined to fail as suggested by some scholars before and after the introduction of the euro, notwithstanding they dramatically limited the efficiency of the EMU.

1 – Conflictual cooperation and the limits of European intergovernmentalism

If we renounce the epic representation of European integration as a long and unstoppable ride toward "an ever closer union", the idea that the initial phase of European integration was the other face of a failure becomes acceptable. The European Coal and Steel Community and the European Economic Community should be defined alternatively as failures in terms of broader cooperation or successful in aggregating a few countries. Neither of the two associations joined all (or at least a significant part) of the members of the European Payments Union. It was the French need to control vital raw materials and to kerb German military potential to inspire the original team of founders that joined in the ECSC (Milward 1992, p. 369 and 385). The six founders settled, in the same way, the atomic energy problem; this was an economic opportunity for the USA and France that European fragmentation and conflictuality put at risk.

Similarly, the rise of the EEC was the result of the different attitudes of Continental Western Europe and the UK toward convertibility and free trade. In the meantime, attempts to create a political framework for the rising European core failed. So integration in the 1950s appears to have been a sequence of failures that created alternative opportunities to solve some of the most urgent problems.

The same goes for monetary integration since the late 1970s. The European Monetary System arose from the failure of broader cooperation among European countries and between them and the United States to save, rebuild or substitute the Bretton Woods system. So the EMS became a second-best solution after more extensive international cooperation was no longer viable.

This disenchanted picture of European integration has the advantage of explaining the origins of at least the first original sins of the EMU. The success of the first European communities derived from the complementarity of their member states' economies and the presence of a political leadership capable of attracting and coordinating members in particular fields in which political and economic needs may join for mutual convenience. Besides, coordinating a few economic sectors in a few countries during a period of sustained economic expansion and monetary stability due to the Bretton Woods system and the American predominance was relatively easy. So both the economic and political sustainability of European integration was granted. However, from the early 1970s, enlargements reduced cohesion and the convergence of national interests, while the introduction of new policies in the communitarian framework increased governance complexity. Also, the growth of economic sectors under European control augmented the effectiveness of crossed vetoes in communitarian negotiations. So coordinating a larger group of members with divergent interests and more opportunities to act as veto players undermined the effectiveness of the integrative choice. Finally, deeper monetary integration magnified the political impact of European integration. Thus, the dichotomy between currency management and democratic practice reappeared, repurposing the legitimacy dilemma.

Another relevant factor complicated European economic coordination. In fact, after the first oil shock, the competitiveness and economic strength of member states diverged and Germany emerged as the economic leader in the area while the UK and Italy faced a deep crisis. This situation changed national priorities and brought into question the affordability of the weaker countries when involved in international cooperation activities as in the case of the Monetary Snake. Also, divergence in economic performances created asymmetries in negotiation power and favoured the rise of hegemonic or almost hegemonic positions for Germany and France that made negotiation unbalanced and addressed the integrative process toward priorities that are those of hegemons. The result was an asymmetrical intergovernmentalism in which the most influential countries can impose their rules but have to face the resistance of the weaker countries in implementing them.

This "conflictual cooperation" characterises the whole integration process and continues today to shape European national politics and inter-EU relations. In other words, the intergovernmental nature of many decisions is not sufficient to guarantee the implementation at national level of European policies and rules. This gap can be explained by the national-centred nature of politics in the European Union. Governments' continuity in power depends on national electors, and ruling parties need to pay priority attention to them. So losers in intergovernmental negotiation can delay or sabotage the full implementation of those intergovernmental choices that can endanger their power at home. This problem emerged after Maastricht and was magnified by the introduction of the euro.

Conflictual cooperation induces a rethinking of the traditional intergovernmental approach. Intergovernmentalists explain decision-making in the EU as the result of member states' negotiations. However, their analysis ends with the adoption of the decision. The experience of monetary integration and the emerging governance gap show that the implementation is important as well as the decision-making phase, and that an intergovernmental approach needs to take care of it because implementation became the real battlefield for the intergovernmental negotiations' losers. Those who failed to prevail in intergovernmental negotiation will try to use their role as the national implementer of communitarian decisions to mitigate the impact of adverse decisions and unwelcome rules on the domestic structure of power that allows them to stay in charge. In other words, losers' ability to resist is part of the intergovernmental process because they can use this strength to renegotiate their position and obligations or to obtain a flexible interpretation of the rules. So the traditional function of guaranteeing the implementation of agreements assigned to supranational institutions by many theories of European integration depends on the effectiveness of the governance system, i.e. the ability of supranational institutions to impose the respect of rules established with intergovernmental agreements. These rules must also be implementable.

2 – The EMU as a non-optimal currency area and the debate on EMU sustainability

One of the most relevant problems discussed before and after the introduction of the single currency deals with the economic viability of the EMU and its sustainability for those member states with weaker economic structures.

Many economists and some politicians addressed this problem to support their critics and hostility against European monetary integration, emphasising the non-optimality of the EMU as a currency area.

When the EMU became a realistic perspective, economic theory was poorly equipped for debating monetary integration. The only theoretical framework available was the Optimum Currency Areas approach introduced mainly by Robert Mundell in the 1950s and put aside in the 1970s when monetary integration became a marginal topic for economic theory (Mundell 1961; McKinnon 1963, p. 717–725; Kenen 1969). When European monetary integration returned as a hot topic in the 1990s, the OCA theoretical framework was recovered and applied to the rising EMU.[1]

From the early 1990s, it was clear that the EMU was not an optimal currency area because it lacked the features identified by economics as being essential for a working OCA. Labour mobility was limited by linguistic fragmentation and different attitudes toward immigration in the area. Also, the EMU members' economies are inhomogeneous and complementary to each other. So the area was at risk of asymmetric shocks. Moreover, the absence of a European fiscal policy capable of facing these shocks and of redistributing resources endangers the cohesion and survival of the whole EMU structure. Today, the OCA theory continues to be central to the criticism of European monetary integration, and some authors explain the crisis of the EMU with the EMU inconsistency with the OCA precepts.

The following chapter will show that the reasons for, and the mechanisms of, the EMU crisis of the late 2000s and early 2010s were not those anticipated by the OCA theory. This conclusion suggests dismissing the OCA approach, at least as a tool for explaining the rise of the EMU crisis. However, this is not enough to demonstrate that ignoring the alarms inspired by the OCA theory in the 1990s was a reasonable political choice at that time. Also, it is essential to understand whether the proponents of the EMU underesti-

[1] For a general overview of the OCA theory, see Horvath 2003; Dellas and Tavlas 2009.

mated the incontestable suboptimality of the EMU as a currency area and if this "original sin" contributed to the bad design and governance gap of the EMU.

The OCA debate is only one part of the general discussion on EMU sustainability. More specifically, it was the academic debate during the period between Maastricht and the adoption of the single currency to focus mainly on OCAs. Instead, OCA theory poorly attracted the attention of those scholars and politicians who had studied the feasibility of European monetary integration since the 1960s. The abstract nature of the OCA theory in the 1950s and 1960s and the subsequent rise of the endogenous OCA theory probably made its theoretical prescriptions irrelevant for EMU planning.[2] Also, monetary integration planners considered the solution of the main problems identified by OCA theory (workers and capital mobility, asymmetrical shocks and eventually fiscal transfers) to be automatically granted by the integration process. Freedom of movement for employees and capital are two of the "fundamental freedoms" included in the Treaty of Rome and considered pillars of monetary integration. So their introduction and implementation were seen as an essential component of monetary integration itself. On the other hand, convergence was the primary strategy for guaranteeing the sustainability of monetary integration and was supposed to kerb the impact of asymmetrical shocks. In addition, there were proposals to create shock absorbers in the form of a European Unemployment Fund to face the consequences of adjustments and convergence in weaker countries or the impact of asymmetrical shocks (Marjolin report, p. 34; *idem*, Annex 1, p. 1).

During the initial debate on monetary union (approximately 1960s–1970s), there were good reasons to pay limited attention to OCA theory inside the European institutions. All

[2] The endogenous OCA theory (Frankel and Rose 1996) suggests that the creation of a monetary union generates the condition for a progressive advancement of the new currency area toward optimality.

changed in the 1990s. At the end of the decade when criteria for admission into the EMU and its governance were adopted, there were good reasons to doubt the effectiveness of convergence and mobility of production factors in avoiding risks anticipated by OCA theory supporters. The EMS crisis in the early 1990s showed the difficulties weaker countries had in surviving in a fixed exchange rate regime and how convergence was economically and politically painful for many countries. Also, the Maastricht Treaty and the Stability and Growth Pact did not include any of those stabilisers suggested by early planners of European monetary integration to cope with unemployment and other negative consequences of monetary unification. So the reasons to ignore OCA alerts lost validity, and this explains why various economists in the 1990s expressed their concern and pessimistic view about the sustainability of the EMU. Many of them, mainly Americans (Jonung and Drea 2009), referred to the OCA theory and the suboptimality of the EMU area to discourage further steps toward monetary integration or to suggest adjustments in the rules for managing the common currency. Some European economists also contested monetary integration and alerted their governments to the perils of surrendering monetary sovereignty. One example is a manifesto published by some German economists at the end of the 1990s to challenge the introduction of the single currency (Kösters et al. 1998).

The nature of the choice of monetary integration can also explain the inadequate attention devoted to monetary integration critics. Notwithstanding money concerns the economic field, the launch of the EMU was mainly a political decision. So the suboptimality of the EMU area was a second-order problem to face after the political effort to unify monetary policies in the whole EMU area was completed. In other words, suboptimality and its consequences were the price to pay for an ambitious political project that could not be delayed if it was to be successful.

The political nature of the EMU project is not enough to justify the inadequate attention paid to the economic limits of the project. However, the economic theory of the 1990s and the concern about the impact of monetary integration on member states' economies were not sufficient to demonstrate that the EMU is not sustainable in the short and mid term. So it was plausible that the EMU could work at least for a while until the expected political union came about or that a suboptimal EMU could be an acceptable political outcome. However, concern about the EMU's political solidity cannot be ignored because clear signs of inconsistency have often emerged since the 1970s. So the main topic that should have to inspire the debate about EMU sustainability was not economic viability but political sustainability. Few economists expended words on this subject. The principal economist who based his criticism on the EMU's political inconsistency was Rudiger Dornbusch. He saw in member states' egoism, in their conflicting national interests and in the opportunistic strategy of highly indebted countries the reasons for the EMU's lack of political soundness. As a consequence, the EMU in Dornbusch's view would be unmanageable (Dornbusch 1996). This conclusion made Dornbusch the first theorist of the governance gap and the most pessimistic one.

Another famous economist who opposed the EMU in the 1990s is Martin Feldstein. He emphasised the political function of the EMU, which he saw as a strategy for imposing political union and kerbing the influence of national central banks on monetary policy (Feldstein 1997, 2000).

Other scholars adopted a more cautious approach to the political side of the EMU. They acknowledged the political nature of creating the EMU but did not deny its sustainability. Instead, they saw EMU survival as being dependent on the political will of EMU member states to keep alive the monetary union, notwithstanding the relevant economic and political costs they would have to face (Ingram 1969; Cohen 1994; Willet 1999 and 2000).

On the other hand, early EMU planners paid almost no attention to the political sustainability of monetary integration. Until the end of the 1980s, the various reports about monetary integration prepared by officers and consultants of the European institutions focused on technical aspects and limited their intrusion into the political field to institutional arrangements aimed at making the currency union manageable. Only at the end of the 1980s with the Delors report did the problem of EMU governance emerge, and a system of sanctions against member states that did not complain about EMU rules was hypothesised (Delors report, p. 23). The committees' members preferred to skip political considerations, avoiding questioning the central assumption that justified their works; i.e. the real willingness of member states to cooperate forever, independently of the costs of monetary integration. This was an ideological assumption probably inspired by the communitarian context in which those studies had been prepared. However, it cannot be excluded that, at least in the 1970s, EMU planners feared the unaffordability of some governments or the poor effectiveness of intergovernmental governance.

3 – A neo-liberal Europe of bankers? The EMU legitimacy gap

The third original sin of the EMU deals with the nature of the political design that inspired monetary integration. After the signature of the Maastricht Treaty, the EU was accused of being mainly oriented toward financial matters and inspired by a neo-liberal project to outflank national government and democracy. The vanishing of concrete perspectives of political union enforced this view of the EU as a "subversive" and anti-democratic construction and undermined its legitimacy.

Today, this original sin remains the most influential in terms of inspiring opposition to the EMU and the EU. Anti-Europeanists and Eurosceptic political parties and movements, as well as intellectuals, emphasise the democratic and legitimacy gap of the European Union to support their clamours for EMU abandonment or EU reforms (*see* chapter 9).

Certainly, the core of the Maastricht Treaty insisted on technical aspects and created a technocratic framework mainly oriented toward monetary matters. Also, the treaty implementation appeared in the media to be mainly focused on rigid parameters and managed by technocrats who were entirely indifferent to national politics and the costs suffered by member states. This image reinforced the negative perception of monetary integration and fuelled suspicions about the subversive nature of the EMU as a neo-liberal project aimed at restricting workers' rights and dismantling the welfare state. However, the matter is more complicated than this, and we need to distinguish the three components of the problem.

The first component regards the technical nature of the EMU. In this case, there are few doubts that monetary integration was conceived initially mainly as a technical matter. It was only in the late 1990s with the Amsterdam Treaty and the agreement on the Stability and Growth Pact that the economic and political impacts of convergence and integration were included in the monetary integration framework. In fact, the increasing unemployment rate and the electors' dissatisfaction with the consequences of the convergence policies induced the new French Prime Minister, Jospin, to ask for an enhancement in the economic growth dimension of the EU economic governance. This was a first signal of the problematic impact of monetary integration into member states' domestic policy (Dyson and Featherstone 1999, p. 8).

The second component, the neo-liberal nature of European monetary integration, is more ambiguous. Many authors support this view of monetary integration or, at least, suggest that neo-liberalism inspired the project and the criteria adopted to implement it (Redwood 1997; Scharpf 1997 and 1999; Wylie 2002; Crowley 2002; Brown 2004; Blyth 2013). However, only some of them see the EMU as a deliberate subversive plan to impose neo-liberalism in Europe. Others suggest that the final design of the EMU derived from negotiation among states with different economic systems and the results depended on the German success in imposing its system. So the EMU and the institution that manages European monetary policy, the European Central Bank, derived from the prevalence of German ordo-liberalism and not from a deliberate neo-liberal project.[3] This thesis seems to be supported by the analysis of the reports about monetary integration that appeared from the early 1960s. At that time, neo-liberalism was not a policy option. Nevertheless, convergence, indebtedness, budget deficit and inflation, the core criteria of the Stability and Growth Pact, were the main elements to keep under control to establish a working monetary union.[4] So it seems that there was no long-term neo-liberal project at work. Instead, there were elements recurrently identified as essential to keeping stable and manageable a monetary union not inscribed in a political union. It was the German predominance in imposing its ordo-liberal approach to monetary union that shaped the ECB and oriented the convergence of European economies toward a German-like model. Also, when the EMU was finalised, neo-liberalism was the dominant paradigm, and this addressed and justified neo-liberal technical solutions to problems identified decades before as well as the suspicions about the neo-liberal nature of the EMU.

[3] Ordo-liberalism is a version of classic liberalism in which the role of the state is granting the condition for a working market. So the main function of the state action is creating an institutional and legal structure capable of supporting the market, instead of searching for more invasive policies like the keynesian ones and addressed to specific macroeconomic targets like the employment rate (Bonefeld 2012; Nedergaard and Snaith 2015, p. 1096–1097).

[4] The Germans, the finance minister Waigel in particular, insisted on the establishment of strict rules for maintaining budget discipline after the introduction of the euro. An agreement at the Amsterdam European Council (June 1997) introduced the Stability and Growth Pact (Dyson and Featherstone 1999, p. 789).

The third component of the problem is the democracy and legitimacy gap. This is probably the most complicated aspect because it derives in part from the other two components. In fact, the technocratic nature of monetary integration and the obligation to respect convergence criteria offered to both central bankers and governments the opportunity to shape the national path toward monetary integration imposing reforms and rules unwelcomed by electors and hard to have approved in the usual conditions. Central bankers aimed at being independent from the government to free themselves and national monetary policy from political conditioning. In some instances, such as in the Italian case, central bankers saw in monetary integration the opportunity to impose on politicians powerful external constraints capable of inducing transformation that sclerotic institutions and political systems are unable to realise (Dyson, Featherstone and Michalopoulos 1996; Dyson and Featherstone 1999, p. 485-507; Sbragia 2001). So monetary integration and central bankers' ambitions negatively influenced the perception of EMU legitimacy and stressed the predominant role assigned to banking matters.

Technocrats and governments were responsible for one part of the monetary integration legitimacy gap. However, there were also structural problems concerning a legitimacy and democracy gap derived from the unresolved conflict between efficient economic governance and the democratic method, a conflict that emerged in the early 1920s and remains unresolved.

4 – Original sins and governance gap

The original sins described in the previous sections generated the governance gap here proposed as the primary structural problem of the EMU.

The poor planning of the EMU, conflictual cooperation, the irreconcilability of national economic interests and strict application of convergence parameters for EMU admission all contributed to undermining the effectiveness of the EMU governance framework agreed in the 1990s. Moreover, the ambiguous and inefficient sanctions system made EMU governance almost ineffective even before monetary unification. This system was probably deliberately conceived in this way to avoid rapid and efficient application of sanctions procedures that could endanger national sovereignty and strengthen too much the European Commission. Instead, the sanctions system was under the Council's control, meaning that the enforceability of EMU governance remained intergovernmental.

Thus, the mechanisms that characterise conflictual cooperation undermined the effectiveness of EU governance and enlarged the governance gap created by the weak rules and inconsistent sanctions system introduced by the Stability and Growth Pact. The inefficiency of this system became more and more evident in the 2000s. So the governance gap added to the original sins of the EMU and became one of them, probably the worst. However, it resulted from poor planning and excessively optimistic expectations regarding member states' willingness to accept in full the impact of external constraints on domestic politics. This meant that the governance gap was not an insurmountable obstacle to monetary integration derived from the structural limits of the European economy. So the problem was not deciding on monetary integration but failing to create an efficient set of rules and sanctions before selecting the members admitted into the EMU and introducing the euro. This general failure was probably an individual success for some members that searched for a governance system capable of compelling all to respect EMU rules except themselves. So it derived from both the distrust between member countries and the attempts of France and Germany to create a loophole for themselves if needed as happened in the early 2000s. In other words, EMU governance was initially conceived as asymmetric, probably to balance the "friendly" application of admission criteria to those countries that otherwise had no chance of joining the EMU.

The intergovernmental approach to EMU governance and the asymmetric nature of the sanctions system was not the only explanation for the governance gap. Another element that contributed to the gap was the wrong perception of the structural impact of monetary integration on the European financial system. The next chapter will show that monetary integration in the 2000s changed financial fluxes and created interdependency that could be avoided with better economic governance. However, the consequences and the problems generated by these interdependencies was underestimated or ignored by EMU governance planners. They focused their attention only on monetary and budgetary parameters and neglected other parameters that indirectly influence convergence and financial stability. When this gap became evident at the end of the 2000s, it was too late to remedy the damages created by poor governance.

Chapter 5

What Has Not Worked in the EMU?

The debate about the sustainability and effectiveness of the European common currency stagnated in the early 2000s after the euro started to circulate. However, some problems emerged immediately after the introduction of the new currency. Prices increased in some member countries.[1] And depreciation of the euro exchange rate with the US dollar occurred.[2] These problems created disappointment and a first wave of disaffection toward the new currency among European citizens, particularly in those countries that faced a significant increase in prices for consumer goods just after the substitution of national currencies with the euro. However, in a few years the euro was accepted by almost all people, except for a few Eurosceptics or anti-Europeanists that found popular discontent during the early phase of euro circulation an attractive issue for inserting anti-euro propos-

[1] In some EMU member countries the prices of certain goods and services increased significantly when the euro began to circulate. It was mainly Southern European countries that suffered this specific kind of inflation, sometimes called "perceived inflation", because the increase in prices as measured by the statistical offices showed no signs of inflationistic flames. It was the inability or unwillingness of some governments to permit some sellers to profit from the confusion created by the change of currency in circulation that led to increased prices during the conversion from national currencies to the euro. However, this kind of price increase was perceived bitterly by many consumers.

[2] The euro/US dollar exchange rate was 1.18 on the first day of the euro's existence (January 1st 1999). During the next three years the euro rate depreciated and remained under 0.90 until early 2002.

als in their political message.[3] In the meantime, free circulation into the Schengen area associated with a single currency in the EMU area reinforced the European identity of many citizens, particularly well-educated people and professionals who frequently travelled between EMU countries.

Finally, monetary unification and the wrong perception of full affordability of national banking systems and sovereign debts favoured a more profound interconnection among domestic financial structures, and massive capital flows toward Southern and Eastern Europe (Hobza and Zeugner 2014). These flows favoured a quick and extensive integration among the member states' financial systems. As a consequence, a fragile and unmanaged European financial system emerged. This system flourished on the grounds of the certainty of EMU irrevocability, the convenience at that time and the belief in the member states' ability to keep the EMU operative.

When the international crisis arrived in Europe in the late 2000s, the picture drawn above deteriorated dramatically. All three pillars of the euro's consensus (acceptance, common identity and affordability) started to creak. Together, the problematic euro sustainability in particular member states, European financial interconnection and the impact of the international crisis generated a process we will call the "euro crisis" in reference to something more complex than the simple sovereign debt crisis that affected the EMU area in the early 2010s usually called the "eurozone crisis". The euro crisis and the complex and contradictory way in which the EU faced it reverberated on the whole European construction, the citizens' perception of the EU functions and its representation by political parties. This impact contributed to generating a general crisis of the European ideal, here called "the crisis of Europe".

Then, the criticisms against the European common currency were revamped, reinforced by the hostility addressed toward

[3] This was the case with the Lega Nord (today just Lega) in Italy, which in the early 2000s adopted anti-euro attitudes in searching for consensus among those voters who were suffering due to the increases in goods prices.

the solution proposed for stabilising the economic system of those EMU member countries mostly affected by the crisis. Many of these criticisms were based on the idea of the unsustainability of the EMU and the euro for weaker countries, the absurdity of austerity and debt reduction policies as a solution to face the economic crisis, and the need to dismiss the common currency for some or all member countries.

This chapter will analyse the rise of the eurozone crisis and try to explain its real dynamic and causes, as well as the impact it had on EMU economic sustainability.

1 – The fragile basis of monetary integration during the early years of the EMU

A frequent error to avoid when discussing the euro crisis regards its origins. It did not originate only from the international crisis. The latter merely acted as a catalyst for a growing crisis in the EMU that was evident from the mid-2000s. However, this crisis was a governance crisis as well as an economic and structural crisis. In other words, a governance gap emerged due to a lack of rules and compelling powers in the EU Commission's hands and an insufficient number of parameters to evaluate the real performances and convergence of member states' economies. This gap undermined the EMU's evolution and favoured the rise of intra-EMU imbalances years before the international financial crisis arrived to amplify the EMU problems.

The first signals of the EMU's poor governability emerged just before the introduction of the single currency, in particular during the convergence phase when the time arrived to decide on the first wave of members admitted into the EMU. Admittance requirements were relaxed to permit the inclusion of countries incapable of respecting the convergence criteria reducing their public debt. Moreover, some of these countries adopted temporary measures to fit the convergence criteria and to simulate convergence toward the other members' fundamental economic parameters. This was the case with Portugal, which reduced its debt just by benefiting from the interest rate reduction on its bonds generated by the prospect of EMU membership (Blavoukos and Pagoulatos 2008, p. 239). Italy also benefited from this reduction while cutting its deficit and debt using the so-called "tax for Europe" introduced by the Prodi government as an *una tantum* measure (Dyson and Featherstone 1999, p. 8). Today it is well known that Greece adopted some accounting tricks to appear to respect the convergence criteria and obtain membership in 2000 (Featherstone 2011, p. 199).

The following tables show in detail the dynamics described above. During the period 1997–2004 Italy reduced its payments for interests of approximately 40%. Greece, Ireland, Portugal and Spain also benefited from reduced interest payments. However, for Germany and France, this reduction was limited or non-existent. In the meantime, Italy, Spain and Ireland reduced their debts significantly as a percentage of GDP while both France and Germany slightly increased them, probably because of the damages caused by the adverse weather conditions in 2003–2004. So the impact of monetary unification on governments' budgets in the early years of the EMU mainly favoured the GIIPS countries.

The initial advantage granted by the reduction of interest on public debt did not activate a working mechanism for a structural debt reduction and fiscal consolidation in Southern Europe, apart from Spain (Blavoukos and Pagoulatos 2008, p. 239–241). In Italy, part of the debt ratio reduction probably depended on reforms that moved expensive services (e.g. sanitary assistance) from the central state to the regions. Many of the Southern European members of the EMU used interest reduction to keep their old political-economical structure based on clientelism and inefficient and pervasive bureaucracies operative. This tactic enabled the survival of the existent power structure, i.e. the conglomeration of political relations that led to consensus for decades and enabled the national ruling elites to remain in power.

Spain adopted a different strategy and opted for a fiscal consolidation policy using structural measures to cut public expenditure. These actions resulted from agreements with trade unions (Blavoukos and Pagoulatos 2008, p. 241) and avoided the tensions that emerged from, say, the conflictual political environment in Italy, particularly after Berlusconi's coalition regained power in 2001.

The reduction of interest rates facilitated public debt sale for those countries that offered interests slightly higher than those paid by Germany and the other Northern European countries due to the perception of a uniform level of risk for securities issued by all the EMU countries.

Higher interest incentives touched both the public and the private credit sector, and cheap money moved toward countries with strong economic growth but weak financial markets. This was the case with Ireland and Spain, where the growing economy and a real estate boom attracted capital from Central and Northern Europe. Later, Cyprus enlarged its financial sector and became an offshore financial centre for non-EMU depositors, particularly the Russians (Georgiou 2013, p. 61). These three countries, which did not have the problem of massive public debt, developed a dangerous fragility in their financial sector, in part because of the growing interconnection of European financial markets. Moreover, the banking system of some EMU member countries benefited from their improved affordability and collected cheap money from Central and Northern Europe to reinvest in Eastern Europe at higher interest rates. This strategy increased the fragility of the newly interconnected EU financial system.

Table 5.1 – Government consolidated gross debt (% of GDP)

	1995	1996	1997	1998	1999	2000	2001	2002	2003	2004
Cyprus	47.8	49.1	53.0	54.7	54.8	54.9	56.5	59.7	63.1	64.1
France	55.8	59.7	61.1	61.0	60.2	58.6	58.1	60.0	64.1	65.7
Germany	54.7	57.5	58.7	59.5	60.0	58.9	57.7	59.4	63.1	64.8
Greece	99.0	101.3	99.5	97.4	98.9	104.9	107.1	104.9	101.5	102.9
Ireland	78.6	69.9	61.6	51.5	46.6	36.1	33.2	30.6	29.9	28.2
Italy	116.9	116.3	113.8	110.8	109.7	105.1	104.7	101.9	100.5	100.1
Portugal	58.3	59.5	55.2	51.8	51.0	50.3	53.4	56.2	58.7	62.0
Spain	61.7	65.6	64.4	62.5	60.9	58.0	54.2	51.3	47.6	45.3

Source: Eurostat http://appsso.eurostat.ec.europa.eu/nui/submitViewTableAction.do

Table 5.2 – General government interest payments (millions of euro)

	1995	1996	1997	1998	1999	2000	2001	2002	2003	2004
Cyprus	141	174	193	261	277	337	361	353	415	415
France	40,309	43,235	43,404	43,609	41,099	41,715	44,608	45,609	44,823	45,808
Germany	68,161	67,336	65,314	66,198	62,791	66,390	65,510	65,099	64,623	63,221
Greece	11,193	11,787	10,525	9,936	10,611	9,798	9,566	9,103	8,761	9,269
Ireland	2,718	2,625	2,706	2,691	2,190	2,107	1,757	1,788	1,770	1,709
Italy	99,789	114,238	100,242	89,024	74,956	75,964	79,045	73,420	69,144	66,723
Portugal	5,039	4,666	3,958	3,475	3,523	3,864	4,060	4,045	3,885	3,894
Spain	23,150	25,402	23,562	22,396	20,316	20,424	20,690	19,693	18,468	17,101

Source: Eurostat http://appsso.eurostat.ec.europa.eu/nui/submitViewTableAction.do

Table 5.3 – EMU convergence criterion: bond yields

	1999	2000	2001	2002	2003	2004	2005	2006	2007	2008	2009
Belgium	4.75	5.59	5.13	4.99	4.18	4.15	3.43	3.81	4.33	4.42	3.90
Denmark	4.91	5.64	5.08	5.06	4.31	4.30	3.40	3.81	4.29	4.28	3.59
Germany	4.49	5.26	4.80	4.78	4.07	4.04	3.35	3.76	4.22	3.98	3.22
Ireland	4.71	5.51	5.01	5.01	4.13	4.08	3.33	3.77	4.31	4.53	5.23
Greece	6.30	6.10	5.30	5.12	4.27	4.26	3.59	4.07	4.50	4.80	5.17
Spain	4.73	5.53	5.12	4.96	4.12	4.10	3.39	3.78	4.31	4.37	3.98
France	4.61	5.39	4.94	4.86	4.13	4.10	3.41	3.80	4.30	4.23	3.65
Italy	4.73	5.58	5.19	5.03	4.25	4.26	3.56	4.05	4.49	4.68	4.31
Cyprus	--	--	7.62	5.70	4.74	5.80	5.16	4.13	4.48	4.60	4.60
Luxembourg	4.66	5.52	4.86	4.70	3.32	2.84	2.41	3.30	4.46	4.61	4.23
Netherlands	4.63	5.40	4.96	4.89	4.12	4.10	3.37	3.78	4.29	4.23	3.69
Austria	4.68	5.56	5.08	4.96	4.14	4.13	3.39	3.80	4.30	4.36	3.94
Portugal	4.78	5.59	5.16	5.01	4.18	4.14	3.44	3.91	4.42	4.52	4.21
Finland	4.72	5.48	5.04	4.98	4.13	4.11	3.35	3.78	4.29	4.29	3.74

Source: Eurostat, http://appsso.eurostat.ec.europa.eu

Table 5.4 – Yearly variation in financial sector passivity (non-consolidated; percentage change from previous period)

	2001	2002	2003	2004	2005	2006	2007	2008
Germany	5.4	1.0	3.1	3.9	6.3	4.8	8.2	4.6
Ireland	--	10.5	22.5	20.1	35.1	21.6	9.6	6.5
Greece	1.0	0.1	9.4	8.6	17.0	14.3	22.2	4.4
Spain	7.6	5.5	16.8	16.3	25.3	20.0	16.8	3.8
France	4.8	1.3	6.8	9.9	15.0	15.3	12.8	2.1
Italy	-3.0	3.4	11.7	7.3	12.1	10.4	0.6	-1.5
Cyprus	8.0	2.6	11.8	20.2	34.1	29.5	27.2	115.6
Portugal	8.5	3.0	11.1	6.4	10.7	13.8	10.2	4.4

Source: http://ec.europa.eu/eurostat/web/macroeconomic-imbalances-procedure/indicators (updated version January 2019)

Table 5.5 – Private sector consolidated debt (% of GDP)

	2001	2002	2003	2004	2005	2006	2007
Germany	123.1	122.1	122.9	118.9	117.0	114.0	110.9
Ireland	139.3	137.4	141.3	149.5	170.1	190.6	198.1
Greece	60.0	63.8	67.9	73.6	85.7	92.5	101.5
Spain	109.8	116.4	126.3	137.6	154.6	177.6	191.5
France	103.8	103.8	103.8	105.2	109.6	112.9	115.9
Italy	79.7	82.7	86.3	89.8	96.0	102.2	109.7
Portugal	149.8	155.9	162.0	165.8	171.4	176.5	185.0

Source: http://ec.europa.eu/eurostat/web/macroeconomic-imbalances-procedure/indicators (updated version January 2019)

Central and Northern EMU members gained almost nothing from the interest rate reduction of the early 2000s and suffered capital outflows toward those EMU countries that offered higher interest levels. In the meantime, Germany had to face a problematic reduction in competitiveness that required painful reforms, particularly in the job market where the government agreed a wage containment policy with trade unions. This agreement created the so-called "mini jobs", sometimes considered a crucial element in the recovery of German competitivity (Lapavitsas et al. 2010, p. 322 and 336–341; Young and Semmler 2011). So in the early years of monetary unification in many EMU member states, those conditions that increased the impact of the international financial crisis in the late 2000s either appeared or were strengthened. The following tables show the genesis of some critical imbalances in the EMU. Tables 5.6, 5.7 and 5.8 depict the progressive but rapid deterioration of competitiveness in Southern EMU countries. Both wages and inflation increased more rapidly in those countries than in Germany. So Germany regained the competitivity lost during the late 1990s and neutralised the effect of the decrease in interest that favoured its Southern competitors, particularly Italy. In other words, the growing intra-EU trade surplus of Germany and the Netherlands derived, at least in part, from the inability of GIIPS countries to control internal economic variables. As a consequence, they lost the advantages and the opportunities gained from monetary unification.

Table 5.6 – Three-year variation of nominal unit labour cost (%)

	2001	2002	2003	2004	2005	2006	2007	2008
Germany	1.4	1.4	1.9	1.3	0.0	-2.9	-2.9	-0.1
Ireland	10.1	9.7	12.3	8.4	12.3	10.9	13.9	17.8
Greece	6.9	12.8	14.6	14.5	14.2	10.0	11.0	7.4
Spain	7.9	9.1	9.7	9.4	9.6	10.0	11.3	13.7
France	4.3	6.4	7.3	5.8	4.9	4.7	5.5	6.3
Italy	5.6	7.8	11.9	11.0	9.2	7.0	6.5	8.5
Portugal	11.5	11.9	11.1	7.1	7.4	4.3	5.1	4.5

Source: http://ec.europa.eu/eurostat/web/macroeconomic-imbalances-procedure/indicators (updated version January 2019)

Table 5.7 – Inflation: consumer prices (%)

	2002	2003	2004	2005	2006	2007	2008
Germany	1.42	1.03	1.67	1.55	1.58	2.30	2.63
France	1.92	2.11	2.13	1.74	1.68	1.49	2.81
Spain	3.07	3.04	3.04	3.37	3.52	2.79	4.08
Greece	3.63	3.53	2.90	3.55	3.20	2.90	4.15
Ireland	4.65	3.48	2.19	2.43	3.94	4.88	4.05
Italy	2.46	2.68	2.22	2.00	2.07	1.82	3.38
Portugal	3.55	3.28	2.36	2.29	2.74	2.81	2.59
EU	2.31	2.10	2.26	2.48	2.60	2.63	4.20
Euro area	2.63	2.39	2.26	2.48	2.59	2.44	4.07

Source: International Monetary Fund, International Financial Statistics and data files

Table 5.8 – Intra-EU28 trade by member state (total products, trade balance in million euro)

	2004	2005	2006	2007	2008	2009	2010
Belgium	22,988	21,730	23,238	27,543	25,205	22,312	20,637
Germany	96,072	100,549	103,046	128,591	112,063	73,457	69,348
Ireland	20,272	19,498	14,965	13,514	13,826	21,433	20,443
Greece	-19,484	-18,659	-19,716	-22,587	-23,234	-19,847	-15,081
Spain	-31,767	-36,742	-40,390	-47,972	-36,211	-17,109	-13,626
France	-23,470	-36,885	-39,599	-52,063	-64,373	-63,130	-74,655
Italy	-765	831	1,356	8,130	10,172	-1,912	-7,348
Cyprus	-2,563	-2,656	-3,047	-3,615	-4,153	-3,470	-3,853
Netherlands	93,201	116,460	130,973	137,473	152,806	120,833	153,407
Portugal	-11,020	-14,855	-15,492	-16,351	-19,086	-16,479	-16,687

Source: Eurostat, http://ec.europa.eu/eurostat/tgm/table.do? tab=table&init =1&plugin=1&language=en&pcode=tet00047

Notwithstanding the advantages gained by their admission into the EMU, many countries did not solve their structural economic problems. The Italian economic decline that started in the early 1990s continued, and growth stagnated yet again before the rise of the international crisis. Greece and Portugal remained peripheral economies and were unable to develop a competitive industrial sector. Meanwhile, Spain, Ireland and Cyprus developed a fragile financial sector excessively involved in real estate investments or financial intermediation. On the other hand, French and German banks expanded their financial activities by investing in derivatives and sovereign bonds, and providing capital to foreign banks involved in financing the housing boom. In the meantime, higher inflation and reduced competitiveness in Southern Europe, again induced by cheap money arriving from Central and Northern Europe, widened the economic gap between Northern and Southern Europe and created a vicious circle in which the Southern European trade deficit became structural and only further credit from Central-Northern Europe could cover it (Sinn 2014a).

So the whole EMU economic crisis can be divided into two phases, with the international financial crisis being a milestone. The first was a "pre-crisis" crisis in which imbalances arose, and the EU institutions were unable to contrast them due to the lack of both economic governance tools and the will to use the existing ones. In the second phase, which we call "the crisis after the crisis", the combined impact of internal weaknesses and the international financial crisis created a dramatic deterioration of the EMU's economic and budgetary conditions. So the existing governance tools became inadequate for facing the crisis, even if efficiently used. On the other hand, the chaotic situation that resulted from uncoordinated national anti-crisis policies and later from the panic generated by the sovereign debt crisis hindered rapid empowerment of effective, credible and coordinated governance. The latter was needed to face a general EMU crisis that magnified the pre-crisis weaknesses of the system and made it exponentially more difficult to recover control of the national budget and macroeconomic policies.

On the road toward the sovereign debt crisis, the countries most involved followed two different paths, as shown in the following figure. These paths diverged during the convergence period and the early years of EMU membership.

Fig. 5.1 – The genesis of the sovereign debt crisis.

Those countries that avoided structural reforms and did not realise a stable fiscal adjustment experienced precarious public finances and were severely touched by reduced competitiveness and the fall in fiscal revenue caused by the international crisis. The other countries, which entered the EMU by arranging stable fiscal adjustments, benefited from the growing financial integration in the EMU area. They expanded the activities of their financial and banking systems by collecting money abroad and reinvesting that money in the domestic private sector (mainly buildings and mortgages in the cases of Ireland and Spain), or expanding their banking activities abroad (as in the case of Cyprus). So when the sovereign debt crisis started, the two groups of countries had different problems to solve and needed different kinds of support. The financially weak countries only needed financial assistance and a restructuring of their banking system, which meant that external support could solve many of the problems. The politically weak countries, on the other hand, required a more complex set of support measures and internal reforms that mainly depended on the national governments in trouble. These reforms proved difficult to adopt and created political tensions that made overcoming the crisis problematic.

2 – *Facing the eurozone crisis*

When the international crisis arrived in Europe, the fragility of the EMU emerged, and the traditional mechanism of the financial drain in a time of crisis exacerbated the problems of each country. Almost all the major EMU countries had to support their banking system by saving illiquid banks or financing them. Moreover, those banking systems that were more involved in the real estate boom had to face a rising rate of insolvency among householders. Also, economic marginality or decline combined with a credit crunch aggravated the gap and Southern EMU countries' dependence on Central and Northern EMU member states. The capital drain exacerbated all these problems because international banks and financial centres retired capital or cut credit to recover liquidity. Within a couple of years, the banking crisis became a sovereign debt crisis when banks' rescue and fiscal revenue reduction magnified the risk of sovereign default in Southern Europe.

The rise of the so-called "sovereign debt crisis" was a turning point for the EMU. It started when the Greek crisis spread to the rest of Southern Europe and Ireland and put at risk the whole EMU and the survival of the euro. The core of this crisis was Greece and its bankrupting government. For years the Greek government hid the real extent of the state budget deficit. When, finally, in October 2009 the new finance minister Papakonstantinou revealed the real extent of the Greek deficit and the deficit/GDP ratio, which amounted to 12.5%, the Greek bonds' rating sank and the interest rate on Greek debt rose consistently (Featherstone 2011, p. 200). In May 2010, after a request for assistance from the Greek government, the EU Commission and the International Monetary Fund launched a rescue plan for Greece, offering a 110 billion euro emergency fund and asking for a drastic cut in government expenses (Katsikas 2012, p. 50). The austerity policy introduced by the government led to wild protests.

Meanwhile, Ireland and Portugal also faced problems and asked for EU support. So a 78 billion euro rescue plan for Portugal was activated in May (Gorjão 2012, p. 66), and 85 billion euros were devoted to the rescue plan for Ireland requested in November (Degryse 2012, p. 33; Shambaugh 2012, p. 191). Unfortunately, the first rescue plan for Greece was too small for the dramatic crisis of that country and a new rescue plan had to be developed, increasing the funds to 219 billion euros in July 2011 and to 240 billion euros in February 2012 (Katsikas 2012, p. 51). Notwithstanding the rescue plans, the sovereign debt crisis spread to other countries in Southern Europe. Both Spain and Cyprus suffered for their links with the financial markets of Portugal and Greece, respectively. In addition, both countries had overexpanded and overexposed banking systems that the government was unable to support because of the collapse of the bond market and the massive needs of the banks they had to rescue. In June 2012, the Spanish government asked the EU for financial support. A 100 billion euro loan guaranteed by the government was arranged for saving the Spanish banks. In March 2013, Cyprus also obtained a rescue plan for saving its financial system. However, the price to pay was very high because a tax on deposits over 100,000 euros was imposed (Georgiou 2013, p. 60 and 63).

The peak of the sovereign debt crisis arrived when the price of the Italian bonds started to fall in summer 2011 and the risk of Italian bankruptcy became real. Italy was the third-biggest economy in the EU and its collapse could have been devastating for the whole eurozone (Jones 2012; Hopkin 2012). However, a rescue plan for Italy was unfeasible due to the country's enormous public debt. A new and complex approach was needed to face such a dangerous crisis. In the end, it was the famous speech by Mario Draghi, who declared in June 2012 that the euro would be saved "whatever it takes", that stopped the most acute phase of the sovereign debt crisis and enabled the EMU financial system to be stabilised.

After the outbreak of the Greek crisis, it became evident that having the same currency and the same rules to respect does not mean that all member governments' bonds have the same level of risk. This perception also suggested that the bonds of other EMU countries could be less reliable than expected, particularly those issued by highly indebted countries or countries in deep financial crisis. In fact, banking support or the rescuing of banks "too big to fail" could only be arranged by the governments and this required the issuing of new public debt. However, focusing only on sovereign debts is misleading. In many cases, the banking sector and its expansion as a consequence of monetary integration was the real driver of the crisis. This was certainly the case with Spain, Ireland and Cyprus. All three countries expanded their financial system by being involved in speculative business. In Spain and Ireland, it was the real estate sector that attracted funds due to the constant increase in house prices. So a speculative bubble arose, as happened in the USA. All these countries also suffered the consequences of their involvement in their neighbours' financial system. Spanish banks funded the Portuguese economy while Irish banks drew funds from the UK financial market. Consequently, the Portuguese crisis reduced the financial soundness of banks in Spain,[4] while the Irish banks suffered for the retirement of British capital. A similar linkage existed between the financial markets of Cyprus and Greece. The main banks in Cyprus collected huge amounts of money from outside the EU. It was mainly Russians that used banks in Cyprus as an offshore banking system, and a relevant flow of money arrived there to escape from Russia and avoid "embarrassing questions" about the origin of that wealth. However, such a high level of depositing required profitable investment opportunities. The main banks in Cyprus found such opportunities by investing in Greeks bonds. They also expanded their banking network in Greece. This exposed them to the collapse of the Greek economy in the early 2010s (Georgiou 2013, p. 59–60). The Greek banks also expanded their activities to the Balkan areas, particularly to those countries that were not members of the EMU. In fact, Greek banks were able to collect cheap money from the EMU's financial markets and lend it to those countries where the interest rates were still high. Unfortunately, this role as an intermediary banking system led to the Greek banks being exposed to capital drain from the main EMU financial centres, as happened with the international crisis of the late 2000s (Pagoulatos and Triantopoulos 2009, p. 42–43). So for those countries that benefited from rescue plans or financial assistance, the sovereign debt crisis had a relevant financial component and was not just a matter of public debt.

Liquidity and a crisis of confidence resulted in a capital drain from the debtor countries. Initially, this drain mainly regarded short-term funds and passed through the ECB and

---

[4] The rescue plan for Portugal probably also aimed to support Spanish banks involved in the Portuguese banking system.

the TARGET2 system.[5] This system absorbed the capital flows through the increase of positive and negative balances as depicted in the following graphs. In practice, capital flows resulted in a dramatic and symmetrical increase of both the debts of capital losers and the credits of capital takers with the ECB. These balances were tiny until the end of 2007 because creditors' surpluses were reinvested in inter-bank credits and the bonds of Southern EMU countries. When the international crisis activated capital drain mechanisms, the balance equilibrium disappeared and they rose continually from early 2009. They skyrocketed at the beginning of 2011, reaching a peak in mid-2012. After that peak, the balances decreased until early 2015 when the start of the Quantitative Easing programme fuelled a new take-off in TARGET2 balances.[6]

The symmetrical structure of the TARGET2 balances (Fig. 5.2) is crucial for understanding the crisis. A distinct group of countries accumulated positive balances inside the system and these balances were almost the equivalents of the negative balances accumulated by another distinct group of countries. The creditors' group included Germany, the Netherlands, Luxembourg and Finland, while in the debtors' group we find Greece, Italy, Ireland, Portugal and Spain. So the TARGET2 balance structure repeats the dual structure of the EMU and the fracture between Central-Northern and Southern EMU countries.

[5] The Trans-European Automated Real-Time Gross Settlement Express Transfer System 2 (TARGET2) is the system used by the ECB and the national central banks to manage the intra-EU money transfer. It was created in November 2007 and replaced the TARGET system created in 1999 (Bindseil and König 2011, 3; Sinn 2014a, p. 176–196).

[6] The Quantitative Easing is a monetary policy tool used to increase liquidity in the system buying bonds in the secondary market and to reduce interest rates on banking loans. This helps families increase consumption. In practice, a Quantitative Easing programme creates money to stimulate the economy. In the meantime, the Quantitative Easing launched by the ECB in January 2015 supported the price of bonds on the secondary market and stopped the sovereign debt crisis (Hodson 2015, p. 153).

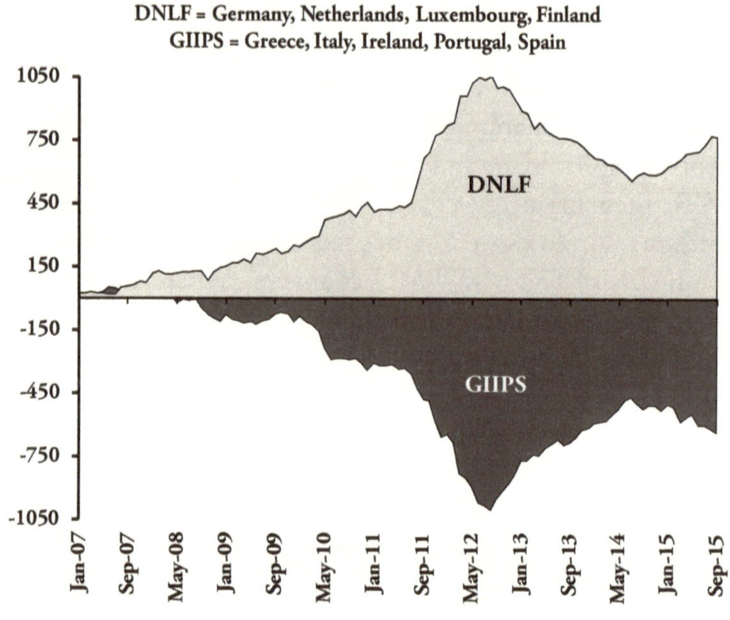

Fig. 5.2 – TARGET2 balances regrouped (billions of euro).

Source: Euro Crisis Monitor, Institute of Empirical Economic Research, Osnabrück University (elaborated from the central banks' balance sheets)

The analysis of the TARGET2 balances of single countries (Fig. 5.3) offers a more detailed picture of the process. The predominance of Germany emerges as a creditor country for the whole period while the peak of 2012 is mainly due to the dramatic increase in Italian and Spanish debtor balances. The concomitant peak in German creditor balances suggests that the sovereign debt crisis before mid-2011 was mainly a drain on German short-term funds from countries in trouble. Later, it became a sudden and massive sale of Italian and Spanish bonds.[7] This conclusion implies that both economic and political motivation worsened and made the sovereign debt crisis

[7] The whole process is explained in detail in Minenna, Boi and Verzella (2016, p. 122–172).

more dramatic. Also, the impact of the "German financial retreat" emphasises the relevance of German singularity and its internal economic policy impact on the rest of the EMU. The following graph roughly estimates the capital movements during the period 2006–2012.

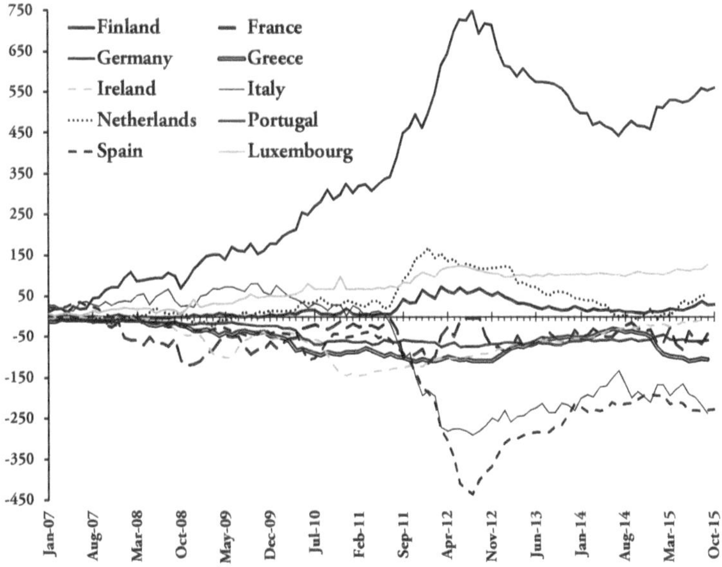

Fig. 5.3 – TARGET2 balances (billions of euro).

Source: Euro Crisis Monitor, Institute of Empirical Economic Research, Osnabrück University (elaborated from the central banks' balance sheets)

The most relevant information in chart regards the magnitude and direction of net capital flux. Germany was the leading capital giver. Benelux was an intermediary that collected capitals from Germany and France and redistributed them to GIPS (Greece, Italy, Portugal and Spain) countries and the UK. France acted in a similar way attracting funds from Germany and the rest of the non-European world. Finally, the UK collected funds from Benelux and GIPS. Part of the funds from GIPS represents internal capital flight escaping from countries in trouble.

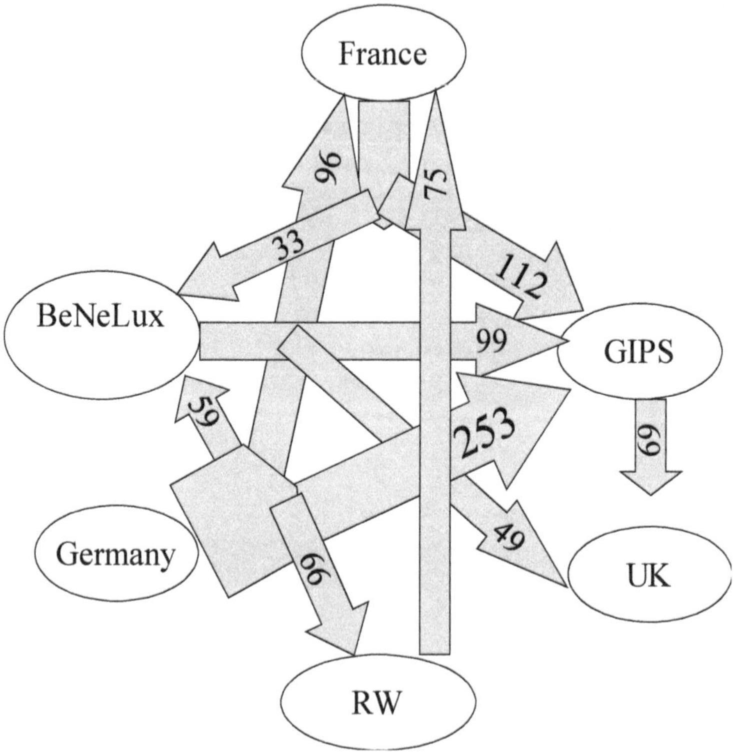

Fig. 5.4 – Net capital flux 2007–2012 (billions of euro).

Source: Elaboration from Hobza and Zeugner 2014

The eurozone crisis was contrasted with various arrangements. It is important to distinguish between the impact of the international financial crisis and the rising sovereign debt crisis. In the early years, the most significant problem was the liquidity reduction of the larger banks due to the American financial crisis and the block of the interbank money market. This problem required the intervention of both governments and the ECB. The governments supported their banks and funded some problematic banking rescues.[8] However, the ECB

[8] These were the famous cases of the French bank Dexia, the German

granted credits to banks as direct credit or via the LTRO channel.[9] Between mid-2008 and mid-2010, German and French banks were the primary collectors of ESCB credit.[10] However, in early 2009, credit to these banks decreased. In mid-2011, credit to French, Italian and Spanish banks increased while credit to German banks remained stable and low.

In 2012, LTRO credits granted liquidity to many EMU banks. However, LTRO credit contributed poorly to solving the credit crunch problem. Instead, the funds permitted repatriation of state bonds and repurchase of the banks' obligations (Minenna, Boi and Verzella 2016, p. 142–172). The following Table 5.9 shows the progressive increase in debt securities held by banks. It is evident that Italian and Spanish banks started to accumulate debt securities in 2009. However, it was during the period 2011–2013 that debt repatriation became massive.

The TARGET2 peak in 2011–2012 probably funded the nationalisation of state bonds and other securities. When other tools for bond market stabilisation became operative (e.g. the European Financial Stabilisation Mechanism), the nationalisation flows stopped and TARGET2 balances decreased. However, the transfer of state bonds in domestic banks' portfolios magnified the already existing vicious link between banks and governments. In fact, the governments needed sta-

---

Landersbanks and Hypo Real Estate, and the Anglo-Irish Bank (Sinn 2014a, p. 57–58). Many other banks required and obtained the support of their governments.

[9] Longer-Term Refinancing Operations (LTROs) are cheap loans (three-year loans with a 1% rate of interest) granted by the ECB to European banks to avoid the credit crunch or the collapse of certain banking systems (House of Lords 2014, p. 48).

[10] It is important to distinguish between the actions of the national central banks and those of the ECB. In some cases, the national central banks of the most troubled countries accepted as collateral for loans low-quality commercial papers to grant liquidity to their national system. It is not clear how independently they took these decisions and the extent to which the ECB supported them (Sinn 2014a).

bility in the bond market, and the interest rate on bonds depended on the offering of bonds on the secondary market. So if banks keep bonds in their portfolios, the spread between interest rates remains low. On the other hand, banks need liquidity, and they can only keep a large number of bonds in their portfolios if someone other than the market can grant them liquidity. This can only be the ESCB accepting bonds as collateral or buying bonds. Finally, with a huge quantity of government bonds in their portfolios, banks' balance sheets, profits and affordability depend on bond price and rating.

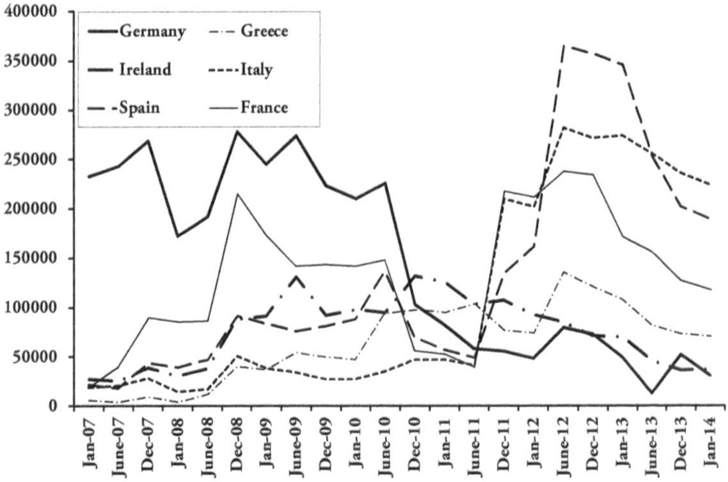

Fig. 5.5 – Lending to eurozone credit institutions related to monetary policy operations denominated in euro (millions).

Notes: All series show the month-end values except for Spain where the monthly average of daily data is reported. All series exclude potential ELA credit.

Sources: Individual central banks; www.eurocrisis.com

Table 5.9 – Debt securities held: outstanding amounts at the end of the period toward the general government (stocks, millions of euro, last quarterly data)

	2006	2007	2008	2009	2010	2011	2012	2013	2014
Italy	121,880	123,747	133,927	170,018	214,739	229,444	349,068	402,636	423,585
Spain	85,839	94,432	112,213	173,561	168,401	202,182	254,085	270,542	310,169
Greece	30,979	24,341	24,233	35,043	46,085	45,939	19,604	12,667	12,398
Cyprus	4,259	4,256	5,541	12,134	15,669	9,030	6,484	5,326	4,651
Portugal	5,804	5,446	5,748	15,161	27,031	25,992	34,936	37,298	38,132
Ireland	62,571	53,894	57,253	64,344	35,979	34,558	44,837	42,407	50,216
Germany	281,176	249,602	232,025	263,084	321,064	292,773	335,870	342,800	362,856
France	313,678	325,780	321,822	337,262	313,974	199,283	254,891	249,477	276,266

Source: ECB, Statistical Data Warehouse, http://sdw.ecb.europa.eu/ browseSelection.do?removeItem =&BS_COUNT_SECTOR=2100&ec=&rc=&oc=&df=true&BS_ITEM=A30&BS_ITEM=A30&DATA_TYPE=1&DATA_TYPE=1&DATASET=0&dc=&node=bbn5449&pb=&activeTab=&trans=N

The entire process of EMU stabilisation can be depicted as in the following graph. It explains how the ECB faced the eurozone crisis by reorganising the whole EMU financial system and restructuring it as a less integrated system through the renationalisation of bonds and the neutralisation of money flows. Later, new tools for stabilising the financial market and the secondary market for bonds were introduced. This strategy allowed the collapse of the whole EMU financial system to be avoided and made the ECB the critical actor in managing the EMU.

The ECB intervention generated the renationalisation of the public debt, probably as a condition imposed on banks in need of funds. ECB loans also offered banks the opportunity to consolidate their financial position by repurchasing their obligations. However, both the ECB intervention and the rescue packages for countries in trouble required austerity policies in those countries and this worsened the economic crisis and made recovery more problematic.

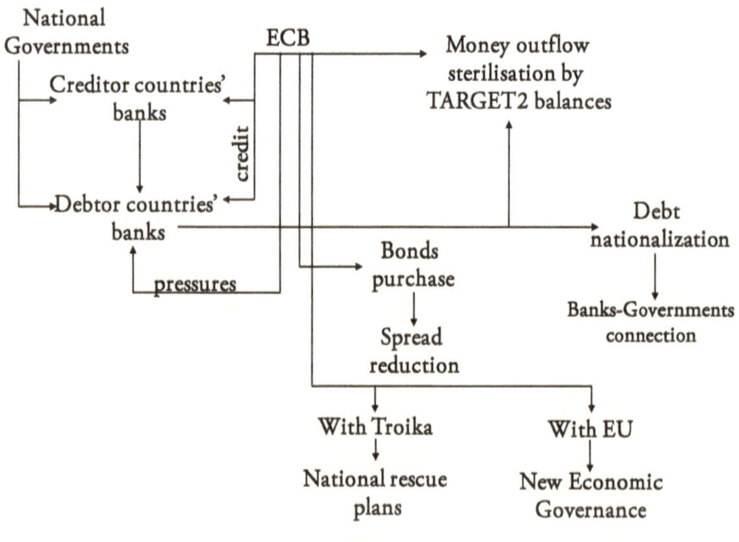

Fig. 5.6 – The ECB strategy to stabilise the EMU financial structure

The ECB action is outlined better in the following figure. It summarises the mechanism that fosters the whole EMU crisis. The international crises activated the banking crises in Europe. The latter resulted in credit reduction, capital flows and banking rescues that augmented public debts. Economic growth declined as a consequence of the credit crunch, while the mounting sovereign debt crisis and the austerity policies imposed by EU rules and ECB conditionality affected growth. Bankruptcies, frozen and irrecoverable loans, and the devaluation of assets reverberated on banks and fed the banking crisis.

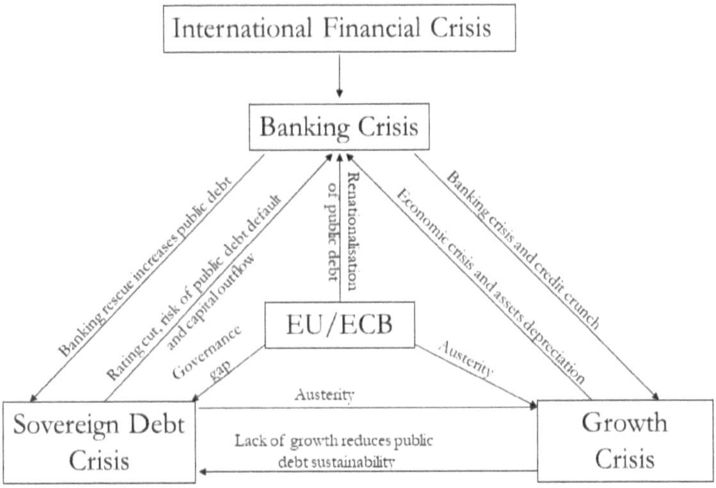

Fig. 5.7 – The propagation channels of the international financial crisis in the European Union.

Source: Elaboration from Shambaugh 2012

3 – The origin of the ECB's predominant role in crisis management

The reconstruction of the EMU financial structure rescue during the sovereign debt crisis depicted above suggests some reflections. The first regards the beneficiaries of the rescue.

It is evident that all EMU members benefited from the rescue. However, German banks benefited more. These banks were the most involved in financial intermediation inside the EMU financial system. Northern banks (mainly German and Dutch banks) in the early 2000s probably "believed" in EMU solidity and affordability and profited from all the opportunities they had to increase their business. However, they were heavily exposed to GIIPS countries whose default could drive creditor banks into bankruptcy. ECB loans granted them liquidity, and the sterilisation of capital flows in the TARGET2 system moved problematic credits from countries in trouble to an obscure and entirely affordable section of the ESCB. So the situation of creditor banks improved, enabling them to avoid bankruptcy.

However, debtor countries were relieved by the risk of default and most of them benefited by interest reduction after that, during the crisis, interest rates on public bonds become unsustainable for their budget. The way in which the ECB faced the EMU crisis required sacrifices and coherence with the logic of the ECB strategy. It was a short-term logic in which EMU members had to work to consolidate the fragile alternative financial structure arranged by the ECB. This meant that there was no space for countercyclical economic policies or national expansive budget policies to face the economic crisis. The only options to defend the newly reached financial stability were keeping frozen the TARGET2 creditor balances and prioritising fiscal adjustment in debtor countries, mainly through austerity policies. This logic differs from the explanations proposed by many EMU critics and anti-EU movements. The main faults of the ECB monetary policy are its emergency nature and its short-term perspective and not the ambition to destroy democracy and the welfare state in Europe, as suggested by many supporters of euro abandonment. The ECB strategy negatively touches both Northern and Southern EMU countries. However, both pay the price for their past choices, and this is the price to avoid the collapse of the whole EMU financial system.

The strategy adopted by the ECB has at least two problematic consequencces. The first regards the economic policies for facing the crisis. The ECB is not entitled to create long-term economic policies, and it is not required to coordinate monetary policy with national or European economic policies. This means that financial stability is the ECB's predominant objective notwithstanding it collides with mid-term solutions to contrast the economic slump. The latter is not a primary task for the ECB, at least in its statute. Moreover, no effective counter-crisis policy can be pursued by either national governments or the EU in the absence of financial stability and a working financial system. This means that, in every case, financial stabilisation is the first step in facing the crisis. The ECB took this step. Unfortunately, it does not have the right or the capability to take the steps that had to follow and national governments in some cases proved to be unable to fulfil their task as the leading economic policymakers.

The second problematic consequence of the ECB strategy is that in the new EMU financial system redrafted by the ECB, the latter has a crucial political role in addressing national budget policies and economic reforms. This political role depends on the relationship between governments, banks and the ECB depicted above. In this relationship, the ECB has the power to lead unsubordinated governments and banks close to bankruptcy as happened in Greece in summer 2015.[11] This

[11] In January 2015, the Syriza party won the Greek elections. Its leader, Tsipras, created a government in coalition with a small anti-euro party. The political programme of the new government included a drastic revision of the agreements signed with the so-called "Troika" formed by the IMF, the ECB and the EU Commission. After tensions and a stalemate in the negotiations to avoid Greece defaulting, Tsipras organised a referendum on a draft agreement with Troika. The agreement was rejected by popular vote. Meanwhile, the emergency liquidity granted by the ECB to the Greek banks was suspended and the latter had to restrict payments and cash machines' liquidity. An interesting (not neutral) reconstruction of the events has been provided by Varoufakis (2017).

possibility is an informal coercive force of a political nature not included in the power surrendered by EMU member states to the ECB. Instead, this authority derives from the structure of the EMU financial system rearranged by the ECB to face the sovereign debt crisis.

The rise of the political role of the ECB was not coincidental. The ECB was probably inspired in developing its intervention strategy by the need to create a coercive tool for addressing the action of governments. In this way, the ECB created an informal governance system that it leads. This system took the place of the almost non-existent economic governance system of the 2000s. Today it supports the growing new economic governance created in the early 2010s and still partially ineffective.

The legitimacy of the ECB's informal predominance is debatable. The topic of legitimacy and the impact of the new economic governance will be discussed in the following chapters. However, it is crucial to understand that the rise of the ECB's political role resulted from the inability shown by the EU institutions to counter the crisis. In the absence of efficient coercive tools at the disposal of the EU institutions, the ECB created a mechanism that granted it governance and political power mainly confined to the economic field. In other words, the ECB strategically contextualised monetary policy and amplified its political impact using technical advantages it was entirely legitimate to use.

Notwithstanding the dramatic course of EMU crises and the vast number of problems that emerged in the early years of its existence, a large number of the arguments used in the 1990s against the monetary union appear to be unfounded, in particular the argumentation inspired by the OCA theory. The most significant problems and factors of fragility identified above (financial flows, excessive expansion and the growing connection of ungoverned financial systems, real estate and derivatives speculation, the lack of economic convergence) were not those indicated by the OCA theory and its supporters. Also, those scholars who today see in the EMU crisis the "revenge of OCA theory" (Krugman 2013) or just its confirmation forget that the international financial crisis of the late 2000s did not primarily create an asymmetrical shock. In other words, the international crisis was not the event the OCA theorists identified as the critical mechanism capable of inducing the collapse of a non-optimal currency area, i.e. an asymmetrical shock. Instead, it was an almost symmetrical shock that touched *in primis* the same sector (the financial one) throughout the EMU area, and that emphasised the weaker elements in each member state's economy. Also, before the crises, the items that made the economic structure of the EMU area fragile were not the lack of capital or labour mobility, nor the trade balance, i.e. the crucial factors identified by the OCA theory. Instead, this fragility derived from the lack of governance that permitted a chaotic and ungoverned integration. The adoption of a broad and complex set of new rules in the 2010s, the so-called "new European economic governance", which we will analyse in the next chapter, demonstrates that it was possible to manage better and more pervasively the consolidation of monetary integration in the EMU area. However, the symmetrical nature of the crisis made the lack of a central European government a minor factor in facing it, at least on the budgetary side. In fact, there were few opportunities to balance the crisis impact with fiscal transfers precisely because the fall in fiscal revenues was symmetrical in the whole area as a consequence of the international crisis. So one of the leading corrective factors a European state could offer to counterbalance the non-optimality of the EMU currency area would be inapplicable.

As specified above, this conclusion works only for the budgetary side. If a central government existed for the EMU area, it could coordinate better the efforts to face the crisis and the use of monetary policy to help the weaker countries emerge from the crisis. Moreover, if this European government had existed since the early years of the currency union, it could have acted to avoid the rise of some elements that amplified the crisis like the real estate boom or the overexpansion of the financial sector. The latter is an obvious conclusion, notwithstanding there is evidence that the governments in the USA, Great Britain, France and Germany did not realise the severity of these risks and did not act to correct these problems until the international economic crisis forced them to act. So the existence of a European state would not have led to better management of the pre-crisis period. Probably, a broader and better governance of the EMU area could be realised with or without a European government. So the problem was not the existence of a European state, but the real ability to manage the EMU and to coordinate macroeconomic policies in the area. The only advantage a European government should have had was the power to impose its rules on all the member states, at least if this hypothetic European state was not a confederation or a weak federation, i.e. the two most likely forms the European state could assume. Because of the absence of a European government, the ECB had to assume a political role limited to new sectors in which it had the power to act. This explains the peculiarity and the limited effectiveness of the reaction to the eurozone crisis.

Summarising, the two main problems that affected the new EMU area were the wrong perception of the risks derived from an unmanaged integration and the inability to coordinate EMU members toward economic convergence and debt reduction. So, as predicted by Dornbusch (1996), the crucial weakness of the EMU project was on the political side. This problem emerges when analysing the economic measures taken to face the crisis.

Chapter 6

The New European Economic Governance

After the signing of the Maastricht Treaty, two main and closely connected problems emerged for monetary integration. The first was fostering economic convergence among member states' economies. The convergence of the leading economic parameters may have allowed the problems created by the lack of common fiscal policy for the whole eurozone to be partially resolved. In other words, convergence was the "magic" tool chosen by the euro planners for enabling economic integration and avoiding political integration. So, until 2008, economic convergence remained the main, perhaps the only, strategy pursued to keep the euro operative without creating Europe. Making economic convergence the pivotal strategy to make the EMU work was a political choice. This strategy made it possible to limit the surrendering of sovereignty in "purely political fields" while creating and consolidating a common currency, i.e. avoiding creating a European government and fiscal solidarity. It was this strategy that failed, not monetary integration. Stable inflation, interest and exchange rates (until the introduction of fixed exchange rates in 1999), and balanced government budgets became the primary objective for the rising eurozone. These objectives and the respect for specific parameters were the core of the so-called "Stability and Growth Pact" (SGP), i.e. the primary economic governance tool in the hands of the European institutions until the end of the 2000s.

The second problem was economic governance, in particular the ability of EU institutions to control and drive EMU member states to implement and respect the Stability and Growth Pact. Economic governance is the place where technical and political matters join and frequently collide. Unfortunately, EMU founders limited the role of economic governance to few and inefficient instruments and relied mainly on convergence. This choice allowed the political fragility of the EMU to be hidden, at least until governing the EMU efficiently became an unavoidable necessity.

Economic convergence and economic governance are interrelated problems because the former depends mainly on the second while the latter for two decades was aimed mainly at achieving the former. The euro crisis demonstrated that the whole architecture of monetary integration is at risk in the absence of a complex and intrusive system of economic governance capable of addressing the economic policy of all the EMU member states and guaranteeing convergence. Unfortunately, this intrusiveness has a negative impact on domestic policies and politics in almost all EMU countries. The tight limits to internal and democratically decided policies are often perceived as an attack on democracy and national sovereignty by both leftist and extreme right parties and movements. So, in the late 2000s, the deepening of monetary integration and the rise of a more stringent and intrusive European economic governance shaped the faith in the whole integration process, changing its priorities, the EU institutional structure and citizens' attitudes toward the EU and its values. A "European identity crisis" followed.

We will discuss the political dimension of this identity crisis in the third part of this book. However, it is essential to understand immediately that today EMU governance is the core problem for European integration. EU delegitimisation derives mainly from the rejection of stricter financial supervision of domestic policies in the EU member states. The single currency became the negative symbol of the European Union's invasiveness. So rising anti-Europeanism, as well as anti-eurism,[1] are directly fed by the enforcement and effectiveness of the new economic governance, i.e. the sum of new rules and practices introduced to face the EMU crisis. These rules and practices collide with the values and declared aims of European integration. They had been perceived by many European citizens and depicted by EU opponents as a betrayal of those values. This contrast contributed to the rise of a broader crisis of European integration that involved not only the euro and the EU economic structure but also the idea of European unity.

This book explains part of the "wider crisis" of European integration with the concept of a "governance gap". In other words, we will place the responsibility of the "wider crisis" on the failure of a convergence-oriented strategy, the lack of governance instruments the EU suffered in the 2000s and the delay in filling this gap. This delay produced damages plugged with emergency measures that created bitter political tension and disenchantment in the European population. At the same time, these damages undermined consensus for further steps in European integration and restricted the range of policies pursuable for that aim.

Ascribing such a relevant role to the governance gap has significant theoretical consequences. First, it means dismissing the economic approach centred on EMU sustainability and focused on the eurozone's governability. More specifically, focusing on the governance gap means rejecting the approach of optimal currency areas and the use of that theory made by many economists and almost all EMU opponents. In contrast, the governance gap approach suggests that the EMU can work as a currency area, notwithstanding it is not an optimal

[1] We distinguish between anti-Europeanism and anti-eurism. The latter is a more specific kind of anti-Europeanism that focuses on monetary integration and the common currency as the main problem for member states' economy and democracy.

one. However, in the absence of a central European government, the EMU needs to be governed by an invasive, efficient and coordinated system of governance. Today, this system does not exist yet, and the rise of populist parties and anti-euro attitudes widespread in many member states put at risk the possibility of completing and consolidating the system.

Second, the governance gap approach stresses the responsibility of member states for making the EMU unstable and inefficient. So this approach partly rejects criticism against EU institutions for the EMU crisis. Instead, it emphasises the costs of poor fiscal and political discipline on the part of member states. However, member states' responsibility is individual as well as collective. The weak governance system of the early 2000s resulted from collective choices made by the member states. They tried to limit sovereignty surrender, abandoning EMU governance and economic convergence for almost voluntary compliance, notwithstanding past experiences demonstrated the poor affordability of some problematic countries.

Third, the governance gap approach implies that member states are fundamentally hostile to political integration. This makes the latter the last best choice for them and offers another element that contrasts with the idea of political integration predominance that has inspired many theorists of European integration since the 1950s.

1 – The EMU governance in the early 2000s

The governance gap originated with the EMU itself. The Maastricht Treaty missed the introduction of governance tools and effective coercive means. During the 1990s, the main leverage to obtain the respects the obligations imposed by the Maastricht Treaty was the possibility of denying admission in the final stage of the EMU. In the treaty, monetary governance relied mainly on the well-known convergence criteria, and there was no "corrective arm" for imposing sanctions, just the risk for non-complying countries of being excluded from the first wave of admission into the EMU.

It was only when the Treaty of Amsterdam introduced the Stability and Growth Pact that EMU economic governance appeared.[2] The SGP included a "preventive arm" and a "corrective arm". The former provided an instrument to identify and correct deviations from the convergence criteria and indicates Medium-Term Budgetary Objectives (MTOs) to gain or maintain fiscal stability. The corrective arm, on the other hand, introduced the excessive deficit procedure and provided the power to inflict fines on the member countries that do not respect the budgetary criteria and the EU calls for correction (Mortensen 2013).

The SGP was reformed in 2005 and integrated after 2010 with other norms that reinforced both the preventive and the corrective arm.[3] Today, it remains the core of EMU governance. However, reforms and integration testify to its problematic enforcement and its poor effectiveness during the early stage of the existence of the common currency.

After introducing the euro, EMU governance showed its inefficiency (Heipertz and Verdun 2010 and 2004; Talani 2008). The existing rules proved to be insufficient to face the problems created by the lack of a shared economic and fiscal policy for the whole EMU area. Also, the coercive power of EU institutions was too scarce to be used against member states. Adopting sanctions needed a complicated decisional process in which political considerations might prevail on the need for an efficient instrument of economic governance for the EMU. A well-known example of the troubled governance of the EMU was the failure of the European Commission to have sanctions

[2] For the specific contents and parameters of the SGP see Table 6.2.

[3] The core point of the 2005 SGP reform was a less restrictive interpretation of the 3% limit for the budget/GDP ratio. That limit was no more compelling for those countries with a debt/GDP ratio under the limit of 60% (Talani 2008).

against France and Germany approved by the Council of the European Union in 2004–2005. In that case, the uncertainty about the effectiveness of the SGP corrective arm became evident. In particular, it emerged that corrective procedures are not almost automatic tools, but a politically mediated process in which *do ut des* arrangements can outflank the SGP rules while reducing the SGP credibility itself (Dutzler and Hable 2005). Finally, the 2005 reform of the SGP made it more flexible but seemed like a loosening of the fiscal rules in favour of some member states, without a corresponding reinforcement of the corrective instruments at the disposal of the EU. That reform probably reinforced the moral hazard attitude of some governments. They saw the reform as an initial step toward more flexible management of EMU governance having faith in future flexibility to their advantage.

Another aspect of the governance gap after the Maastricht Treaty was the scarce coordination between "governances". The term "governance" indicates a unified system of governance that applies poorly to the management of economic matters in the European Union, at least until the 2010s and the introduction of the so-called "new economic governance". So we must distinguish at least between "economic governance" and "monetary governance". While the SGP was the core of monetary governance, the Broad Economic Policy Guidelines (BEPGs) were the constitutive pillar of the rest of economic governance.

The BEPGs had been introduced by the Maastricht Treaty and adopted yearly from 1993 until 2002. Since 2003 they have been revised every three years and have the legal form of recommendations, i.e. a legislative act that suggests unbinding actions (Degryse 2012). So member states adopt or reject the new BEPGs using the Open Method of Coordination (OMC),[4] and the practice of "comply or explain".

[4] The Open Method of Coordination was introduced with the Lisbon

In 1997, the European Employment Strategy contained in the Amsterdam Treaty was merged with the BEPGs as part of a new kind of EU economic governance in which employment had more relevance than before. A new set of guidelines called "Employment Guidelines" (EGs) integrated the EU economic governance system (Goetschy 1999; Palpant 2006; Raveaud 2007). One year later, the EU economic governance also included environmental matters. The so-called "Cardiff Process" connected environment protection and European policies. Taking care of environmental matters, it became an obligation for EU policymakers (Unfried 2000). Finally, in 2005, the BEPGs and EGs were joined together in a single set of 24 guidelines. Six of them deal with macroeconomic policy, ten with microeconomic policy and the remaining eight with employment. The OMC also touched on poverty, pensions and health matters joined together in the single field of social protection.

Economic convergence, monetary governance and economic policy coordination by the OMC were the pillars of the EU economic governance from the 1990s until the end of the 2000s. Unfortunately, all three pillars were weak and easily cracked. The limits of the SGP application in the 2000s have been depicted above. These limits added to the poor application of the convergence criteria in the late 1990s when admission into the EMU was decided.

2 – The governance gap and the crisis of the EMU

When the world economic crisis started, in particular after the Lehman Brothers collapse, EMU governance became still

Strategy in the March 2000 European Council. It consists in establishing guidelines and timetables to reach short-, medium- and long-term goals. These guidelines have to be translated into national and regional policies following indicators and benchmarks identified at European level. One of the most relevant aspects of the OMC is its non-compelling nature (Dehousse 2003; Radaelli 2003).

more problematic. Many countries failed to fulfil the SGP criteria, and the Excessive Deficit Procedure was ineffective and unsafe for regaining stability and convergence, as well as being impossible to apply to so many countries.[5] Moreover, the crisis revealed the existence of other problems that resulted from monetary integration and that needed to be considered in EMU governance. One of these problems was the unavoidable need to include a more comprehensive list of macroeconomic objectives in the EMU's economic governance. The economic crisis and the different reactions of member states to macroeconomic imbalances showed that convergence is not just a matter of fiscal discipline and inflation containment. Rather, it needs macroeconomic coordination and a more comprehensive set of parameters than the SGP ones. The crisis in Southern Europe and Ireland demonstrated that many elements contribute to undermining economic convergence, which for decades was the basis of the whole strategy for economic and monetary integration. The unemployment rate, house pricing, intra-EU trade, capital flows and other more technical parameters proved to be essential for convergence and useful indicators for anticipating imbalances.[6]

[5] From 2008 to 2013, Excessive Deficit Procedures (EDPs) were applied against many of the EU member countries. At the end of 2014, there were procedures still open against the UK (since 2008), Spain (since 2009), Greece (since 2009), Ireland (since 2009), France (since 2009), Poland (since 2009), Slovenia (since 2009), Portugal (since 2009), Cyprus (since 2010), Malta (since 2013) and Croatia (since 2013). In 2014, procedures against the Czech Republic (2009–2014), Slovakia (2010–2014), Austria (2009–2014), Denmark (2010–2014), Belgium (2010–2014) and the Netherlands (2010–2014) were closed. During the period 2009–2013, EDPs were opened and closed against Italy (2009–2013), Bulgaria (2010–2012), Germany (2009–2012), Finland (2010–2013), Latvia (2009–2013), Lithuania (2009–2013) and Romania (2009–2013). http://ec.europa.eu/economy_finance/economic_governance/sgp/corrective_arm/index_en.htm.

[6] The relevance of some parameters emerged from the analysis of the GIIPS crisis and its genesis (e.g. house prices and capital flows for Spain and Ireland, competitiveness for Italy).

On the other hand, their role in generating the euro crisis demonstrates that the fiscal-centred approach based on budget stability, debt containment and convergence adopted since Maastricht does not work. In fact, that approach does not consider the internal dynamics generated by monetary integration and the need to govern them.

Finally, the rise of the eurozone crisis made apparent the need for procedures and instruments to face emergencies and systemic imbalances. Moreover, implementation and coercive tools for imposing accomplishment on troubled governments became indispensable. Later, the need for a more sophisticated approach to economic governance and EMU monetary policy emerged. As a consequence, the vision of the 2000s of the ECB monetary policy and the "ideology of convergence" was inadequate for the new needs of the EMU.

In 2010–2011, the ineffectiveness and the limits of EU economic governance in addressing member states induced the EU institutions to establish a new set of rules that dramatically reduced economic policy alternatives for national governments, particularly for the most troubled ones.

The essential norms to face the crisis and empower the EMU economic governance were included in the so-called "Six-pack" (2011) and "Two-pack" (2013) sets of norms. The Six-pack introduced two significant innovations: the European semester and the reverse qualified majority as a method for deciding on sanctions.

The European semester is the core of the new EU economic governance. It is a sequence where member states present budget drafts and action plans to fulfil EU duties in terms of the economic and budgetary policy. EU institutions, mainly the Commission, interact with member states, warning them about missing goals and dues and, if needed, impose sanctions against them irrespective of their obligations. So most of the new EU economic and monetary governance is carried out during the European semester.

The reverse qualified majority empowered the EU coercive capability. It imposed a qualified majority to block sanctions, not to approve them as happened before. In this case, too, EU institutions draw from the emergence of the EMU governance gap a lesson to ameliorate the management of the common currency, enforcing the SGP corrective arm and increasing the effectiveness of the EU coercive tools. However, launching an infraction procedure still requires a qualified majority. This rule counterbalances the strength of the EU institutions and risks undermining the effectiveness of the new economic governance (Fernandes 2014).

The Six-pack also introduced a new enforcement regime against member states that do not respect economic governance rules. Also, the Six-pack imposed on countries that exceeded the 60% of GDP rule for public debt a 5% yearly cut in the excessive quota, including in the *acquis communautaire*, a rule previously introduced by the so-called "Fiscal Compact". Finally, it introduced new instruments for so-called "macroeconomic governance", in particular macroeconomic scoreboards and an early warning system to call member states to make readjustments to their economic policies.

The macroeconomic scoreboards are not the only parameters considered for macroeconomic governance. There are additional indicators established by Article 4.4 of EU Regulation no. 1176/2011.[7] Scoreboards and additional indicators are regularly

[7] The list of additional indicators is as follows: Real GDP, Gross Fixed Capital Formation, Gross Domestic Expenditure on Research and Development (GERD), Net Lending-Borrowing, Current plus Capital Account, Net External Debt, Inward FDI (flows and stocks), Net Trade Balance of Energy Products, Real Effective Exchange Rate (Euro Area trading partners), Terms of Trade (goods and services), Share of OECD Exports, Labour Productivity, Nominal Unit Labour Cost Index, Nominal House Price Index, Residential Construction, Private Debt (non-consolidated), Financial Sector Leverage (debt-to-equity), Employment, Activity Rate (15–64 years) (% of total population in the same age group), Long-term Unemployment Rate (% of active population

reviewed by a working group of the Economic Policy Committee named "LIME" jointly with member states and the ECB. These are crucial innovations because, probably for the first time, the EU aims to coordinate national economic policies referring to parameters other than the Stability and Growth Pact ones.

The Two-pack introduced technical elements such as a common budgetary timeline and other rules for interaction with member states that receive financial aid.

The European Semester rule, Six-pack and Two-pack are communitarian rules, but the new economic governance also includes intergovernmental treaties that integrate (sometimes anticipating) the new communitarian rules and make more stringent the constraints for the most problematic member states. These treaties are the Euro Plus and the Fiscal Compact.

In the Euro Plus Pact, the central prescription is the so-called "golden rule", i.e. the obligation to keep the public budget in balance by constitutional rule.[8] The Fiscal Compact prescribes a balanced budget as well. It also demands a 5% annual reduction of the excessive public debt and a structural deficit equal to or lower than 0.5% (1.0% for countries with a public debt lower than 60% of GDP).[9]

---

in the same age group), Youth Unemployment Rate (% of active population in the same age group), Young People Neither in Employment nor in Education and Training (% total population), People at Risk of Poverty or Social Exclusion rate (% total population), People at Risk of Poverty after Social Transfer Rate (% total population), Severely Materially Deprived People (% total population), People Living in Households with Very Low Work Intensity (% total population).

[8] More precisely, the Euro Plus Pact states that "participating member states commit to translating EU fiscal rules as set out in the Stability and Growth Pact into national legislation. Member states will retain the choice of the specific national legal vehicle to be used but will make sure that it has a sufficiently strong binding and durable nature (e.g. constitution or framework law)" (European Council 2011, p. 19). Only Italy and Spain inserted the golden rule in their constitutions.

[9] The Financial Times Lexicon defines structural deficit as follows: "A

Table 6.1 – Macroeconomic scoreboards, thresholds and monitoring function of the scoreboard

Scoreboard	Threshold	Function
External imbalances and competitiveness		
3-year backward moving average of the current account balance as a per cent of GDP	+6% and -4%	A high value means the country depends heavily on export. The reverse for low values.
Net international investment position as a per cent of GDP	-35%	A high value means that the country is heavily indebted to foreigners. The reverse for low values.
5-year percentage change in export market shares measured in values	6%	This shows if the country augmented or diminished export as a % of total commerce. It is an indicator of change in economic competitiveness.
3-year percentage change in nominal unit labour cost	+9% (EACs) +12% (no EACs)	This is an indicator of change in competitiveness due to a change in labour costs.
3-year percentage change in the real effective exchange rates based on HICP/CPI deflators, relative to 41 other industrial countries	-/+5% (EACs) -/+11% (no EACs)	A high value indicates poor competitiveness of exported products. The reverse for low values.
Internal imbalances		
Private sector debt (consolidated) in % of GDP	133%	This shows the total debt of the private sector (firms, families). A high value suggests excessive credit demand by private actors.
Private sector credit flow in % of GDP	15%	A high value suggests a liquidity crisis or excessive credit to the private sector.

budget deficit that results from a fundamental imbalance in government receipts and expenditures, as opposed to one based on one-off or short-term factors. A government budget deficit occurs when a government spends more than it receives in tax revenue, while a structural deficit is when a budget deficit persists for some time." http://lexicon.ft.com/Term?term=structural-deficit

Year-on-year changes in house prices relative to a Eurostat consumption deflator	6%	This influences rent prices and family budget.
General government sector debt in % of GDP	60%	This is one of the main parameters of the SGP. Excessive debt is considered to endanger financial stability and the ability of the government to face fluctuation in international capital markets and interest rates.
A 3-year backward moving average of the unemployment rate	10%	This shows a trend in unemployment in the mid term
Year-on-year changes in total financial sector liabilities	16.5%	This indicates potential speculative booms
3-year change in the activity rate	-0.2%	This shows a trend in the mid term for the economically active population aged 15–64 in relation to the total population of the same age.
3-year change in the long-term unemployment rate	+0.5%	This shows a trend in the mid term for the share of unemployed persons for one year or more in the active population in the labour market (15–74 years old).
3-year change in the youth unemployment rate	+2%	This shows a trend in the mid term for the unemployment rate of persons aged 15 to 24 as a percentage of the labour force of the same age group.

Legend: EAC = Eurozone Countries

Source: https://ec.europa.eu/info/business-economy-euro/economic-and-fiscal-policy-coordination/eu-economic-governance-monitoring-prevention-correction/macroeconomic-imbalance-procedure/scoreboard_en; https://ec.europa.eu/eurostat/cache/metadata/FR/tipsun10_esms.htm; https://ec.europa.eu/eurostat/web/macroeconomic-imbalances-procedure/indicators

Table 6.2 – Contents of the normative pillars of the EMU economic governance

Treaty	Contents	Main Juridical Sources
Stability and Growth Pact	Inflation max 1.5% more than the average of the three countries with the lower inflation rate Deficit max 3% of GDP (if public debt is higher than 60% of GDP) Public debt max 60% of GDP Long-term interest rates max 2% more than the average of the three countries with the lowest inflation rate	Articles 212 and 126 of Treaty on the Functioning of the European Union (TFEU); Council Regulation (EC) No. 1466/97 of 7 July 1997 on the strengthening of the surveillance of budgetary positions and the surveillance and coordination of economic policies; Council Regulation (EC) No. 1467/97 of 7 July 1997 on speeding up and clarifying the implementation of the excessive deficit procedure; Council Regulation (EC) No. 1055/2005 of 27 June 2005 amending Regulation (EC) No. 1466/97 on the strengthening of the surveillance of budgetary positions and the surveillance and coordination of economic policies; Council Regulation (EC) No. 1056/2005 of 27 June 2005 amending Regulation (EC) No. 1467/97 on speeding up and clarifying the implementation of the excessive deficit procedure.
Six-pack	European Semester Reverse qualified majority Obligation to reduce the debt quota exceeding 60% of GDP (at least 5% yearly) Expenditure benchmark. This imposes a cap on annual expense growth Preventive recommendation to reduce macroeconomic imbalances New enforcement regime. Sanctions are applied in three steps. First, after the first alert, a forced deposit (remunerated with interest) is imposed.	Regulation (EU) No. 1173/2011 of the European Parliament and of the Council of 16 November 2011 on the effective enforcement of budgetary surveillance in the euro area; Regulation (EU) No. 1174/2011 of the European Parliament and of the Council of 16 November 2011 on enforcement measures to correct excessive macroeconomic imbalances in the euro area; Regulation (EU) No. 1175/2011 of the European Parliament and of the Council of 16 November 2011 amending Council Regulation (EC) No. 1466/97 on the strengthening of the surveillance of budgetary positions and the surveillance and coordination of economic policies; Council Regulation (EU) No. 1177/2011 of 8 November 2011 amending Regulation (EC) No. 1467/97 on speeding up and clarifying the implementation of the excessive deficit procedure; Regulation (EU) No. 1176/2011 of the European Parliament and of the Council of 16 November 2011 on the prevention and correction of macroeconomic imbalances; Directive 2011/85/EU – requirements for euro area countries' budgets.

Six-pack	If the member state enforces no significant actions, a second alert is issued, and the forced deposit is no longer remunerated with interest. Finally, if the second alert does not induce the member state to correct its position either the sum deposited becomes a fine. Early warning system based on macroeconomic scoreboards Obligation to present Medium-term Budgetary Objectives (MTOs) revised every three years	
Two-pack	This defines specific rules for reinforced monitoring of member states experiencing financial difficulties, those interested in rescue plans in particular It establishes a common budgetary timeline. Member states must present their government budget draft to the European Commission within the deadline established by the collective timeline	Regulation (EU) No. 472/2013 of the European Parliament and of the Council of 21 May 2013 on the strengthening of economic and budgetary surveillance of member states in the euro area experiencing or threatened with serious difficulties with respect to their financial stability; Regulation (EU) No. 473/2013 of the European Parliament and of the Council of 21 May 2013 on common provisions for monitoring and assessing draft budgetary plans and ensuring the correction of excessive deficit of the member states in the euro area.

Euro Plus	Budget balance rule to be inserted in higher-level national laws (golden rule)	European Council 24–25 March 2011.
TSCG (Fiscal Compact))	Obligation to keep the government budget in balance or surplus and insertion of this rule in the national legislation or Constitution Obligation to reduce the debt quota exceeding 60% of GNP by 5% each year Maximum structural deficit admissible for countries with a public debt that exceeds 60% of the GDP: 0.5% at market prices (1% if public debt does not exceed 60%)	Treaty on Stability, Coordination and Governance in the Economic Monetary Union.

Sources: https://eur-lex.europa.eu/; https://www.consilium.europa.eu

Most of the procedures introduced by the new economic governance and some existing ones reformed and adapted to the new system had been regrouped and coordinated in the European Semester framework. The following figure shows the step sequence of the European Semester.

The European Semester has three phases. It starts with a preliminary phase in which two different analyses are carried out by the European Commission. The first analysis regards budgetary and structural policies, while the second deals with macroeconomic imbalances. During the preparatory phase, the European Commission analyses the previous year's situation and its follow-up, including the correct implementation of the policies and correction agreed during the previous European Semester. In this phase, each member state prepares and submits to the European Commission a national reform programme and a three-year budget plan called a "stability programme" for the member states of the eurozone, and a convergence programme for the others.

The budget and structural analysis result in an annual growth survey being sent to the Council of the European Union and the European Council. Both the institutions spend phase one of the European Semester analysing the annual growth survey. The Council of the EU draws conclusions about the survey and submits them to the European Council. In contrast, the European Parliament provides opinions to the European Council about the Employment Guidelines. After having evaluated the survey, the Council of the EU's conclusions and the opinions expressed by the European Parliament, the European Council provides policy orientation to the member states.

In the macroeconomic imbalances analytic line, an alert mechanism report identifies countries at risk of macroeconomic imbalances. An in-depth review of the economic conditions for those countries follows. The European Commission uses these reviews to evaluate the objectives and plans outlined by member states at the start of phase two, while also considering the draft budget plans for the following year that member states have to submit by October 15th.

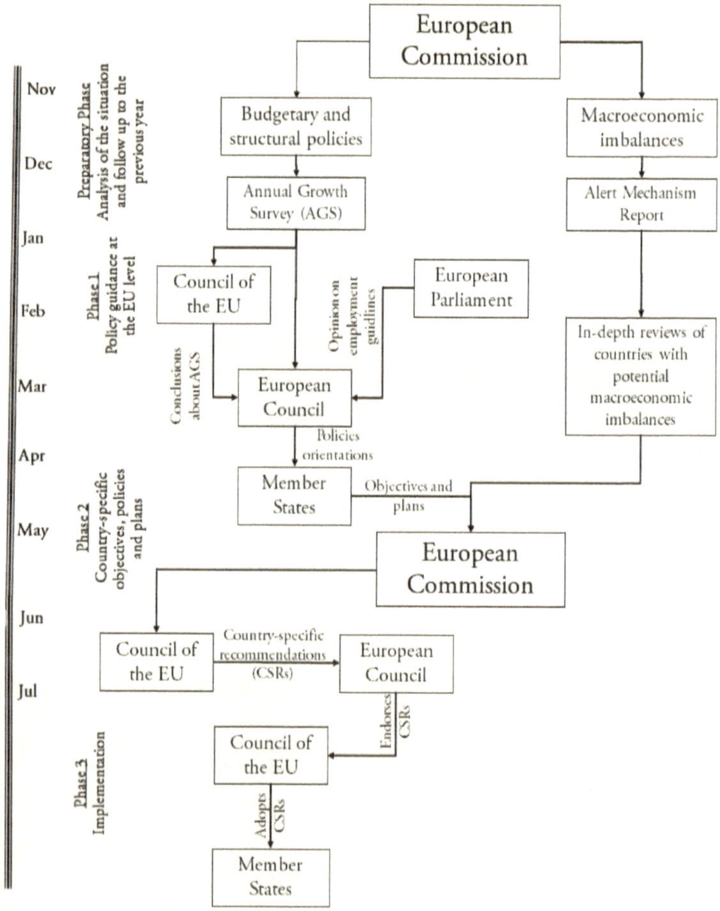

Fig. 6.1 – The European Semester

Source: Council of the European Union 2013

Then, the European Commission prepares a first draft of Country-Specific Recommendations and submits them to the Council of the European Union. When the latter and the European Commission agree on a final draft of the Country-Specific Recommendations, the draft arrives at the European Council. If it endorses them, the recommendations are adopted by the Council and transmitted to the member states. This starts the implementation phase (or phase three) in which member states have to adapt their domestic budget policy to the recommendations.

Analysis of both budgetary and macroeconomic imbalances can generate sanctions as part of the two corrective lines of action respectively called Excessive Deficit Procedure (EDP) and Excessive Imbalances Procedure (EIP).[10]

4 – Does the new European economic governance work?

The introduction of the macroeconomic scoreboards and the strict economic coordination determined by the European Semester procedure created a framework for managing the member states' economies and for pushing ahead with convergence and parameter-oriented economic policies. However, it seems this stricter cooperation did not solve the main divergencies among member states' economies.

[10] The Excessive Deficit Procedure is defined by Article 126 of the Treaty on the Functioning of the European Union. The Excessive Imbalances Procedure, on the other hand, derived from the Six-pack, or more precisely from Regulation (EU) no. 1176/2011 of 16 November 2011: "On the prevention and correction of macroeconomic imbalances". https://ec.europa.eu/info/business-economy-euro/economic-and-fiscal-policy-coordination/eu-economic-governance-monitoring-prevention-correction/stability-and-growth-pact/corrective-arm-excessive-deficit-procedure_en; https://ec.europa.eu/info/ business-economy-euro-0/economic-and-fiscal-policy-coordination/eu-economic-governance-monitoring-prevention-correction/macroeconomic-imbalance-procedure_en

The following Table 6.3, shows the deviations from the macroeconomic scoreboards of both the larger and the main problematic EMU member states.[11] The data start with the last year before the adoption of the macroeconomic scoreboards. The table shows that economic governance remains a problematic matter. There are at least four elements in the data to support this conclusion. First, for some scoreboards there are relevant divergencies mainly affecting the most troubled countries of the EMU. Divergencies in the net investment position and the private sector debt remain relevant notwithstanding the latter shows a trend toward reduction of divergence from the scoreboard (apart from France). Second, debt remains the most diffused and relevant case of deviation and the reduction of excessive debt is not generalised. Comparing the first two years in the data series, only Germany and Ireland show a decrease in deviation from the threshold. Greece still has an enormous deviation while Spain, Italy, Portugal and France show increases or an irrelevant reduction in deviation. Third, the gap between the German economy and the economies of the GIIPS countries remain wide, with Germany being very close in respect to all the macroeconomic scoreboards in 2017. Fourth, when all the countries under analysis show improvements in reducing divergencies from the scoreboards, it remains uncertain whether these depend on better economic governance. The Irish performance in regaining export market shares as well as the containment of house prices seems to be more the consequence of external macroeconomic conditions than the result of supranational governance.

The dynamic of macroeconomic scoreboard deviation also depends on two other elements that suggest a poor performance of European economic governance. First, the introduc-

[11] The data in Table 6.3 refer to France, Germany, Greece, Ireland, Italy, Spain and Portugal. Sometimes, one or more of these countries are omitted from those scoreboards where they have no deviation from the admitted range or scoreboard.

tion of flexibility and mid-term perspectives (three- or five-year-long adjustments) made economic scoreboards less stringent for member states' governments. Cases of negotiations and huge flexibility conceded to problematic countries (e.g. Italy) show that economic governance constraints had been applied softly and politically mediated. Also, the introduction of a specific interpretation of traditional parameters of EU economic governance like budget deficit enabled an increase in flexibility in economic governance negotiation.[12]

Second, the impact of ECB monetary policy, the Quantitative Easing in particular, increased structural imbalances inside the EMU, especially the internal balance of payments divergence between Germany on one side and Italy and Spain on the other. This emerges from the following figures, Figs 6.2 and 6.3. After a reduction during the period 2012–2014, TARGET2 balances rear up and continue to increase until today. So it is clear that the main internal imbalance of the EMU is still far from being solved. The concomitance between the new rise of TARGET2 balances and the start of the Quantitative Easing suggests a relation between the increase in liquidity and the increase in divergence between member countries inside the system.[13]

---

[12] The budget deficit considered in economic governance is the so-called "structural budget deficit", i.e. the deficit depurated of the impact of the economic crises. If calculated as before, a budget deficit is an almost certain amount while a structural budget deficit is open to interpretation and the complex and politicised calculations that made negotiation during the European Semester a smooth job.

[13] The official explanation proposed by the Bundesbank and the Central Bank of the Netherlands for the TARGET2 increase in balances after the introduction of the Quantitative Easing deal with the bonds' purchase done by peripheral central banks. So this increase seems dependent on technical reasons instead of imbalances in the internal commercial and financial flows (Dor 2016, p. 6). However, Dor suggests this explanation does not work for Italy (*idem*, p. 6–7).

Table 6.3 – Macroeconomic scoreboard deviations from thresholds

a) *External imbalances and competitiveness*

	2011	2012	2013	2014	2015	2016	2017
Current account balance – 3-year average							
Germany	0.0	0.2	0.6	1.1	1.7	2.3	2.4
Greece	-7.2	-4.4	-1.3	0.0	0.0	0.0	0.0
Portugal	-4.9	-2.0	0.0	0.0	0.0	0.0	0.0
Net international investment position – annual data % of gross domestic product (GDP)							
Ireland	-104.1	-102.7	-98.3	-129.3	-163.7	-135.7	-114.3
Greece	-53.8	-80.9	-95.4	-96.9	-101.1	-104.7	-107.5
Spain	-56.9	-54.9	-60.2	-63.0	-54.5	-50.3	-48.8
Portugal	-65.7	-81.5	-81.3	-83.6	-78.2	-70.5	-69.9
Export market shares – 5-year % change goods and services							
Germany	0.0	0.0	0.0	0.0	0.0	0.0	0.5
Ireland	0.0	0.0	0.0	0.0	31.8	52.7	58.4
Spain	0.0	0.0	0.0	0.0	0.0	0.0	3.8
Portugal	0.0	0.0	0.0	0.0	0.0	0.0	8.6
Nominal unit labour cost – 3-year % change							
None							
Real effective exchange rate (42 trading partners, based on HICP/CPI) % change (t/t-3)							
Germany	0.0	-4.0	0.0	0.0	0.0	0.0	0.0
Ireland	-4.6	-7.2	0.0	0.0	-1.4	-2.0	-1.2
Greece	0.0	0.0	0.0	-0.6	-0.6	0.0	0.0
Spain	0.0	-0.3	0.0	0.0	0.0	0.0	0.0
France	0.0	-2.8	0.0	0.0	0.0	0.0	0.0
Italy	0.0	-1.2	0.0	0.0	0.0	0.0	0.0

b) *Internal imbalances*

	2011	2012	2013	2014	2015	2016	2017
Private sector debt, consolidated – % of GDP							
Ireland	141.0	146.6	134.7	145.3	173	150.3	110.6
Spain	63.4	55.0	44.2	32.8	21.8	13.8	5.8
France	2.3	5.3	4.4	8.5	9.8	13.6	15.2
Portugal	71.1	77.3	69.4	57.5	46.4	36.3	29.2
Private sector credit flow, consolidated – % GDP							
Ireland	1.4	0.0	0.0	0.0	0.0	0.0	0.0

House price index, deflated – annual average rate of change							
Ireland	0.0	0.0	0.0	9.1	5.0	0.6	3.5
Portugal	0.0	0.0	0.0	0.0	0.0	0.1	1.9
General government gross debt (EDP concept), consolidated – annual data							
Germany	18.6	19.9	17.4	14.5	10.8	7.9	3.9
Ireland	50.9	59.9	59.7	44.1	16.8	13.4	8.4
Greece	112.1	99.6	117.4	118.9	115.9	118.5	116.1
Spain	9.5	25.7	35.5	40.4	39.3	39.0	38.1
France	27.8	30.6	33.4	34.9	35.6	38.2	38.5
Italy	56.5	63.4	69.0	71.8	71.6	71.4	71.2
Portugal	51.4	66.2	69.0	70.6	68.8	69.2	64.8
Unemployment rate – 3-year average							
Ireland	4.2	5.2	4.9	3.7	1.9	0.1	0.0
Greece	3.4	8.4	13.3	16.2	16.3	15.0	13.3
Spain	9.7	12	14.1	15.1	14.2	12.1	9.6
France	0.0	0.0	0.0	0.1	0.3	0.3	0.0
Italy	0.0	0.0	0.4	1.8	2.2	2.1	1.6
Portugal	1.9	3.6	5.0	5.4	4.4	2.6	0.9
Total financial sector liabilities, non-consolidated – annual data % change on previous period							
Ireland	0.0	0.0	0.0	3.0	0.0	0.0	0.0
Activity rate – % of total population aged 15–64 % point change (t/t-3)							
Ireland	-3.4	-1.7	0.0	0.0	0.0	0.0	0.0
Greece	0.0	0.0	-0.1	0.0	0.0	0.0	0.0
Spain	0.0	0.0	0.0	0.0	0.0	0.0	-0.1
Italy	-0.6	0.0	0.0	0.0	0.0	0.0	0.0
Portugal	-0.1	0.0	-0.5	-0.2	0.0	0.0	0.0
Long-term unemployment rate, % of active population aged 15–74							
Greece	0.0	0.6	2.8	0.7	0.0	0.0	0.0
Youth unemployment rate – % of active population aged 15–24 % point change (t/t-3)							
Ireland	14.1	4.3	0.0	0.0	0.0	0.0	0.0
Greece	20.8	27.6	23.3	5.7	0.0	0.0	0.0
Spain	19.7	13.2	12.0	5.0	0.0	0.0	0.0
France	1.6	0.0	0.0	0.0	0.0	0.0	0.0
Italy	6.0	8.0	10.1	11.5	3.0	0.0	0.0
Portugal	6.6	10.7	7.9	2.5	0.0	0.0	0.0

Sources: ECB Statistical Data Warehouse

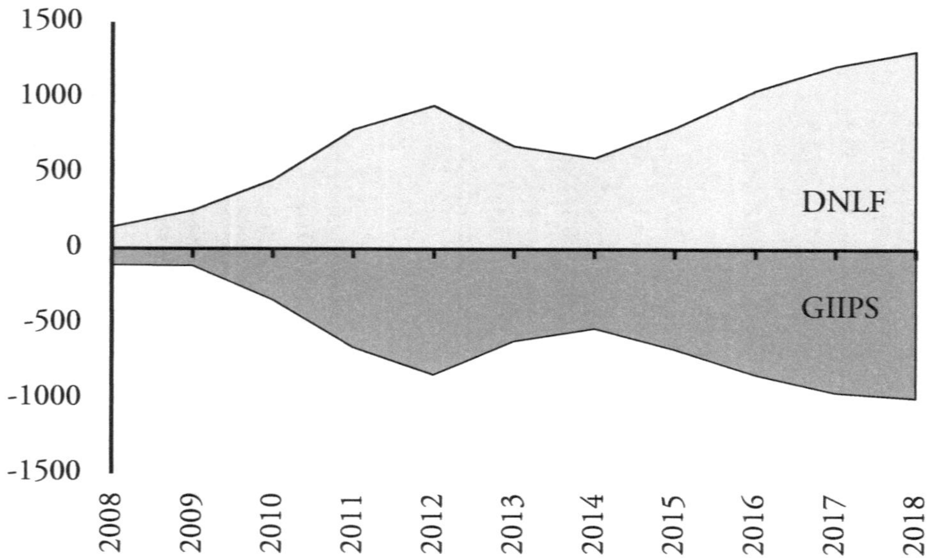

Fig. 6.2 – TARGET2 regrouped balances 2008–2018 (billions of euro).

Sources: ECB Statistical Data Warehouse

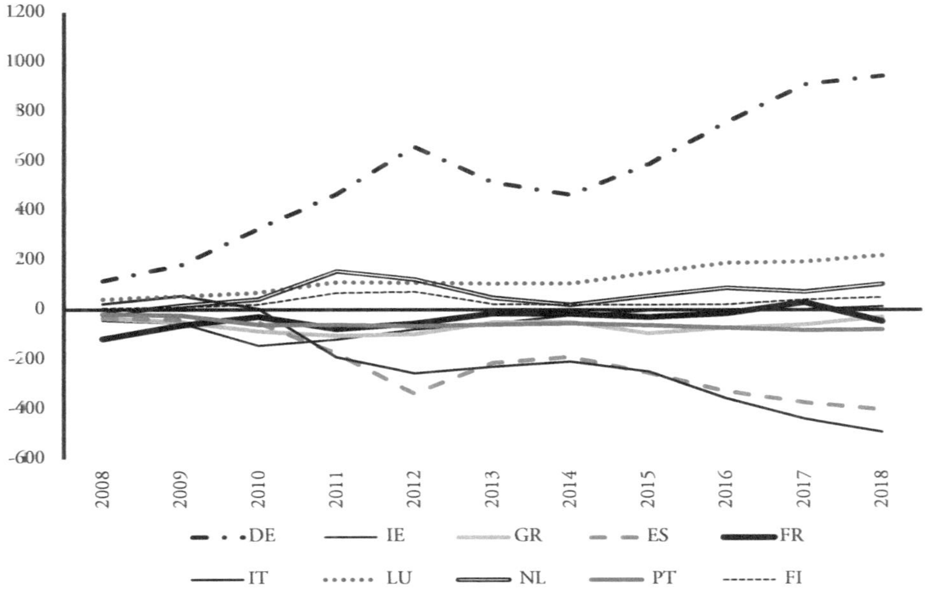

Fig. 6.3 – TARGET2 balances 2008–2018 (billions of euro).

Sources: ECB Statistical Data Warehouse

The analysis of the new economic governance effectiveness proposed above shows that governance architecture and monetary policy are closely connected. While rules and supervisory activities aim to address macroeconomic variables, monetary policy also has a relevant impact on the same variables, notwithstanding monetary and governance objectives are not fully coordinated and sometimes divergent. The cases of Quantitative Easing and TARGET2 balances are emblematic. Both the monetary policy tools facilitated the outflanking of stringent economic constraints by the most troubled countries. On the other hand, the monetary policy of the ECB limited the impact of the European governance and the rigidity of its instrument and procedure, thereby permitting the recovery or survival of the most troubled countries and, worse still, of their obsolete economic and administrative structures.

PART III

THE POLITICS OF THE EMU

Chapter 7

Power and EU Institutional Structure in Times of Crisis

The eurozone crisis induced a reshaping and reinforcement of the EU economic governance while also changing the balance of power between EU institutions and introducing new entities and new actors into the governance arena. This occurred by reinforcing the supervisory and sanctioning power of EU institutions, mainly the EU Commission, and creating new organisations and supervisory agencies. Finally, new actors such as the Euro Group and the Council of the Euro Area were involved in EU economic governance.[1] In the meantime, the implementation of the Lisbon Treaty favoured this kind of evolution toward a more active economic governance actuated by a more complex set of institutions. On the other hand, the need for further advancement in economic governance to consolidate the euro area stability drew the EU institutions toward plans that dramatically collide with the member states' autonomy and democratic government.

[1] The Euro Group joins together the finance ministers of the euro area countries, the ECB governor and representatives of the EU Commission. The Council of the Euro Area joins together the heads of state and governments of the euro area countries, organises two informal meetings each year and elects a president with a two-and-a-half-year mandate (Sadeleer 2012).

1 – Changing the EU institutional architecture to manage the euro

New EU norms on economic governance and macroeconomic coordination were not the only solutions adopted to face the crisis. While the European institutions introduced the new economic governance, the member states tried to face the crisis using "emergency" intergovernmental agreements. The most important were the Euro Plus Pact (European Council 2011) and the Treaty on Stability, Coordination and Governance in the Economic and Monetary Union, usually called "Fiscal Compact" or TSCG (2012).

Intergovernmental treaties and EU norms were not enough to face the sovereign debt crisis and the potential crises that may arise in the EMU in the future. So when the Greek crisis started, it became evident that the ECB could not outflank the no-bailout rule of the Maastricht Treaty,[2] and that a simple intergovernmental loan to Greece was not sufficient to solve its problems. Moreover, other countries were affected by the rising sovereign debt crisis and needed financial support. The EU did not have a set of intervention instruments with which to face a systemic crisis. Then, in 2010, EMU member states created some "emergency" financial institutions. The first one was the European Financial Stabilisation Mechanism (EFSM), a sort of budget line granted by the EU budget with a lending capacity of € 60 billion. It allowed support for Ireland and Portugal but was too small to face the rising sovereign debt crisis in Italy and Spain. So EMU member states created the European Financial Stability Facility (EFSF), a private company they owned. It had a lending capacity of €

[2] The no-bailout rule (or clause) derived from Article 125 of the Lisbon Treaty, but it was originally introduced with the Treaty of Rome. It excludes the possibility that EU member states might assume the commitments of other member states. This rule is crucial in avoiding the rescue of bankrupted member states by the governments of other EU members.

440 billion to use for granting loans and also for purchaseing member states' bonds on the primary market.

The introduction of bond purchasing operations was the chief innovation at that time and showed that the critical problem was no longer the Greek crisis but the incoming general sovereign debt crisis in Southern EMU member states. Furthermore, this innovation made the EFSF the "additional arm" of EMU economic governance. This arm was capable of outflanking the no-bailout rule that stops the ECB supporting member states' bond prices (Gocaj and Meunier 2013; European Central Bank 2011). Both the EFSM and the EFSF had a limited duration (until the end of 2013). However, the sovereign debt crisis experience and the rise of a more complex system of EU economic governance suggested creating a stable instrument for crisis management. Meanwhile, ECB governors (mainly Draghi) used the crucial role of the ECB in the financial system to expand the European System of Central Banks' (ESCB) intervention machinery to lead and to interpret the ECB mandate flexibly, particularly in the field of bond purchase and as lenders of last resort.

The European Stability Mechanism (ESM) was established under the ECB auspices and became the principal tool for supporting EMU member states in financial trouble (Gocaj and Meunier, 2013). It took the place of the funds created just after the start of the sovereign debt crisis and replicated the strategy initially adopted by the ECB to purchase government bonds on the secondary market to stabilise their price and freeze their flows. However, this strategy became an official activity carried out by a formal institution such as the EMS. In practice, there was an upgrade of the ECB strategy from informal to formal governance level. Today the ESM may be considered the core instrument for managing the sovereign debt crisis in the EMU area and part of the European monetary governance set of instruments.

The sovereign debt crisis also revealed the fragility of the whole EU financial and banking sector. This induced the European Council to reinforce and integrate the supervisory architecture for those sectors creating in 2011 the European Systemic Risk Board (ESRB) and three new supervisory agencies named the European Banking Authority (EBA), the European Securities and Market Authority (ESMA), and the European Insurance and Occupational Pension Authority (EIOPA) (European Central Bank 2011). These were the initial steps toward the European Banking Union, a supervision and resolution system managed by the ECB and based on three pillars: the Single Supervisory Mechanism (SSM), the Single Resolution Mechanism (SRM) and the European Deposit Insurance Scheme (EDIS).[3] The SSM was established by Council Regulation 1024/2013 to supervise banks in the eurozone and other EU countries using the European Banking Authority. The SRM rose under Regulation 806/2014 to ensure an orderly resolution of bankruptcies for banks in those EU countries that participate in the Banking Union. Finally, the EDIS aims to create a European system to deal with banks' insolvency and grant to depositor of banks in bankruptcy to recover at least 100,000 euros. While the first two pillars were created after 2014 and 2016, respectively, the EDIS is still under discussion and opposition has been raised against its establishment (Brunsden 2017).

The following figure shows the entire institutional transformation process resulting from the reaction to the euro crisis. The original structure of the EU economic governance was not dismantled, just extensively integrated. New rules, procedures, methods, agencies and actors became parts of it. In oth-

[3] See https://ec.europa.eu/info/business-economy-euro/banking-and-finance/banking-union/single-supervisory-mechanism_en; https://ec.europa.eu/info/business-economy-euro/banking-and-finance/banking-union/single-resolution-mechanism_en; https://ec.europa.eu/info/business-economy-euro/banking-and-finance/banking-union/european-deposit-insurance-scheme_en; https:// ec.europa.eu/info/business-economy-euro/banking-and-finance/banking-union/single-supervisory-mechanism_en

er words, a more substantial number of policymakers had at their disposal a more significant number of policy tools.

Another substantial change regards the complexity of the EU economic governance network. More actors with more instruments generated a more complicated policy network and made policy design more sophisticated due to a broader choice among policy tools and their combinations. Also, new opportunities to combine formal and informal governance emerged. This evolution is evident in the ECB case.

2 – The rise of the ECB's "informal" economic governance

The governance gap in the 2000s and during the sovereign debt crisis, as well as the impossibility of arranging quickly new entities and new treaties to empower the EU and make EU institutions capable of saving the crumbling EMU, forced an increase in intergovernmental cooperation. However, intergovernmental arrangements were not enough to manage the technicalities and the immediacy of the EMU problems, particularly the increasing banking illiquidity and the sovereign debt crisis in Southern Europe. Also, the rise of the NEG and the empowerment of some EU institutions were not enough to force recalcitrant member states to comply with old and new rules.

The European Central Bank, supported by the European System of Central Banks, emerged as the only European institution capable of acting rapidly and efficiently, particularly after the nomination of the new governor, Mario Draghi. Being in charge of monetary policy and commercial paper discounts, the ECB had the power to address the banks of the EMU member countries. However, its most important prerogative was the blackmail power derived from its pivotal role in arranging day-by-day solutions to guarantee banks' liquidity and support the government bond market.

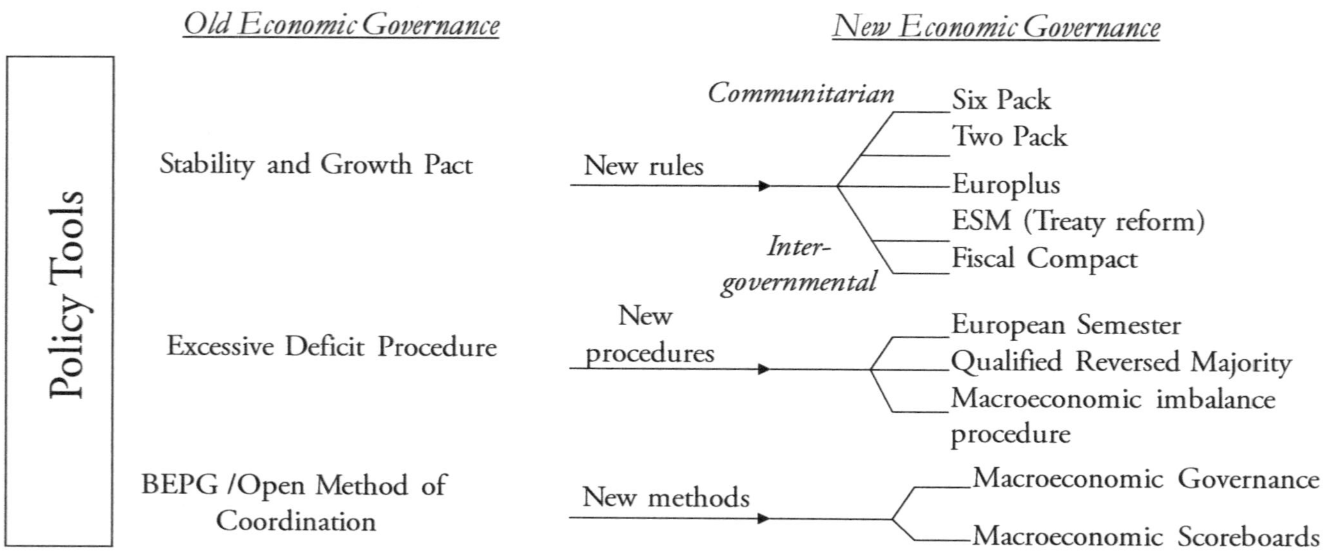

Fig. 7.1a – The evolution of the EMU economic governance.

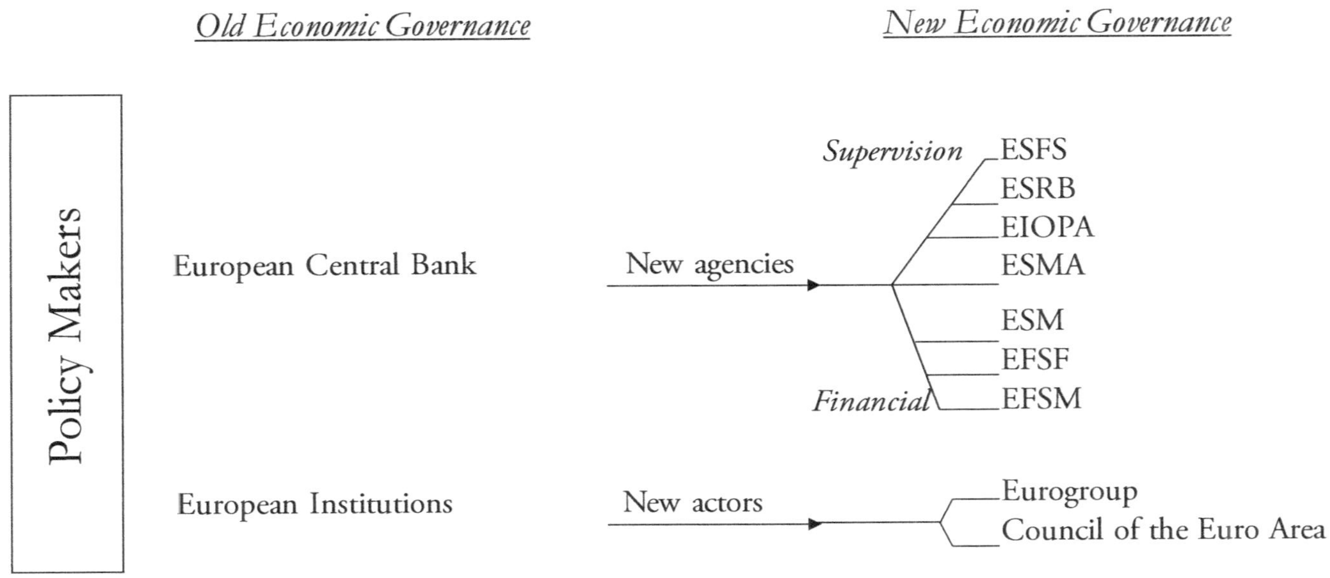

Fig. 7.b – The evolution of the EMU economic governance.

The liquidity and solvability of commercial banks in many EMU countries depended on the ECB's acceptance of these bonds as collateral for loans. This meant that if the ECB refused to accept sovereign bonds as collateral, many banks, particularly those from the most troubled countries, would be bankrupt.

The ECB power increased after the first months of the sovereign debt crisis when it funded commercial banks to buy domestic bonds in the secondary market. The ECB aimed to stabilise bond prices and to reduce the interest rates charged to the weaker countries. However, it could not ignore the high power it gained from public debt renationalisation. In fact, this process reinforced the banks-government link, which the ECB could use to exert political pressures.

Another instrument used by the ECB and the ESCB to face the crisis was the TARGET2 system. The ESCB accepted the accumulation of unpaid balances in the TARGET2 system by the Southern European countries involved in the sovereign debt crisis. Thus, the TARGET2 system became a sort of expansion basin capable of neutralising the impressive capital flow generated by the crisis. However, by acting in this way, the ECB changed the whole nature of the TARGET2 system, transforming a merely technical tool into a powerful instrument of monetary policy. Finally, the ECB lowered the standards for accepting commercial paper as collateral. In other words, national central banks were permitted to use low-quality collateral for granting loans from the ECB (Sinn 2014a, p. 150–154). This favoured the most troubled banking systems in EMU countries.[4]

The interaction between the ECB and the national central banks of the EMU member states is an exciting topic in need of a more in-depth analysis. The real balance of power inside the ESCB remains unclear. Probably, NCBs have more indepen-

[4] Varoufakis (2017) confirms that when he was Greece's Finance Minister, he had to sign a government endorsement of the main Greek banks' commercial bills to be used as collateral for the ECB credit.

dence than expected in implementing monetary policy at the domestic level. On the other hand, NCBs had been charged with a large part of the losses risk in some monetary interventions, as in the case of quantitative easing.[5] This suggests that the ECB perceives the danger of exiting the euro for some member states, as well as the potential consequences of excessive autonomy of national central banks. We must bear in mind that the governors of the national central banks are nominated by the government and could be subjected to pressures from it.

The strategy it pursued made the ECB the centre of the "European informal governance", a system of relationships based on the ECB's blackmail discretionary power and the pivotal role it has in every temporary or long-term strategy to face the EMU crisis. Moreover, the ECB became the only EU institution that has enough coercive power to compel member states' governments to implement EU rules and accept political pressures. So both the other EU institutions and core member states need "borrowing power" from the ECB. This contributed significantly to the ECB's empowerment. Finally, using the TARGET2 system to freeze capital flows made the ECB the primary guarantor of credit balance payment for creditor countries. This role permitted the ECB to resist pressures from the most powerful member countries, Germany first and foremost.

The matter of informality in European governance cannot be limited to the concept of "blackmailing". The latter is a poor scientific definition, and it hides the complexity of the transformation induced by the euro crisis. So it is preferable to refer to the concept of "informal governance".

From the early 2000s, informal governance became a relevant concept in the literature. In particular, scholars devoted

[5] The rules established for ECB Quantitative Easing assign to the national central banks the profits derived from their operation on national bonds. However, this also implies that losses (as in the case of exiting the EMU) will be charged to the national central bank. See Claeys, Leandro and Mandra (2015).

attention to the role of informal governance in international organisations such as the International Monetary Fund and the European Union (Christiansen and Piattoni 2003; Puetter 2004; Chwieroth 2013; Stone 2013; Christiansen and Neuhold 2013; Kleine 2013). Also, the analysis of multilevel governance became crucial for EU studies, and informal governance emerged as a critical tool for making multilevel governance work. In fact, some authors focus on the relationship between informal governance and decision-making and emphasise the opportunities granted by informal governance to create informal arenas where actors can negotiate more freely, avoiding the boundaries of formal arenas (Puetter 2004; Conrad 2006; Christiansen and Neuhold 2013, p. 1197).

Different authors define informal governance in different ways. Puetter defines informal governance as the influence of a group of actors on policy formulation using informal agreements between the group's members capable of supporting these agreements when acting in formal arenas (Puetter 2004, p. 857). Christiansen and Piattoni stress the importance of informal governance in permitting access to decision-making to policy actors otherwise excluded from decision-making processes (Christiansen and Piattoni 2003, p. 6). Other authors link informal governance to unwritten rules capable of modifying or replacing entirely formal norms usually implemented outside the official channels (Helmke and Levitsky 2004; Stone 2013).

In the literature on informal governance, there are useful elements for analysing the ECB action during a crisis. The first element deals with the relationship between formal and informal governance. Many authors consider informal governance to be a useful complement to formal governance. They suggest that informal governance facilitates formal governance and helps negotiations as it offers an informal and more flexible environment where agreements can be made and decisions taken to transfer into formal institutions (Puetter 2004; Kleine 2013, p. 46 and 49).

Other elements discussed in the literature regard power and empowerment. The literature suggests that informal governance works both in symmetric arenas (where actors are almost peers) and asymmetric arenas (where some actors are more powerful than others or predominant) (Kleine 2013, p. 249; Stone 2013, p. 133;). However, governance is a dynamic process, and the power balance can change, causing the empowerment of one or more actors. This also happens in informal governance, probably more rapidly than in formal governance. In fact, in informal governance, what matters is the real power of an actor, not just the power assigned by formal rules and treaties. So actors in informal arenas can use (or gain) "informal power" they do not have or cannot use in formal arenas (Stone 2013, p. 125).

Informal governance, informal power and empowerment are the three most important concepts the literature offers to analyse the ECB role and action in facing the euro crisis and supporting the new economic governance. ECB acted widely in the informal arena, shaping economic governance using the informal power granted by its "technical" policy tools (e.g. Emergency Liquidity Assistance or ELA and the TARGET2 system). Formal and informal ECB empowerment followed as a consequence of its role in facing the crisis, the lack of governance tools among the other EU institutions and the poor effectiveness of intergovernmental governance. Later, ECB empowerment moved from the informal to the formal arena. Moreover, some "technical devices" used by the ECB to face the crisis were substituted by new policy tools capable of acting in the formal arena. So the ECB used its "technical devices" in designing policies to save the EMU and reform the European financial system. However, by turning technical devices into policy instruments, the ECB expanded its action range in policy sectors in which, formally, it has no power to intervene. In fact, due to the general governance gap and the specific limits to the ECB activities (e.g. the no bail-out rule), the ECB had no instrument to efficiently implement a supranational monetary policy in a time of crisis. Also, the ECB's informal governance permitted the ECB to dictate the economic policy and reforms to the most troubled countries in the EMU. This opportunity has thrown the ECB into high politics, i.e. the field it was created to avoid.

3 – Who saved the euro? Institutional evolution and the limits of the "new intergovernmental" approach to the EMU crisis

The new political role of the ECB generated a new set of political questions about its legitimacy, transparency and accountability. Also, other questions arose about the further enhancement of EMU governance and the future EU institutional order. The first set of matters directly affects the EU political sphere, particularly democracy and the whole legitimacy of the European supranational structure. We will discuss this in the following chapter. The second set of matters, on the other hand, affects the future of EMU governance directly. However, this same future depends on the interaction between member states and European institutions and who leads the decision-making process.

Studying the way in which the euro crisis has been faced is beneficial in understanding who leads the EU transformation process. In fact, member states and European institutions faced the crisis mainly using two different approaches. Intergovernmental treaties were the main instruments used by member states in the early phases of the crisis to respond quickly to the stressful situation. Indeed, the core of the NEG was the slower but more coherent answer offered by the EU institutions.

Intergovernmental treaties and the NEG rules are partially redundant. This redundancy suggests contraposition or delayed coordination between member states and EU institutions on strategies for facing the crisis. More specifically, an intergovernmental and a communitarian approach to the crisis appeared. This dichotomy was replicated in scientific literature, feeding a debate between supporters of the so-called "new intergovernmentalism" and those scholars who emphasise the empowerment of new and old EU institutions as a consequence of the crisis. We will refer to these scholars' approach as "new institutionalism", notwithstanding this term does not exist in the literature.

We need to distinguish between the general perception of intergovernmentalism and the specific literature that introduces the concept of "new intergovernmentalism". Intergovernmental negotiations and treaties in the initial phase of the EMU crisis, as well as the predominant role of Germany and France, reinforced the widespread perception that national governments lead the EU. Many authors embed this perception in their works after 2009–2010, revitalising the traditional intergovernmental approach. However, Puetter, Bickerton and Hodson identify a specific process they define "new intergovernmentalism" and depict a path that started after Maastricht. In their view, after Maastricht, member state policy coordination became the core of the integration process. So integration advanced mainly through delegating functions to new agencies and institutions instead of empowering the existing ones (Bickerton, Hodson and Puetter 2015a; *idem* 2015b, p. 704–705). This strategy permitted member states to continue integration, avoiding further supranationalism. The new intergovernmentalists do not deny the empowerment of some EU institutions. However, they see this empowerment as marginal or functional according to the national government's rule. Bickerton et al. admit that the Fiscal Compact strengthened the European Commission just a bit (Bickerton, Hodson and Puetter 2015b, p. 704). Also, Puetter introduces the concept of "deliberative intergovernmentalism" to emphasise the increased importance of the European Council since the crisis. In her view, it became something like a "*Gouvernment Economique*" of the European Union (Puetter 2012, p. 174). This evolution seems to be the empowerment of a European institution, notwithstanding Kunstein and Wessels who suggest that the Euro Summit emerged as a potential rival of the European Council (Kunstein and Wessels 2013, p. 6). However, in the new intergovernmental perspective, it is an intergovernmental process realised inside European institutions.

Some authors have contested the new intergovernmentalism. In particular, Schimmelfennig suggests it adds nothing to the traditional intergovernmental approach (Schimmelfennig 2015b). Other scholars suggest different approaches mainly focused on the EU's institutional framework transformation and the changing balance of power among them. So these authors, whom we call "new institutionalists", propose a specific perspective to analyse the European Union's institutional evolution and a view of EU institutions' empowerment that is more optimistic than those suggested by the new intergovernmentalists. Their approach to institutional evolution derives from the work of Streeck and Thelen (Streeck and Thelen 2005). These authors propose two concepts called "layering" and "redirection" adopted by Salines et al. to analyse the evolution of the EU institutional system. The latter identifies layering processes in the adding of new institutional elements and redirection processes in directing existing institutions toward new objectives and functions. So they see the assumption by the ECB of a new supervisory role as an example of redirection. Instead, they interpret the creation of the European Systemic Risk Board as a case of layering (Salines, Glöckler and Truchlewski 2012, p. 669–70).

Notwithstanding this representation of the ECB transformation seems simplistic in the light of the analysis we proposed in the previous section of this chapter, it does not collide necessarily with the new intergovernmental one. In fact, the reconstruction of the transformation process is almost the same. However, the authors referred to here as "new institutionalists" emphasise the empowerment of the EU institutions as the main result of the crisis, while new intergovernmentalists suggest the crisis aggravated their marginalisation.

The new institutionalist authors analyse how the crisis and the new economic governance changed the role and power of the different EU institutions. In particular, the European Parliament, the European Commission and the European Central Bank attracted the attention of these scholars. Ritterberger stresses the role played by the economic dialogue introduced by the Six-pack and the Two-pack in the empowerment of the European Parliament. In the meantime, he suggests that the crisis has not changed the consolidated practices of the EU parliamentarisation (Ritterberger 2014, p. 1175 and 1180–1181). On the other hand, Kohler thinks that parliamentarisation dramatically increased the European Parliament's functions and its role in policymaking (Koheler 2014). According to Dinan, Parliament empowerment had been facilitated by the Lisbon Treaty and the ability of the Parliament leaders, mainly President Schultz, to address the Lisbon Treaty interpretation in a favourable way for the Parliament (Dinan 2014, p. 121). Finally, there are few doubts that the rise of the new economic governance gave the European Commission new and broader powers, at least in the economic policy field (Kunstain and Wessels 2013, p. 9).

Another consequence of the crisis and the changing roles of the European institutions was the rise of new relationship patterns between each of them and others. One relevant case deals with the stricter connection between the European Parliament and the European Central Bank. From the early 2000s, the latter offered something like a "voluntary accountability" to the European Parliament aimed at gaining more democratic legitimacy (Jabko 2003; *idem* 2010). Instead, the relationship between the ECB and the European Commission became stricter inside the Troika and because of the crucial role of the ECB in the EU rescue activities since the Greek crisis.

The picture that emerged from the literature review above showed a more complicated institutional transformation than the single empowerment or re-emergence of the intergovernmental management of the EU. In fact, as a result of intergovernmental choices and because of the European institutions' efforts to gain power, the influence of the latter has increased no less than that of the member states and intergovernmental councils. Of course, the nature of empowerment and its dimensions is different for each institution. The ECB expanded both its field of action and the range of instruments at its disposal. On the other hand, the Commission augmented its technical functions mainly as a consequence of the new economic governance. Finally, the Parliament gained political visibility by acting as the only European institution directly legitimated by the electors and by "lending" its legitimacy to other institutions and gaining influence.

4 – The domestic structure of power and destructive Europeanisation in EMU member countries

The reshaping of the EU institutional structure and the different kinds of empowerment also changed the relationship between the EU institutions and the member states. The augmented invasiveness of the Commission's supervision, the new constraints imposed by the intergovernmental treaties, tensions between member states on European policies and the increase in rules make the inter-level relationship the real core of the EU politics after the crisis. Notwithstanding the relevance of member states' action and the weakness demonstrated by the Commission during the early phase of the crisis, intergovernmental management of the EU pays the price of divisions and divergent interests that weaken dramatically the ability of member states' governments to agree on a shared line on many topics. So delegating functions to the European institutions became the only way to consolidate agreements and hopes to have their respect granted. This is particularly true for those agreements reached thanks to the momentary predominance of one or a few countries that impose rules but are not sure they will be able to continue to bc predominant. Thus, the new economic governance and its application became a battlefield where the first-hour winners defend their gains and losers fight to regain what they lost. In fact, some governments hindered the application of agreements they subscribed to or delayed their application, calling for flexible application and for making political pressures that directly threatened the political cohesion of the European Union. This was the case with the problematic negotiation between the Troika and the first Greek government led by Tsipras, the Portuguese decision to dismiss the economic policy lines suggested by the Commission, and the tensions with the Italian governments led by Renzi and later by Conte. So those who see intuitively a reinforcement of governments and intergovernmental methodology as a consequence of the crisis underestimate the impact of contrasts between national governments in diminishing intergovernmental cohesion and reducing the impact of the intergovernmental governance of the EU. Also, the rise in power of new parties not involved in the previous decades' negotiations for European integration magnified tensions.

Conflicts between the EU institutions and member states may be explained by moving from the traditional intergovernmental approach to European integration in which governments and interstate negotiations are the core of intra-EU relations to a post-functionalist view of the integrative process of domestic politics in member states (Hooghe and Marks 2009). The post-functionalist approach contests the claim that states monopolise the representation of their citizens in international relations, a claim that is the basis of intergovernmentalism (Marks, Hooghe and Blank 1996; Hooghe and Marks 2009, p. 2). Indeed, domestic patterns of conflict assume a crucial role in influencing governments' attitudes toward integration (Hooghe and Marks 2009, p. 2). However, interest groups and economic issues are not the only to define domestic acceptance or opposition to supranational rule as in the traditional neo-functionalist approach. In Hooghe and Marks's view, it is the community that determines the attitude toward integration. This makes community identity and domestic politicisation of EU issues the reasons for the shift from the so-called "permissive consensus" that allowed governments to agree to the initial steps toward European Union creation to the "constraining dissensus" that arose with the domestic politicisation of the European Union issues. It is this constraining dissensus that generates tensions between member states and hinders the path toward further integration in Europe because politicisation of European integration changed the decision-making process (Hooghe and Marks 2009, p. 5 and 8). In other words, decision-making moved from a restricted elite of politicians to mass politics and this shift made elements such as identity and national perception of EU matters the core for attitudes of member states' citizens toward European integration constraining mainstream parties in their political programmes. Bartolini suggests that national political elites became the victims of those constraints they created and imposed on their countries, voters and in the end on themselves (Bartolini 2004, p. 190; Bartolini 2006). Finally, progress in European integration reinforced the relevance of non-economic issues. This disadvantaged mainstream parties traditionally structured on the right-left axis while it created consensus for populist (often Eurosceptic) parties (Hooghe and Marks 2009, p. 13 and 18) that used identity issues to feed opposition to the EU and further integration.

The post-functionalist explanation of the changing attitude toward European integration and its impact on member states' domestic politics fits well with the post-crisis period. The growing anti-Europeanism seems proportional to the impact of the new economic governance on member states' domestic politics and this confirms the post-functionalist explanation of the evolution of European integration. However, the study of monetary integration and its impact on mainstream parties' and governments' attitudes toward the EU suggests that something has been missed in the post-functionalist analysis. This is particularly evident in the most troubled countries, such as Greece and Italy.

One of the most relevant processes activated by European integration and dramatically accelerated by monetary integration is "destructive Europeanisation" – a kind of Europeanisation that impacted destructively on domestic politics in those member states that fit poorly with the requirement of the integrative process. While the literature insists on Europeanisation as a transformative phenomenon and focuses mainly on those changes that support European integration (Cowless, Caporaso and Risse 2001), the experiences of countries like Italy and Greece demonstrate that Europeanisation can result in the destruction of existent equilibria without an effective transformation of domestic political and economic structures that make them fit with the European standards.

Destructive Europeanisation is particularly problematic in those countries where the power structure and consensus for the leading parties depend on peculiar arrangements in contrast to the EU practices, deficit spending policies and consolidated patronage systems in particular. In fact, the political dimension of deficit spending policies consists of patronage links with electors, entrepreneurs and interest groups. Each of them gains from supporting the leading political elites. Unorganised electors obtain public jobs or admission in private firms through favourite channels that are sometimes crucial for their careers. On the other hand, entrepreneurs accede to public contracts or became suppliers of private firms thanks to the pressures of common political referees. Finally, interest groups obtain different kinds of advantages such as public support for mass employment, keeping obsolete industries operational, a benevolent attitude toward tax evasion, specific privileges for supporting groups and many other kinds of "patronage side payments" like generous pension systems and early-retirement privileges. However, this system depends on access to public resources, in particular to the state budget and public debt. So public expenditure is crucial for hiring people in the public sectors and granting them privileged conditions of work and pensions, keeping at work public industries and some obsolete firms crucial to guarantee massive employment in the area where they work, distributing public contracts for building infrastructures and services, and – last but not least – safeguarding banks that provide credit to politically supported entrepreneurs.

In the meantime, efficient taxation is hindered by other kinds of patronage linkages based on tolerance of tax evasion for small entrepreneurs and house owners. This fiscal laxness negatively influences the state budget balance and makes growing indebtedness a structural trend in those countries where this system prevails. In these countries, Europeanisation has had a destructive impact on the power structures without creating the conditions for a radical transformation in the domestic relationship between politics and the economy.

Since the 1980s, the European integration has imposed a dismantling of some of the pillars that sustained patronage systems. State aid to the private sector, state-owned industries and banks, and, later, public debt became victims of the Europeanisation process. Their disappearance destabilised the structure of power of certain member countries and created a political vacuum in which new actors gained power or changed the exixting power balance between groups and organised interests (Bartolini 2004, p. 184). However, this process undermined "virtuous Europeanisation". In contrast, in those countries mostly touched by the impact of destructive Europeanisation, it created the conditions for growing hostility toward the European Union, resistance against further integration and ephemeral attempts to keep operative or recreate the key features of the collapsing structure of power.

When the 2008 crisis arrived, and the new economic governance made debt cuts and balanced budgets, the fundamental economic objectives for the EU member states, destructive Europeanisation was revamped and its impact fostered anti-Europeism diffusion and a rise in the power of populist parties. Both mainstream parties and new populist parties saw the European Union as an issue to politicise for domestic debate and to include in political programmes. However, criticism toward European institutions did not arrive only through populists. The parties in charge also advanced criticisms and tried to resist EU constraints, on the economic governance side in particular. In fact, these parties drew consensus from consolidated patronage links and the occupation of power centres they had to surrender to apply the new economic governance rules. Meanwhile, deficit spending and debt-oriented policies became unachievable because they contradicted the EMU rules. Meanwhile, these kinds of policies became the core of anti-crisis proposals of anti-EU parties and extreme parties in government coalitions. So, if identity plays a relevant role in the rise and success of the new populist and anti-European parties, it was the structural unfitness of the domestic structure of power and the impact of destructive Europeanisation that explain the crisis of mainstream parties and the real nature of their collapse in some troubled countries.

5 – The future of the European economic governance: from the governance gap to the governance bias?

During the first eight years of the new European economic governance, a triple incongruence emerged between economic governance, monetary policy and the architecture of multi-level governance of the eurozone countries. The increasing contrast between economic governance invasiveness and the hostile attitudes of the most troubled countries added to the inconsistency between the financial stabilisation aims of the

ECB and the convergence objectives of the Commission discussed in the previous chapter. Surprisingly, none of the EU institutions paid sufficient attention to these incongruences and they continued planning a deepening and more invasive economic governance for the future by that time unacceptable in some countries.

The architecture of the existing economic governance and the guidelines for its enhancement derive from a sequence of documents and reports that culminated in the so-called "Five Presidents Report" (European Commission 2015). The latter recovers and reorganises the core of some crucial documents that shaped the new economic governance in its early phase. There is a continuous line from the early documents that started the debate on the new economic governance, such as the documents of the ECB on reinforcing the economic governance in the eurozone (European Central Bank 2010), the EU Commission report on economic policy coordination (European Commission 2010a) and the report on strengthening the EU economic governance submitted to the Council at the end of 2010 (Task force on economic governance 2010). All these documents were followed in 2012 by two other reports, usually known as the "Blueprint" and the "Van Rompuy Report" (European Commission 2012a; *idem* 2012b).

The Five President Report recovers many ideas from the previous documents and summarises the steps proposed for completing the EMU in a three-stage path to make progress on four fronts:[6] towards a genuine economic union, towards a

[6] The three-phase structure is common to many documents on economic governance planning. Both the Blueprint and the Van Rompuy Report (sometimes called the "Four Presidents Report") propose a governance development plan in three phases. The first document divides proposals into short-term, mid-term and long-term proposals. On the other hand, the Van Rompuy Report suggest three periods (2012–2013, 2013–2014 and post-2014) in which the proposals have to be implemented (European Commission 2012a; *idem* 2012b).

financial union, towards a fiscal union and towards a political union (European Commission 2015, p. 4–5). The three stages cover the period from 2015 to 2025 and propose a road map with specific objectives for each of the four fronts (*idem*, p. 20–21). Two other documents, both announced in the Five President Report, the White Paper on the Future of Europe and the Reflection Paper on the Deepening of the Monetary Union (European Commission 2017a; *idem* 2017b), confirmed the main guidelines and aims of the European economic governance for the future anticipated in the Five Presidents Report. So the Report can be considered the key document in analysing the EU plans for the future of governance. Moreover, it depicts clearly the political rationale of those reforms and the changes required in the EU and national institutions to have an effective economic governance.

The most surprising characteristic of the Report is the inconsistency of the political side. Almost all the Report's proposals aim to consolidate the EMU and create new instruments and entities to make economic governance more effective. This requires member states to surrender further powers to the EU and accept more constrictive rules and the empowerment of enforcing rules and sanctions. All this shift in power is poorly compensated with a more substantial involvement of the European Parliament and the national parliaments in debating governance (in the European Semester framework in particular) and more transparency in the decision-making process (European Commission 2015, p. 20–21). The fourth front (political union) is not mentioned at all, apart from recalling democratic accountability and legitimacy mainly referred to institutional strengthening. Unfortunately, most of the institutions to reinforce are European institutions, the Eurogroup in particular. The latter is proposed as a new and crucial section of the EU institutional architecture and represents the final predominance of EMU affairs in the new EU context.

The three pillars of the future EU economic governance as depicted in the Five President Report and the following Reflection Paper are convergence, juridical embedding of the governance rules and reinforced macroeconomic conditionality. All of them are linked by a common rationale, i.e. avoiding the political union issue by means of the radicalisation of the technocratic approach to European governance.

Convergence remains the crucial tool for having economic governance without a political government. This is the strategy identified since 1960 and adopted at Maastricht to face the challenge to create a common currency avoiding a common government. There are just a few adjustments, such as the proposal of a single external representative of the eurozone, the transformation of the European Stability Mechanism in the European Monetary Fund and the creation of a European Ministry of Finance. However, these reforms serve only to reinforce economic governance at the expense of member states.

The insertion of governance and intergovernmental treaty rules in national legislation (here called "juridical embedding") is aimed at strengthening the compelling nature of the EMU agreements at national level, as happened with the Fiscal Compact golden rule that Italy and Spain inserted in their Constitutions to grant its enforcement at the peak of the sovereign debt crisis. Consequently, the planned governance for the future EU is still more compelling than today's one and is aimed at restricting further the member states' operative space in economic policies.

Finally, reinforced macroeconomic conditionality is the main deterrent against non-compliance with governance rules. It is something more than the simple macroeconomic conditionality planned since the early 2010s and is limited to the freezing of the payment of cohesion funds for those members that failed to apply the EU rules (Verhelst 2011; Jouen 2015). In the Five President Report and the connected documents, macroeconomic conditionality consists mainly in the exclusion of the non-compliant members from the benefits planned in facing shocks and adjustments in the EMU area. So the impact of this exclusion on the members' economy is more significant than the simple freezing of structural funds and hinders major adjustments in internal and competitive imbalances. Unfortunately, competitiveness and trade deficit are the crucial issues for the structural divide between the Northern and Southern EMU. Meanwhile, these issues remain untouchable in the intergovernmental debate due to the conflicting interests of the two groups of members, mainly Germany on one side, and Italy and Spain on the other. Thus, as happened in the pre-Maastricht era, today's planners of the EMU governance prefer avoiding discussing politically sensitive issues at the price of the political unsustainability of their project.

So the plans for the future of EU economic governance deliberately forget the political limitations of the EMU and risk increasing the internal cleavage between debtor and creditor countries that the reforms of the early 2010s did not fill. Also, the run to stricter and more compelling constraints to national economic and fiscal policies conflicts with the limited abilities of the most troubled members to solve by themselves the gaps that made them poorly comply with the EU rules. So a loop emerges in which an exasperating run toward more efficient and invasive governance makes it less effective. In other words, the governance gap that made governing the EMU impossible before the 2010s became a "governance bias" of the EU institutions that sees stricter governance as the only possible way to manage the euro and avoid EMU dissolution without significant steps toward further political integration democratically legitimised.

In conclusion, governance as conceived in the Five President Report and carried out until the 2019 European elections is in strident contrast to two elements capable of derailing the plan for a "deep and genuine governance" as conceived by EU technocrats. The first point of friction regards democracy and accountability in the EU member states. It is evident that, if effectively applied, the principles of the enhanced new economic governance will empty the domestic sovereignty of the EMU member states again, at least in the field of economic policy. The second point of friction is a consequence of the first, i.e. the rise of strong political opposition against the EU plans for economic governance and more generally against the whole EU. The main manifestations of these contrasting points, the EU democracy deficit and the rise of anti-euro parties, respectively, will be analysed in the next two chapters.

Chapter 8

European Currency and National Democracy

Since the 1980s, the progressive and seemingly unstoppable advancement of European integration has generated concern about its effects on the member states. European integration has increasingly touched values connected with politics, economy and, more recently, welfare. These influences, initially perceived as separate problems, were all connected by the concept of European post-World War II democracy, usually referred to merely as democracy. However, the simple term "democracy" is too generic to correctly depict the political regime predominant in Europe after World War II.

From the 1950s, democracy in Europe was interpreted as a system of values capable of including and coordinating many elements, previously considered independent or in conflict. Universalism and nationalism, free market and state intervention, capitalism and social welfare, freedom and order were combined in a "marvellous" and seemingly eternal political construction based on electoral democracy and enriched with practical compromises elaborated at the end of the war to soften tensions inherited from the inter-war period. European integration was one of these compromises, and it was accepted or tolerated until its effects conflicted with the perceived essence of democracy. This turn happened mainly at the launch of the EMU and the tension became more vehement with the start of the economic crisis and the introduction of the new economic governance. Then, the perils for democracy became the central argument of those who opposed or criticised the EMU as the primary expression of the EU's pervasiveness in domestic affairs.

Some authors claimed that democracy was at risk due to the rise of the European leviathan that oppressed democratic nation states and justified their criticisms against the EMU by the need to defend freedom.[1] On the other hand, supporters of European integration joined the debate in an attempt to demonstrate that the EU and integration are not a threat to democracy or, at least, that they can be enhanced to curb the negative impact they had on it. In both cases, the democratic regime seems like a static monolith on which the EU and the EMU have an effect and to which they cause damage. On the other hand, democracy and the socio-political context in which it rose evolved shaping and being shaped by European integration. So the integration trajectory was influenced by the progressive obsolescence of the models of democracy (Held 1987) that appeared in Europe after the war.

Unfortunately, the evolutionary dimension of democracy is poorly considered by many scholars involved in the debate on the EU and democracy. Yet it is the key to understanding the existing relationship between democracy and European integration. This link is something more complicated than the simple reduction of democracy depicted by Eurosceptics or the causal relationship between monetary integration and democracy emptiness proposed by the opponents of the EMU.

[1] The idea of the EMU (the euro in particular) and its constraints as a threat to democracy in the EMU member states is widespread in the literature against the euro, particularly in social media and the political debate. However, this topic also features in the academic literature. Some examples of authors that deal with this topic are Rodrik (2011), Bagnai (2012), Crum (2013), and Matthijs (2017).

1 – *The European democratic deficit*

While many anti-EU critics focus primarily on the damages caused by the EMU to national democracies since the 1990s, the scientific approach to the relationship between integration and democracy in Europe analyses both the national and supranational dimensions as well as a more extended period of the European integration history. In this perspective, monetary integration is just the last phase of a long-term process, not the origin of the problem. So discussing the impact of the EMU on democracy requires an understanding of the general debate on integration and democracy in Europe.

The starting point of that debate is the concept of the "democratic deficit" of the European Union. Notwithstanding some scholars discussed the effects of integration on European democracy since the late 1950s (Meade 1957; Scitovsky 1957), it was only after the signing of the Maastricht Treaty that the problem gained extensive evidence. In fact, before the acceleration of integration resulted in the Single European Act and later the Maastricht Treaty, the boundaries imposed by the European level of governance on national policies and politics were poorly perceived and did not appear highly invasive of national prerogatives. So the European institutions were legitimated by the "permissive consensus" granted by European citizens who passively accepted them and no democratic deficit was perceived (Hooghe and Marks 2009). This situation changed when new and relevant policies and powers were transferred to the European level. Then, the growing invasiveness of European influence and the limits to member states' choices became more evident and perceived by citizens and politicians.

In 1995, Weiler et al. defined the so-called "standard version" of the democratic deficit concept (Weiler et al. 1995). In their essay, they concentrated on many elements and questions raised by the growing influence of the EU on national policies and politics. Most of these elements re-emerged in the literature that followed and shaped the growing debate on democracy and integration in Europe. Weiler et al. affirmed that European integration enlarged the polity in which decisions affecting citizens were taken. In fact, the European polity included citizens of many countries and all of them influenced choices previously determined only by citizens of the affected member state. Consequently, democracy "diminished" because of the disempowerment of individuals and this process undermined the EU democratic legitimacy (*idem*, 6).[2] Weiler et al. also depicted the dynamics of power redistribution generated by integration. In particular, they stressed the limited ability of national parliaments to check the European decisional processes and the inability of the European Parliament to act in their place (*idem*, 7). Moreover, they showed how in the EU decisional process the national majorities can be subverted if a right government in a member country has to accept decisions taken by a majority of leftist governments at European level and vice versa (*idem*, 9). Finally, they insisted on the problematic perception of the importance of European elections' and the non-emergence of a transnational party system capable of fostering a European political space (*idem*, 8).

In their seminal work, Weiler et al. also introduced a crucial aspect of the subsequent debate on European democracy, namely the no-demos question. They devoted a large part of their essay to discussing a pronunciation of the German Constitutional Court focused on the relationship between demos and parliamentary representation. This discussion was the occasion for presenting the so-called "no-demos theory", which suggests that a European democracy cannot exist without a European demos. If so, the European institutions cannot have the authority and legitimacy of a demos-cratic state, and increasing the role of representative institutions such as the European Parliament without a European demos would dimin-

[2] We will call this phenomenon the "dilution of democracy".

ish the EU legitimacy instead of increasing it (*idem*, 13). Weiler et al. identify two approaches to the no-demos theory: the soft version (the "not yet" approach) and the hard one. While the soft version says that the European demos does not exist yet, but could be created or emerge by itself, the hard one states that a European demos does not exist and is not desirable (*idem*, 13). From the soft version derived other approaches to the democratic deficit problem that search for a way to create a European demos or something equivalent for democratising the EU. In contrast, the hard version is coherent with all those approaches that deny the need to democratise the EU or even the possibility of doing so.

Weiler et al. conclude the article by contesting some basic assumptions that they feel are prevalent in the current debate on the democratic deficit. In particular, they criticise the identification of demos only with the form of demos accepted by the nation states. Also, they suggest that it is not correct to conceive of a democratically legitimate rule-making polity just in national terms and it is equally wrong to imagine that the only form the Union can take is that of the nation state (*idem*, 15). In other words, they suggest that the European Union can be something different from a European nation state and that this "different thing" could be legitimated as democratic by the European demoi instead of a non-existent European Volk.[3] From the idea that demoi can act together in legitimising supranational democracy derives the literature on demoi-cracy that tries to combine the existence of different nation states and demoi with the reality of a democratic or democratising EU.

Notwithstanding many concepts emphasised in Weiler et al. had already been touched on in the literature, their systematic analysis addressed the debate on the democratic deficit in the following years. Some dichotomies that emerged in Weiler et

[3] The word "demoi" is used here as the plural of "demos" and indicates the different demoi that compose the EU.

al. inspired or reinforced different approaches to studying the democracy and integration approach. For example, the no-demos vs demoi dichotomy inspired respectively the debate on the non-existence of a democratic deficit and the real nature of European integration, and the approaches of European demoi-cracy and network democracy. On the other hand, the dichotomy between individual and parliamentary disempowerment and government empowerment anticipated a considerable quantity of research on institutional transformation and accountability as well as studies on the new non-statal forms of the EU. Also, references to diminished democracy and legitimacy echoed the following debates on the legitimacy deficit and quality of democracy. Finally, they anticipated the discussion on democracy in a multilevel system and the national-democracy-centred approach that became predominant in the anti-euro discussion.

After Weiler et al.'s essay, the literature on EU democracy and the democratic deficit flourished, particularly in the early 2000s (Jensen 2009). Then, different currents of thought emerged that we can classify by using their most crucial statement as the discriminator.

A useful discriminator for classifying the different approaches is the attitude toward the democratic deficit. Some authors contested the existence or relevance of the democratic deficit and, as a consequence, the need to correct it. On the other hand, other scholars addressed the democratic deficit as one of the main problems to solve.

While Dahl sees the EU as just an international organisation and extends to it his scepticism about the possibility of being democratic, Moravcsik suggests that the democratic deficit is just a myth (Dahl 1999; Moravcsik 2008). In fact, notwithstanding the EU was not created to be democratic, it has characteristics that make it similar to democracies and it is composed of democratic states. On the other hand, Zweifel and Crombez adopt a comparative approach to confirm that the

EU is similar to the leading democracies in the world, thereby dismissing the existence of a democratic deficit (Zweifel 2002; Crombez 2003). Majone dismisses the democratic deficit as a category mistake suggesting the EU is a regulatory polity that has not to be or become a democracy (Majone 2006). Franchino, meanwhile, focuses on a specific element that supporters of the relevance of the democratic deficit emphasise as clear proof of its existence, namely accountability. Franchino minimises the EU's lack of accountability, stressing that the Council has excellent control of bureaucratic processes and that many decisions delegated to the supranational level return to national authorities for implementation (Franchino 2004, 2005 and 2007).

Other authors insist on the relevance of the democratic deficit and try to explain its causes. Some scholars focus on specific limits of the EU. For example, Decker, and Hix and Follesdal link the democratic deficit with the lack of a European party system (Decker 2002; Follesdal and Hix 2006). Follesdal and Hix (2006) also suggest that the absence of a real parliamentary opposition at the European level is a crucial obstacle to EU democratisation. Habermas sees in the non-existence of transnational media the main problem for the construction of a European public sphere (Habermas 2001). De Beus, on the other hand, sees the rise of a European identity as the *sine qua non* condition for having that public sphere (De Beus 2001). These authors seem to look at the EU as a nation state under formation where it is the lack of those characteristics they consider to be crucial for a democratic nation state to hinder democratisation.

Some scholars emphasise the importance of the degenerative processes activated by European integration and how they magnified the democratic deficit. Papadopoulus identifies in the so-called "blame shift" and the problem it creates for multilevel accountability one of the reasons that made the democratic deficit worse (Papadopoulos 2010). This is an essential element of the whole debate because it stresses the importance of distinguishing between the real democratic deficit and the democratic deficit as perceived by citizens. Meanwhile, Eberlein and Grande maintain that the rise of informal governance methods made the EU less accountable (Eberlein and Grande 2005). Their work also introduces new elements to the debate on integration and democracy and reveals that multilevel governance is a crucial channel in transmitting the impact of integration on democracy. In this case, they are the decisional and implementation methods used to influence that effect.

2 – Facing the democratic deficit

Implicitly or explicitly, many of those authors who identify in specific gaps the causes of the democratic deficit suggest that there are solutions to the problem. However, some scholars reject the possibility of solving the democratic deficit if EU democracy is not developed on the same basis as national democracy. Among them, there are authors with general approaches like Lord and Beetham who retain that to be democratic the EU has to respect the same minimum standard of national democracy (Lord and Beetham 2001). Other authors contest this isomorphic approach and suggest there are no reasons because of a supranational democracy has to be so similar to the national one. Coultrap maintains that a democratic deficit is perceived by those who mainly focus on parliamentary democracy (Coultrap 1999). Both Coultrap and Meny criticise those who suggest the EU has to replicate the national state model (Meny 2002). Instead, they suggest, new paradigms can be invented for the EU. Many scholars have welcomed their suggestion, and new approaches have appeared. The most important is the demoi-cratic approach.

Theorists of demoi-cracy accept the soft version of the no-demos theory and suggest that the EU can be reformed to become demoi-cratic. However, these reforms are not so extreme as to dramatically transform the EU political identity. So they escape the no-demos trap, creating something different they call "demoi" to take the place of the non-existent European demos and recreate the traditional structure of a democratic institutional structure.[4] In their definitions, the demoi include peoples, states and sometimes stakeholders (Hurrelmann 2015, p. 20). So it recovers the conventional approach of the electoral and functional channels of representation. The principal limitation of the demoi-cracy approach consists in its limited applicability. In fact, such a specific structure can be created just in the EU.[5] So demoi-cracy appears to be more a theoretical construction used to outflank the democratic deficit problem than a real form of advanced democracy. In other words, the demoi-cracy approach does not refer to the EU as it is; it describes it as it has to become to avoid the accusation of being non-democratic. Also, the artificial nature of demoi-cracy makes it indistinguishable from a non-democratic structure to citizens' eyes.

Within the anti-isomorphic literature, there is an approach we can call the "transformationalist approach". It focuses mainly on the transformation process that led to the EU as we know it today. It is characterised by a historical perspective in which the evolution of the EU explains the rise of the democratic deficit. The transformationalist approach rejects the iso-

---

[4] Nicolaidis defines demoi-cracy as "a union of peoples, understood both as states and as citizens, who govern together but not as one". Cheneval and Schimmelfennig simply define demoi-cracy as a polity of multiple demoi (Nicolaidis 2013, p. 351; Cheneval and Schimmelfennig p. 2013, 334).

[5] Hurrelmann refers to institutional, sociological and citizenship requirements the EU has to fit to "make demoi-cracy applicable as a normative model for its democratisation". However, Hurrelmann concludes that currently, the EU meets only in part the institutional requirements. Also, in the absence of demoi-cratic citizenship and identity, institutional reforms for demoi-cratisation of the EU risk accentuating the "already existing participatory inequalities among European citizens" (Hurrelmann 2015, p. 23, 26 and 33).

morphism view of global democracy and democratisation as an extension of national democracy and the consequent need to adopt the same structures and principles.

Notwithstanding both Bartolini and Streeck could be included in this category, their work has a general relevance that goes beyond the more straightforward matter of democratic deficit because they propose a long-term analysis of the integration process that found its place in the field of integration theories (Bartolini 2006; Streeck 2014). Here we will focus on the Schimmelfennig analysis of the EU transformation. His approach suggested the term "transformation(alist)" we use to describe the way in which he and other authors explain the EU characteristics (Schimmelfennig 2010). Schimmelfennig rejects the application of traditional democratisation theories to the European Union because these approaches derived almost exclusively from the experience of nation states. Instead, Schimmelfennig emphasises the action of institutional actors in introducing democratic norms in the European Union. This action happened at a critical juncture in the history of the EU and was aimed at granting, or preserving, legitimacy to the integration process (*idem*, 212).[6] So Schimmelfennig distinguishes the origins of EU democratisation he found in the normative process, from the origin of nation states' democracy as explained by the traditional literature on democratisation. Also, he faces the no-demos problem by suggesting a "transformationalist approach" based on normative innovation that explains European democratisation notwithstanding the absence of a European demos (*idem*, 219). Schimmelfennig identifies

[6] Schimmelfennig just writes "to preserve" referring to the legitimacy of integration. However, other scholars show that during the eurozone crisis other institutions acted to increase their legitimacy, for example with voluntary accountability as in the case of the European Central Bank. Also, the new procedures for choosing the presidents of the European Parliament and the European Commission are aimed at increasing the EU democratic legitimacy overall (Jabko 2003).

the reason for the normative evolution in the constitutional conflict among institutional actors that compete for political rights and competences in the EU (*idem*, 222). So the democratic deficit became an instrument for those actors that search for empowerment, and that can refer to democratic values to undermine the legitimacy of the previous structure of the EU inspired by efficiency-driven criteria.

This explanation may be a sort of sophisticated reworking of the original debate on the democratic deficit. In that discussion, Moravcsik and Majone dismissed the democratic deficit as a false problem due to the efficiency-driven criteria that generated the European integration and inspired the functions initially assigned to the European institutions (Majone 1998 and 2002; Moravcsik 2002). On the other hand, authors that contested this dismissal of the democratic deficit problem emphasise the impact of European integration on national-level politics and the legitimacy deficit it caused (Follesdal and Hix 2006). Transformationalist theory recovers the elements that emerged in the debate of the early 2000s and suggests that Moravcsik and Majone were right in describing the original function of the EU institutions, but Follesdal and Hix identified factors that gained political relevance and addressed the following development in the EU institutional evolution and democratisation.

Another classification criterion that became more and more relevant with the rise of the eurozone crisis refers to the importance devoted to European democratisation. In this case, the literature can be divided between those authors who care about EU democratisation and those who mainly care about the effect of European integration (monetary integration included) on the member states' democracies. In fact, a crucial question that remained in the background for years regarded the reason for democratising the EU. Why democratise it? Why bother? This issue was explicitly proposed by Philippe Schmitter, one of the most enthusiastic supporters of EU democratisation. He tried to explain the reasons that suggest the need to democratise the EU, including referring to the impact of Europeanisation on national democracies (Schmitter 2000 and 2003). More specifically, at the end of the 1990s, Schmitter saw in the incoming steps toward enlargement and monetary integration a challenge to the EU that made democratisation a necessity. Also, he notices that growing contestation against domestic democratic rules and practices and the end of "permissive consensus" at the European level require anticipation of the effects of a mounting legitimacy crisis for both national democracies and the EU. Finally, Schmitter suggests that democratisation can replace Monnet's integration engine based on functional spillovers, an engine Schmitter considers to be exhausted (Schmitter 2000). Today we see Schmitter's view as prophetic, but obsolete. He was right in anticipating the incoming crisis of EU and national democracies' legitimacy. However, today it is too late to use EU democratisation as an antidote for the legitimacy crisis, as proposed by Schmitter. So Schmitter's question, "why bother?", remains unanswered or changes to "does it still bother?"

3 – The legitimacy deficit

The theme of democratic deficit is strictly connected to the issue of the EU and EU policy legitimacy, and of a hypothetical legitimacy deficit. In fact, high levels of legitimacy can compensate for the democratic deficit, while low levels of legitimacy make EU democratisation useless or, worse still, dangerous.

The legitimacy issue is crucial for connecting the traditional debate on democracy in the European Union with the new evidence and approaches regarding citizens' attitude toward the EU, the EMU and European integration in general. The "perceptual revolution" in European studies,[7] the spread populism,

[7] We refer to "perceptual revolution" to indicate the growing attention paid by political scientists and sociologists to citizens' feelings toward the EU

and the increased relevance of citizens' attitudes toward the EU and European integration found in legitimacy a more flexible concept than democracy itself. In fact, legitimacy includes the relevance of individual perceptions and cognitive limits better than other approaches in which the normative and procedural elements are preponderant. In other words, if citizens perceive the EU as legitimate, the democratic deficit loses relevance and does not undermine the support for European institutions and integration. On the other hand, if the EU is viewed as illegitimate, anti-EU feelings will grow notwithstanding progress in EU democratisation. So to study the contribution to the anti-EU opposition, what matters is how citizens see the EU and the EMU, rather than how they really are.

As usual, such an important concept as legitimacy has been defined in different ways and debated by a multitude of authors. Stillman accurately describes how legitimacy was determined over the centuries while referring to different countries and different perspectives.[8] However, what is relevant for this book is democratic legitimacy, in Europe, today. In contemporary definitions, the connection between citizens and government is predominantly stated in functional terms. For example,

---

and integration. This turn in European studies depends on two factors. First, new research methodologies and data mining techniques (e.g. sentiment analysis techniques and big data analysis of socials on the Web) permit in-depth analysis of individual perceptions of political phenomena and explain their attitudes and choices referring to these perceptions instead of general categories such as party families, social classes, levels of education and other aggregate indicators used in traditional studies. Second, the rise of collective political behaviours that transcend the traditional classifications and are partly explained by new forms of political participation (mainly by the Internet and the social media) made the individual the key actor to study. So attention to institutional structures, political ideologies and many other elements previously used extensively in electoral studies and social movement analysis moved from the messages transmitted to the individual actors to the perception of these messages by individuals.

[8] An extensive review of authors who have debated legitimacy can be found in Stillman (1974).

Scharpf defines legitimacy as the "sense of normative obligation that helps to ensure voluntary compliance with undesired rules or decisions of governing authorities" (Scharpf 2009, p. 173). Suchman, on the other hand, proposes conceiving legitimacy as "a generalised perception or assumption that the actions of an entity are desirable, proper and appropriate within some socially constructed system of norms, values, beliefs and definitions" (Suchman 1995, p. 574). In general, legitimacy is prevalently interpreted as the mechanism that induces citizens to obey the law and accept governments including in those cases in which laws seem wrong and the government undesirable. This happens because those laws and those governments are perceived to be part of a set of values widely accepted by citizens. The problem remains identifying what these values are.

To solve this problem, a normative, an identity and a utilitarian approach arose in regard to legitimacy. The normative approach identifies a set of procedures, norms and institutional arrangements that define the level of legitimacy of a political entity. In the case of the European Union, this approach generated and oriented the initial debate on the democratic deficit. In fact, that debate centred mainly on the institutional structure of the EU and the democratic nature of the supranational governance. In this case, the set of values that define legitimacy is the set of democratic values and the principles of accountability, responsiveness, people sovereignty and compliance with norms. So legitimacy depends very little on citizens' perceptions because the values and beliefs listed above can be evaluated with objective criteria.

The identity approach focuses on a broader set of values than the basic democratic ones (here called "normative values") and on a more sophisticated interpretation of them. In this case, history, culture and traditions play a relevant role in defining both the values and the way in which they are interpreted. So the same actions of a legitimate and appropriate government in one democratic regime could be perceived as illegitimate in another democratic regime that does not share the same "social" values. This is the case with human rights (e.g. the death penalty) and solidarity values, particularly the welfare state, which are accepted differently in the EU and the USA.

Finally, the utilitarian approach connects legitimacy to citizens' expectations about government action. The latter is legitimate mainly because of its ability to satisfy citizens' requests. This approach was conceived primarily as an input-output dichotomy.[9] Some authors insist on input legitimacy through the active participation of citizens in policy definition and deliberation, while other scholars focus mainly on output legitimacy derived from satisfying outputs of policies implemented by the government.

The three approaches described above may be combined in a more straightforward classification based on just two kinds of legitimacy: legitimacy by acceptance and legitimacy by satisfaction. The first class includes those forms of legitimacy generated by the acceptance (more or less enthusiastic) of the existing norms and institutions. Approval may result from traditions, normative and procedural evaluation, or the lack of alternatives (real or just perceived). On the other hand, legitimacy by satisfaction derives from concrete support for government action both in terms of citizens' involvement in the deliberative process and the adoption of rules suggested "by the people" and concrete outputs resulting from government policies, with or without the citizens' involvement. This classification permits the inclusion of some elements that today appear relevant in studying new forms of delegitimisation of democratic governments or legitimisation of democratically disempowered regimes. Adopting this classification helps to explain fluctuations

[9] This dichotomy was initially proposed in 1970 by Scharpf. A few years later, Stillman echoed the Scharpf approach in adopting a definition of legitimacy wholly based on governmental output (Scharpf 1970, p. 22; Stillman 1974, p. 39).

in legitimacy for the same governments and institutions when commonly shared values, and institutional settings, remain the same. Also, it made it easier to explain cases of inversely proportional relations between output and legitimacy. In fact, rigid definitions of legitimacy poorly explain why the EU moved from permissive consensus to delegitimisation notwithstanding undoubted progress in democratisation. On the other hand, the more flexible concept of legitimacy by acceptance allows the embedding of complementary concepts such as blame shift and individual perception in legitimacy analysis. Similarly, the idea of satisfaction includes personal judgement in output evaluation and enables input and output legitimacy to be combined. So cases in which citizens saw their suggestions accepted and implemented by the government with policies that generated poor results can be explained by personal satisfaction for input responsiveness and blame shift (e.g. against the EU) for poor results

4 – The debate on democracy in the EU after the eurozone crisis

The input-output approach to legitimacy today seems predominant, at least in the literature on the EU. Scharpf, in particular, proposes a narrow interpretation of the legitimacy deficit in the EU. He suggests that the welfare state is the primary legitimising element of the post-war European democracy. European integration, particularly after the introduction of the euro and new economic governance, induced member states to reform and partially dismantle the welfare systems he saw as embedded in the European set of values that determined legitimisation of the European governments (Scharpf 2009).

The chain proposed by Scharpf that links monetary integration, welfare reduction and democracy delegitimisation may work in explaining the way in which the process has been perceived. However, it is not sophisticated enough to describe the real course of the welfare state crisis and the progressive delegitimisation of the EU. The reduction of the welfare state did not result mainly from the EMU. Rather, it started before the introduction of the euro and continued as an element of the evolution process of post-World War II European democracy. So welfare state reduction was on the agenda of European governments for decades, and the EMU became an opportunity to pursue this aim. When the eurozone crisis erupted, cuts in social benefits became the easiest way to quickly face fiscal collapse and respect EMU parameters. However, the most troubled countries had already had almost 20 years to adjust their budget structure to the Maastricht parameters. So it was not because national governments did so that the welfare state entered into crisis; it was because they had not done it before. On the other hand, delegitimisation of the EU also resulted from the way in which national governments and political parties, unable or unwilling to reform their countries, addressed citizens against the EU and discharged to the supranational level and the common currency responsibilities for domestic choices.

The eurozone crisis and the rise of the New Economic Governance revamped the debate on democracy in the EU. This debate moved from the academic field to the political one where a particular emphasis was devoted to the consequences of the EU for national democracies. So the EU democratic deficit lost relevance while the matter of "democracy reduction" became pivotal.

There are at least four different reasons for this change. First, growing anti-Europeanism and Euroscepticism caused the politicisation of the democratic deficit debate. However, this process mainly depended on the impact of the economic crisis on the member states, and this moved the focus from the EU to the national level. So the limits of EU institutional design and its democratic nature lost importance.

Second, the politicisation of the debate on democracy led to a "pragmatic approach" to the matter. So the normative approach used in the previous academic debate left space for a "perception" approach to democracy. The latter emphasised the way in which citizens perceive democracy and its reduction. However, democracy reduction and the perils for democracy were perceived mainly at the national level as a restriction of democratic choices resulting from EU constraints to national policies. This turn in the perception of democracy's problems also influenced the academic debate, and case studies on the impact of EU governance on national democracies flourished.

Third, the use of democracy as an argument for political communication orientated the debate toward those topics that became strategic for EU opponents, the EMU and the euro first and foremost. In fact, after the early years of the euro's circulation, the common currency became the preferred target of all those who opposed integration. They used the euro and the constraints imposed by the Stability and Growth Pact and later by New Economic Governance to explain why economic policies traditionally perceived as sound anti-crisis policies (e.g. deficit spending and popularised Keynesian policies) had been dismissed or rejected. So a complex but efficient discursive construction connected the euro and democracy in anti-Europeanists' political communication. This discursive construction also attracted some scholars who shared the same arguments and the same limitations of anti-EU parties and movements. These limitations mainly regard the ideological nature of economic policies suggested for saving democracy, national sovereignty and, sometimes, European integration.

Fourth, the eurozone crisis strongly affected social and economic structures that heavily contributed to defining the main characteristics of the post-World War II European democracy. Fiscal restraint, budget cuts and financial stabilisation policies endangered welfare state and employment policies, i.e. two of the pillars of democratic legitimacy for European nation states. So the real effects of EU constraints impacted on democracy at the only level in which it exists, namely the national one.

The way in which the EU faced the sovereign debt crisis and the rescue of member states magnified the attractiveness of the democracy reduction approach. In particular, it was the Greek crisis that showed how supranational constraints could emasculate national democracy and sovereignty. Also, the general debate on austerity in times of economic crisis made evident the strict limits within which supranational constraints had confined national economic policies. In both cases, a new threat to national democracy appeared, i.e. the prevalence of specific member states' priorities regarding the democratic choices of the others. In particular, it was Germany that emerged as the leading country capable of orientating European constraints to member states' democratic prerogatives moulding them to the German priorities.

On the other hand, the relevance of the public debt issue and the economic constraints the new generations inherited from the older ones demonstrates that there are other elements to consider in judging the relationship between democracy and European integration. In particular, it is the ability of the supranational level to protect member states' citizens from the excesses and long-term consequences of their democratically elected governments that emerged from the eurozone crisis as a valuable asset that the EU can offer to democracy.[10]

5 – Quality of democracy and policy coordination in the EMU

The same questions that inspire the debate on the EU democratic deficit arise for the EMU. These items may be answered using the same perspectives and approaches that

[10] The case of public debt is particularly relevant as an example of those unpleasant heritages the new generation received from previous generations and governments and stressed by Buchanan in his works. The SGP constraints, and more generally the EU, can grant EU citizens a defence against past policies that compromise their ability to decide democratically the new policies to adopt.

emerged in the democratic deficit debate. However, almost all of this literature assumes that the core problem is the democratic nature or gap of the EU and its institutions. In other words, many authors see EU governance and interference in national politics as an erosion of member states' democracy and try to prove (or refute) that the EU compensated for the decline in democracy at the national level by becoming more democratic or creating new forms of supranational democracy. Our approach is different, and we do not subscribe to the idea that a decline in national democracy is an automatic outcome of sovereignty transfer, either in the case of the EMU or that of European integration.

Many studies on democracy in the EU focus almost exclusively on the electoral mechanism and electoral accountability. So they suggest that a decrease in electoral accountability reduces democracy. Few doubts exist that surrendering sovereignty to the EU makes national governments less accountable. In fact, they are no longer responsible for those policy fields surrendered to the EU level. So voters should not hold national governments accountable for policy outcomes in those areas. Furthermore, clarity of responsibility may be reduced by blame-shifting or blame avoidance tactics to endorse the EU governance and policies they blame for failures and costs (Pierson 1995). Finally, it seems evident that as EU institutions are poorly democratically legitimised, their influence and decisions cannot have a sufficiently democratic nature. So in adopting a mono-dimensional approach centred on electoral accountability, it is undeniable that multilevel governance in general, and EU economic governance in particular, erode democracy at the national level.

However, by adopting a broader approach based on the quality of democracy, which depends on more dimensions than electoral accountability (inter-institutional accountability, responsiveness and the rule of law being the most important), that conclusion becomes less convincing. In fact, reducing electoral accountability does not automatically reduce the quality of democracy because other dimensions may change at the same time as a consequence of electoral accountability reduction compensating for the accountability decrease. For example, what about the case when a reduction in electoral accountability coexists with an increase in responsiveness or the rule of law? In this case, does the quality of member states' democracy get worse? If causal linkages exist between a decline in one dimension and an increase in another, analysis cannot be limited to electoral accountability.

The theoretical problem we aim to introduce at this point is the efficiency of democracy, i.e. the ability of a democratic regime to fulfil the goals wanted by its citizens stably and sustainably. Combining the responsiveness, accountability and sustainability of policies is the crucial need for democracy that emerged from the integration experience. This concept directly challenges the procedural approaches used to define responsiveness and accountability. Sustainability introduces a limit to the people's will that represents the central element in almost all the procedural definitions of democracy and its quality. These definitions mainly originated in the fields of philosophy and law many years before the economy and international economic interdependence became a crucial element in shaping political regimes. Also, the contemporaneous rise and consolidation of nation states and a new concept of nationalism made the nation-state the standard political unit for democracy analysis. So when advanced domestic economies became inextricably interconnected and national politics heavily influenced by exogenous factors, the binomial association between the procedural approach and the nation state became obsolete. This is particularly evident in the European Union case in which domestic politics in member states faces both exogenous and supranational factors. These factors are not entirely exogenous because national governments can influence supranational decisions. So EU affairs affect domestic politics and the quality of democracy. However, these issues are predominantly concentrated in the economic field. So in the EU the relevance of democracy sustainability and the obsolescence of the procedural-national binomial are magnified.

Another element that suggests dismissing the procedural approach to democracy quality is the rise of the "perceptual approach" to democratic legitimacy. In this approach, legitimacy and electoral behaviour mainly depend on the perception that electors have of government action. So the crucial question for explaining their perception of responsiveness regards what matters for electors: the goals reached or the policies adopted to obtain them? In other words, is a more democratic regime in which citizens decide on the best way to gain what they want (procedurally responsive democracy or input democracy) or a system in which citizens decide what they want and achieve it (substantially responsive democracy or output democracy) preferable?

Definitions of responsiveness like that of Przeworski, Stokes and Manin that identify a government as responsive if it adopts policies signalled as preferred by citizens describe without doubt a procedurally responsive democracy in which citizens are free to do badly. However, if we conceive responsiveness as the reception of citizens' aims regarding results instead of policies (substantial responsiveness), the interpretation of the impact of EU economic governance on member states' quality of democracy changes. What matters is whether or not national governments achieve the results that citizens asked for. It is quite intuitive that voters evaluate results, not policies, and choices for electoral punishment or rewards depend on a government's results rather than policy content. So if citizens ask for full employment and economic growth, they will punish or reward the incumbents depending on the employment and growth levels. This will happen independently of the policies adopted to obtain those results (in the absence of adverse collateral effects), or, more importantly, regardless of the level of government that took the most critical decisions to reach the objectives.[11]

Informative asymmetries and limited knowledge make citizens results oriented in the short term. So accountability also depends on short-term results because of the attitudes of electors. This means that citizens' satisfaction, which legitimises a democratic regime, depends on substantial responsiveness.

The distinction between procedural and substantial responsiveness is crucial for evaluating the effect of the EMU on the quality of democracy in member states. Critics of the EMU maintain that the empowerment of EU economic governance caused by the eurozone crisis eroded democracy into the member states. As explained above, by adopting a procedural responsiveness perspective centred on electoral accountability at the national level, their statement is sound. This could not be the case when referring to substantial responsiveness. In fact, in that case, results depend on the interaction between at least two levels of government (national and supranational) So we might imagine a multilevel democracy as a system in which every member state is accountable and (substantially) responsive to both EU institutions and the national electorate. Also, sustainability gains an almost constitutional dimension. In fact, in a substantial responsive perspective implemented in a multilevel system, external constraints imposed by treaties approved by sovereign state governments are politically equivalent to constitutional rules.

To make this crucial statement more explicit and understandable, we introduce the concept of multilevel inter-institutional accountability (MIA). As its name implies, it is a concept strictly linked with inter-institutional accountability. However, if the latter is about same-nation institutions, MIA regards a political environment as being characterised by mul-

[11] This is evident for employment (Rombi 2016).

tilevel governance. From our point of view, MIA acts when national governments can be held to account by the EU's institutions. Moreover, of course, because supranational European institutions might hold governments to account, they need some punishment tools. These kinds of instruments include Early Warning Alerts, Excessive Deficit Procedures, Macroeconomic Imbalance Procedures and other sanctions legitimised by EU governance rules.

However, at this stage, it is necessary to underline that, within the EU context, MIA often acts as a control mechanism used to ensure the member state's fulfilment of the EU's policy priorities. As a result, multilevel inter-institutional accountability seems more robust than its domestic counterpart. This specific characteristic of MIA produces two sizable effects: on the one hand, it makes national electoral accountability more complicated, increasing the distance between the voters and the national government; on the other hand, it stimulates a new kind of responsiveness, which can be called "multilevel responsiveness" (MR). There is MR when a member state is responsive to the demands proceeding from the supranational level. Therefore, in the EU, the classical interpretation of responsive government as "a government attentive to, and influenced by, the voice of the people" is no longer suitable for describing the functioning of modern democracies (Sartori 1976). At least contemporary European governments have to be attentive both to the voters' and the EU institutions' requests. The national governments have delegated to EU institutions authority over policies areas that used to be those of the nation state, like monetary policy or international trade. In regard to those policies fields, national political leaders may, at most, bring their own citizens' requests from within the European institutions. They do not the opportunity to be directly responsive to their voters, simply because the Europeanisation of many policy sectors has removed these policies from the nation state political arena. In those policies areas, national governments, by contrast, have to be responsive towards EU institutions' decisions (multilevel responsiveness) to avoid the enforcement of MIA mechanisms, such as an infringement procedure against them.

From a conceptual perspective, the functioning of MIA and MR create a nation state's almost controlled democracy in which national governments have to be accountable and responsive towards both a national and a supranational principle.

MR in the EU is substantially responsive because it is parameter oriented, which means that the EU prescribes the outcomes and only suggests policy solutions. Sanctions depend fundamentally on the respect of parameters. In this case, responsiveness and accountability depend on both the aims of citizens and the EU. If all or parts of these objectives are coincident, the interaction between levels may generate outcomes that satisfy national electors. In other words, if the EU and voters ask for the same outcomes, MIA and MR may reinforce electoral and inter-institutional accountability, and substantial responsiveness at national level, thereby improving the quality of democracy. Of course, if the EU's and electors' objectives diverge, EU economic governance may be detrimental to the quality of democracy in member states. The following figure depicts the complex network of accountability and responsiveness relations in a multilevel democratic system.

Of course, the remaining dimensions of the quality of democracy are also influenced by multilevel governance. European integration has reinforced many aspects of freedom, and equality has been improved by EU rules against racial, gender and sexual discrimination. On the other hand, other aspects of freedom and equality were negatively influenced by European and monetary integration, as in the field of workers' rights. Finally, there are few doubts that European integration supported the rule of law in member states.

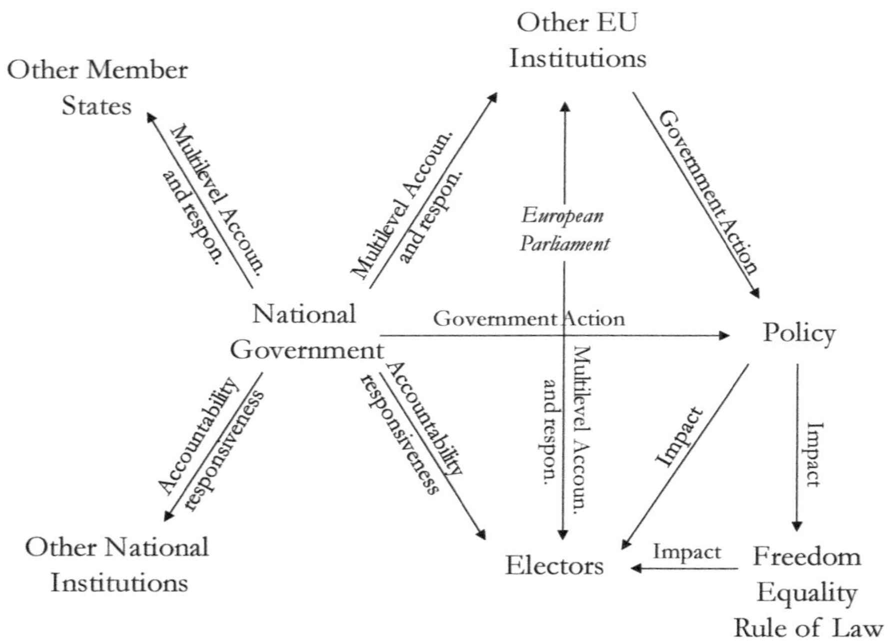

Fig. 8.1 – The quality of democracy in the European multilevel governance system.

Monetary integration and new economic governance had a broad impact on the new structure of multilevel quality of democracy described above. However, this impact did not affect only the traditional form of democracy's quality. Rather, new elements were introduced that changed the nature of democracy's quality in the member states and made specific models of democracy obsolete, and obsolete views of democracy more obsolete. In fact, from the 1990s economic policy sustainability in the mid and long term was required for EMU member states. So both sustainability and time became crucial elements in determining the quality of democracy. In particular, time changed the essence of accountability and responsiveness in economic policies for the EMU member states. Rigid and widely known parameters for the budget deficit and public debt improved the electors' perception of sustainability and long-term effects of economic policies dramatically. Also, these strict parameters counterbalance the short-term preferences and electoral cycle distortions that characterise the economic and budgetary policies preferred by the national government. As a consequence, electors have a more precise perception of "effective" responsiveness and accountability. So while in a procedural approach perspective EU limits to national electors' choices are detrimental to the quality of democracy, in a perceptual-substantive approach EMU rules reinforce accountability and responsiveness at the domestic level because they are capable of integrating them with sustainability criteria.

Chapter 9

The Euro and the EU Identity Crisis

As anticipated in the previous chapters, the EMU and the euro crisis contributed in a decisive way to the so-called "identity crisis" of the EU, i.e. the rejection or apparent betrayal of traditional values attributed to "Europe" as perceived by many European citizens, and the consequent delegitimisation of both the EU institutions and the whole integration process.

This identity crisis had various and relevant consequences for the member states' European politics and the citizens' attitudes toward European integration and the EU. Also, the entire party structure in many EMU member states was affected and sometimes reshaped by the effect of the EU identity crisis. New parties appeared and shared negative attitudes toward the EU and the euro. Some of them gained power in troubled member countries. In the academic field, a bitter debate arose between supporters and opponents of the EU and the EMU, with many economists and sociologists openly contesting the common currency and the policies they saw in its background. New populist parties drew from this debate those elements they needed to build an apparently coherent critique of the EU multilevel system. In this set of beliefs, opposition to the euro gained a pivotal role and allowed these parties to oppose the pro-EU ruling elites and sometimes dismiss them from power.

1 – The European Union identity crisis

The debate on the EU, democracy and the EMU fed the identity crisis and became a crucial element in the delegitimisation process. EU pervasiveness became more evident after the introduction of the common currency while the new economic governance favoured those political actors who referred to the anti-democratic effect of the EU influence and the economic impact of the euro as the leading causes of stagnation and the loss of competitiveness in many EMU countries. Not by chance, the euro became one of the preferred targets for anti-European movements and political parties. So anti-eurism added to anti-Europeanism and Euroscepticism and reinforced them.[1]

Again, it is essential to stress the relevance of "politics as perceived" by citizens to explain their political behaviour. In the previous chapters, we demonstrated that monetary integration is a complicated process shaped by many variables and that supranational governance may reinforce the quality of democracy at the national level. However, the widespread perception of the EU- member states relationship depends on a few elements perceived as relevant and that become pivotal in populistic propaganda, as well as on the very misleading interpretation of essential concepts, democracy first and foremost.

This deviating perception of the EU, the EMU, its political consequences and the deleterious effects of the "European mythology" created decades ago to justify European integration are among the leading causes of today's identity crisis of the EU. However, the evident lack of coherence in the EU structure and objectives fostered a "European identity crisis" that reduced the citizens' support for further integration drastically and represents today the most problematic obstacle for EU development. This lack of coherence depends on the obvious contrast between the so-called "European values" proposed in the traditional representation of the European integration process and the working method of the EU. Solidarity, peace, well-being diffusion, cooperation and advanced democracy have been

[1] We define anti-eurism as the negative attitude toward monetary integration that characterises those persons and parties that propose abandoning the euro.

emphasised in public debate as the fundamental values of European integration and absorbed by European citizens as the reasons for integration. When European armies became involved in armoured conflicts worldwide, financial solidarity was denied and publicly dismissed in financial rescue plans for Greece and other EMU member countries in crisis, democracy was constricted by EU governance, the welfare state was endangered by the austerity policies adopted to cut public debt and the effects of European mythology were dissipated, European citizens saw the EU as it is and this disappointment became a powerful political tool in the hands of EU opponents.

A detailed analysis of the European crisis in the 2010s is not the aim of this book. Relevant literature exists on the different causes of the "crisis of Europe" and the rise of Euroscepticism and anti-Europeanism. This chapter focuses on the contribution of the euro crisis and monetary integration in general to the European identity crisis. Two elements probably contributed most to this crisis. The first was the now evident prevalence of economic and monetary affairs in the integration process. The impact of the introduction of the euro and the pervasiveness of the EMU governance overshadowed the political dimension of integration, i.e. the dimension indicated as being most prevalent in public discourse on European integration. So the image of the EU as a Europe of banks and bankers that prevails on citizens, democracy and solidarity gained ground. The second was the evidence of an unbalanced relationship between EU members and the prevalence of a few members' interests in the collective interests of the EU. This was true in particular for Germany, widely perceived as the almost hegemonic (albeit reluctant) member of the EU, and the only one that gains from the crisis among the other member states.[2]

[2] The German export and current account surplus, as well as the fall of the interest rates on German bonds, suggest that Germany gained from the other EMU members' crisis. Young and Semmeler (2011) reject some of these accusations while Sinn (2014b) and Grimm (2015, 265) estimate

European mythology, a vulgarised perception of the EU's structural problems, and the rise of the populist movement with anti-European policy proposals converged in generating a growing opposition to European integration. Their convergence also favoured the rise of a "counter-mythology" useful for justifying anti-Europeanism and proposals for dismantling the EMU and the EU. These proposals were not only the result of populist reaction to the crisis. Rather, anti-eurism and Euroscepticism were also widespread in the academic environment, which is not immune to the effects of European mythology and other misunderstandings.

The political relevance of the EMU-national democracy relationship and the pivotal role it assumed in political and electoral programmes as well as in policy design makes it one of the most relevant analytic perspectives for this book. However, this relevance exists due to the central role assumed by the topic in political communication and the construction of an ideological-like approach to the matter, not only for its scientific relevance. In other words, we suggest here that most of the literature that stresses the negative impact of the EMU on national democracy is undermined by mono-disciplinary or ideological approaches that address erroneous premises or ambiguous interpretations of concepts and events. Of course, politicians' understanding of the EMU-democracy relationship is also restricted and inspired by ideological factors. However, their opinions and statements are part of the issue to analyse, but outside the analytical framework for scientific analysis. Nevertheless, some scholars and politicians share common ambiguities, probably because of mutual influence.

---

that 40 billion euro was the amount saved by Germany during the period 2010–2014 thanks to the reduction of its bonds' interest rate.

The main questions raised by the democratic deficit debate poorly affect the matter of the relationship between democracy and monetary integration in Europe. Notwithstanding such a complicated relationship as depicted above, many studies and debates on the impact of the EMU on national democracy prevalently suggest a negative impact. The core of this relationship resides in the constraints it creates for democracy in the member states, or at least in the most troubled ones. So the effects generated by European integration and the new economic governance that disempowered procedural accountability and responsiveness at the national level were considered sufficient to justify the claims of the anti-democratic nature of the EMU.

The first and most ambiguous concept used by those authors and politicians who suggest that the EMU negatively influenced democracy is an inadequate or distorted view of democracy itself. Their views generate two kinds of "distorted democracy", here called "irresponsible democracy" (or "democracy without responsibilities") and "sacralised democracy" (or "sacral view of democracy"). Notwithstanding these views were mainly diffused among political leaders and activists, some scholars also share in a more sophisticated way the same views. This applies primarily to scholars who barely distinguish political passions from political analysis.

Irresponsible democracy refers to forms of democracy in which electors are considered free to make their choices without taking into account the consequences of those decisions. In the most radical applications of this concept, just governments are responsible for the consequences of their choices, not the electors that put the government in power. So implicitly, citizens have the right to remain free of charges for their electoral choices. When they pay for their government's mistakes with a reduction of welfare benefits and rights previously gained or with a reduction of policy choices, this is claimed to be undemocratic. Unfortunately, the essence of democracy resides in the electors' right to accountability and responsiveness because electors will suffer or benefit from those policies adopted by those governments that have to be accountable and responsive. The political and academic debate about the Greek crisis is full of this misinterpretation of democracy.

Sacralised democracy refers to a Manichaean vision of the democratic method that imposes its application on all institutional and decisional contexts. In this perspective, the democratic method is sacral because it is considered the only good one, almost perfect and incompatible with non-democratic alternatives, while all other decisional procedures are undemocratic and so unacceptable. This view imposes democratisation of all the institutions and dismissal of those that cannot become democratic. The fiercest political opponents of the EU frequently share this picture in a softer or harder version. Most of them are political leaders. However, some scholars adopt this view, sometimes explicitly and sometimes not, in particular when they target as anti-democratic all those external influences, rules and institutions that limit the range of choices of national electorates. Such a rigid view of democracy transcends the nature of democracy as a political regime confined to specific fields such as political electoral systems, institutional settings and values. Also, this view confuses direct and representative democracy, assuming that direct democracy is the most democratic political system and representative democracy a second-best choice to be sidelined whenever possible. Representative democracy is the European democracy we deal with, while direct democracy is the model preferred by populists but is almost irrelevant in the EU member states' history. There are no reasons to see direct democracy as the natural evolution of representative democracy toward a superior level, as suggested by many populist parties and leaders.

A more sophisticated ambiguity in interpreting the concept of democracy involves the normative-procedural view of democracy and the perception of democracy we discussed above. In this case, the fundamental ambiguity regards what truly matters for democratic legitimacy. For decades, citizens' understanding of democracy has been oriented by political parties and controlled media. Party politics, institutions, norms and procedures as pictured by parties and media shaped the view citizens had of democracy. However, when political parties and ideologies lost ground and influence, and individual access to information became wider and unmediated by political parties, pictures and perceptions of democracy and legitimacy diverged. New forms of independent political participation "from below" make the perception of democracy relevant as well as the institutional structure. Worse still, electoral support and programmes mainly rely on the perception of democracy and legitimacy, not on the constitutive elements of a real democratic regime. This means that perceived democracy is a crucial concept in understanding the evolution of electoral and party politics, at least since the early 2000s. Meanwhile, political discourse and the rhetorical use of the democracy concept concurred in creating an ideological view of democracy in which, at least in the EU, the integration process played a relevant role, usually in a negative light. This evolution escaped unperceived almost entirely by those who predominantly refer to the procedural approach to democracy. Thus, they lost the link between democracy and legitimacy that explains the acceptance and refusal of European integration by national electorates.

Deviant conceptions of democracy are not the only principles and theories misapplied in the debate on the impact of the EMU on national democracy. Other concepts used to criticise the EU action in facing the crisis, its ineffectiveness as a problem solver, and the devastating effects of EU action and EMU rules on member states are austerity and Keynesianism. In these cases, the focus is on the economic policy side, the debate is nation state oriented and it seems convincingly thought out. However, the debate suffers from the same limitations as the previous ones on optimum currency areas and, more generally, almost all the applications of economic and economic policy theories to European integration. More specifically, political activists and some academic authors refer to austerity and its supposed alternative (Keynesianism) without considering the decisional context in which specific choices had to be taken.

The broad debate on austerity and anti-crisis economic policies is particularly meaningful in analysing how economic theory applications had been misconceivingly applied to EU and ECB policies. One of the main accusations made against the EU and the EMU was having been unable to face the crisis and having made it worse by imposing austerity policies. As in the case of democracy, popular and vulgarised interpretation of economic theory played a leading role in addressing public opinion and, surprisingly, the academic debate too. Both the so-called "austerity policies" and the Keynesian policies were decontextualised during the discussion on the eurozone crisis. While austerity has been considered a "perverse" anti-crisis policy, Keynesian policies (usually confused with deficit spending policies) were sold as the immediate solution to the crisis. So austerity appeared as a nonsensical policy imposed by a neo-liberal EU on national governments emasculated by the European norms and ruling nation states deprived of national sovereignty.

We have already explained in this book that this is a simplistic view of the EU's role in the crisis and a misleading reconstruction of the real impact of the EMU on national democracy. In particular, we emphasised how an economic-prone analysis of the eurozone crisis loses entirely the political components that addressed the EU reaction to the crisis and the following choices that were political, not economic, choices. In other words, political rationality is entirely ignored or vulgarised by those who see the optimal solution as the only valid solution to apply. They neglect the fact that almost every political choice is a suboptimal one because it results from compromises and diachronic *du ut des*. So negotiations explain political decisions better than economic theories and optimality criteria. Also, choices depend on the aims pursued by decision-makers. Many authors autonomously assign to political decisions a specific objective while that decision derived by a complex set of interrelated objectives unperceived or neglected by those authors. Thus, most of the literature on the EMU and democracy in the European Union became polluted by oversimplified explanations of the EU's role in constraining democracy and economic policy during the eurozone crisis. Many scholars and politicians saw austerity as an anti-crisis policy imposed by the EU. They forget that the EU is not expected to develop anti-crisis economic policies or industrial policies, apart from in specific cases. Also, in the case of budget policies, the EU does not implement them, it just checks that the member states do it in the right way as agreed in the treaties. So these authors and politicians confuse what derives from the EU and ECB policy with those obligations derived from treaties the member states negotiated and signed. Furthermore, they ignore an element that must appear evident to every expert in political institutions, namely their natural tendency to defend their prerogatives and the institutional context in which they operate. So austerity seems more the consequence of defensive policies that aim to keep operative the EMU framework (the only framework where the EU institutions can work to face the crisis) than an economic policy imposed on the member states. On the other hand, member states know the stability and growth parameters since the 1990s when the member states themselves agreed with them. Austerity is the obvious consequence of their own choice and their inability to reform their administrative and economic structures by moving resources from inefficient and patronage-prone activities to other expenses capable of supporting financial stability and relaunching competitiveness.

On the "Keynesian side", things are worse. Decades before the collapse of the Marxist ideology, Keynesian and pseudo-Keynesian approaches gained a relevant political attractivity for the left and, later, for leftist opposers of the EU. So Keynesian-like economic policies, as well as simplistic views of international and monetary economics, became the ideological background for anti-Europeanists and anti-eurists. When the crisis arrived, decontextualized Keynesianism became an icon for populists and sovereignists who oriented their propaganda and their economic policy proposal. However, the Keynes they have in mind and quote is not the real Keynes or, in the best case scenario, he is today one of the economists died from decades Keynes himself blamed to address misleading economic policies in the 1930s.

3 – The rise of anti-euro parties

Misconceptions and ambiguous analysis had a profound impact on public opinion and political programmes, in particular on those anti-euro and anti-EU parties and movements that rose or emerged during the late 2000s and that became one of the most dangerous threats to the stability of the eurozone in the late 2010s.

Some of these parties were extremist parties founded decades ago that adapted their political discourse and electoral programmes to the new context of the eurozone crisis and the growing discontent among electors (Table 9.1). They were mainly neo-fascist and Marxist-Leninist parties that confirmed their traditional hostility to European integration using new pieces of evidence and argumentations derived from the euro crisis. So their attitudes were easily anticipated, while their poor electoral results were surprising. In fact, well-established extreme-right and extreme-left parties did not gain as many votes as expected, apart from a few cases, such as the Golden Dawn party in Greece (Bistis 2013; Ellinas 2013 and 2015; Toloudis 2014; Grimm 2015).

The parties that benefited most from the crisis were new or reorganised parties that appeared both on the right and the left. Some of them obtained enough electoral support to gain power, as happened with Syriza in Greece (Spourdalakis 2014; Stravakakis and Katsambekis 2014), the Lega and Movimento Cinque Stelle in Italy (Franzosi, Marone and Salvati 2015 Lanzone, Ivaldi and Woods 2017), Podemos in Spain (Kioupkiolis 2016) and the Freiheitliche Partei Österreichs in Austria (Heinisch 2016; Moreau 2018). Others like the Front National in France, Alternative für Deutschland in Germany and the Partij voor de Vrijheid in the Netherlands became the main competitors of the parties in power (Arzheimer 2015; Berbuir, Lewandowsky and Siri 2015; Lanzone and Ivaldi 2016; Schmitt-Beck 2017).

While almost all the parties that gained votes because of the eurozone crisis (both inside and outside the EMU area) shared at least a critical attitude toward the European Union, many parties inside the EMU area adopted a specific negative attitude toward the euro, blaming the monetary union for the crisis and the difficulties experienced in recovering (Table 9.2). So they inserted in their political programmes and speeches the aim to drive their countries out of the euro as the primary economic policy strategy to regain sovereignty and to be able once again to adopt deficit spending policies to enable economic recovery and social justice. So the common currency became a "politicised issue" that magnified the Europeanisation of domestic policy in EMU member states.

Notwithstanding a vast majority of the anti-euro parties consist in small entities with limited electoral support, some of the declared anti-euro parties played a relevant role in some member states' politics (Tables 9.3 and 9.4). This was the case with the Front National, which was capable of arriving at the *ballotage* for the French presidency with its leader Marine Le Pen, and the Lega-Movimento Cinque Stelle coalition in Italy, which gained power and created a government that was ambiguous about attitudes toward the euro. This made the politicisation of the common currency a relevant issue for European policy too. However, the reduced severity of the crisis made anti-eurism less strident in many countries, while those anti-euro parties that wanted to create a government were induced to moderate their anti-eurism and avoid referring to exiting the euro in their political programmes. A list of the main anti-euro parties and their electoral results are presented in the following tables 9.1 to 9.4.[3]

4 – The EMU and the fifth cleavage

The electoral impact of the euro crisis in terms of the diffusion of Euroscepticism and the rise of anti-eurism has been explained mainly by referring to the Rokkan theory of cleavages and the new cleavage theory, i.e. the cleavage between materialist and post-materialist values (Lipset and Rokkan 1967; Inglehart 1977; Flora, Kuhnle and Urwin 1999). More specifically, the new cleavage theory was just the starting point for proposing a new kind of socio-economic fracture generated by the national/transnational or integration/demarcation dichotomy as defined by Kriesi (Kriesi 2007 and 2014). The central element recovered by the so-called "valorial cleavage" between materialism and post-materialism regards voters' attitudes toward globalisation. Some authors explain the rise of the new populist parties (anti-eurist included) in Western Europe as a consequence of the new cleavage, more specifically the positive attitude toward European integration of winners in the globalisation/integration process and the negative attitude of the losers in the same process (Kriesi et al. 2006, 2008 and 2012).

[3] I am grateful to Stefano Rombi for his help in collecting and elaborating the data included in these tables. I remain the only one responsible for errors and omissions.

Table 9.1 – List of the main anti-euro parties in the EMU member states

Country	*Party*	*Name (in English)*	*Name (original)*	*Side*	*Founded*
Austria	FPO	Freedom Austrian Party	Freiheitliche Partei Österreichs	R	1956
Austria	BZO	Alliance for the Future of Austria	Bündnis Zukunft Österreich	R	2005
Austria	T. Stronach	Team Stronach for Austria	Team Stronach	R	2012
Austria	EUSTOP[2]	Eu Stop		R	2014
Austria	REKOS[2]	The Reform Conservatives	Die Reformkonservativen	R	2013
Belgium	VB	Flemish Block	Vlaams Belang	R	2004
Belgium	FN	Front National	Front National	R	1985
Belgium	LDD	Libertarian, Direct, Democratic	Libertair, Direct, Democratisch	R	2007
Belgium	PVDA/PTB	Workers' Party of Belgium	Partij van de Arbeid van België	L	1979
Belgium	DLB[2]	Belgians, Rise Up!	Debout Les Belges!	R	2013
Estonia	EIP[2]	Estonian Independence Party	Eesti Iseseisvuspartei	R	1999
Finland	PS	True Finns Party	Perussuomalaiset	R	1995
France	FN	National Front	Front national	R	1972
France	NPA[2]	New Anticapitalistic Party	Nouveau Parti anticapitaliste	L	2009
France	DLF	France Arise	Debout la France	R	1999
France	LO-LCR	Workers' Struggle - Revolutionary Communist League	Lutte Ouvrière/Ligue communiste révolutionnaire	S	1939
Germany	NPD	National Democratic Party of Germany	Nationaldemokratische Partei Deutschlands	R	1964

Germany	AFD	Alternative for Germany	Alternative für Deutschland	R	2013
Germany	REP[2]	The Republicans	Die Republikaner	R	1983
Greece	KKE	Communist Party of Greece	Kommounistikó Kómma Elládas	L	1918
Greece	LAOS	Popular Orthodox Rally	Laikós Orthódoxos Synagermós	R	2000
Greece	XA	Golden Dawn	Laïkós Sýndesmos – Chrysí Avgí	R	1980
Greece	ANTARSYA[2]	Front of the Greek Anticapitalistic Left	Antikapitalistiki Aristeri Synergasia gia tin Anatropi	L	2009
Greece	EPAM[2]	United Popular Front		N	2011
Ireland	DDI[2]	Direct Democracy Ireland	Direct Democracy Ireland	N	2012
Italy	LN	Northern League	Lega Nord	R	1997
Italy	FN[2]	New Force	Forza nuova	R	1997
Italy	PCL[2]	Workers' Communist Party	Partito comunista dei lavoratori	L	2006
Italy	SC[2]	Critical Left	Sinistra critica	L	2007
Italy	M5S	Five Star Movement	Movimento 5 stelle	N	2009
Italy	FDI	Brothers of Italy	Fratelli d'Italia	R	2012
Luxembourg	KPL[2]	Communist Party of Luxembourg	Kommunistesch Partei Lëtzebuerg	L	1921
Netherlands	PVV	Party for Freedom	Partij voor de Vrijheid	R	2005
Netherlands	AEP[2]	Anti Euro Party			
Portugal	CDU	Unitary Democratic Coalition	Coligação Democrática Unitária	L	1987

Portugal	PCTP/ MRPP	Portuguese Workers' Communist Party/Reorganised Movement of the Party of the Proletariat	Partido Comunista dos Trabalhadores Portugueses/Movimento Reorganizativo do Partido do Proletariado	L	1970
Slovakia	KSS	Communist Party of Slovakia	Komunistická strana Slovenska	L	1992
Slovakia	SNS	Slovak National Party	Slovenská národná strana	R	1989

Notes: [1]. A large number of the parties listed in this table were included in the Chapel Hill Expert Survey and evaluated at 3.5 or less points. Also, these parties included in their electoral programmes an evident anti-euro attitude. So well-known parties like Podemos and Syriza have been not included in this list; [2]. Not included in the Chapel Hill Expert Survey, but openly hostile to the euro.

Sources: for tables 9.1 to 9. 4: R. Bakker et al. 2014, 2015; www.parlgov.org

Table 9.2 – Votes for Eurosceptic parties in elections from 2008 to 2015 (%) and anti-euro (AE) parties' quota[1]

Country	2008		2009		2010		2011		2012		2013		2014		2015	
	Tot.	AE	Tot.	AE	Tot.	AE	Tot.	AE	Tot.	AE	Tot.	AE	Tot.	AE	Tot.	AE
Austria	28.2	28.2	17.3	17.3							29.8		26.3			
Belgium			16.7	16.7	10.7	10.7							11.0[2]	2.2		
Estonia							0.4	0.4					5.3	1.3	8.3	0.2
Finland			9.8	9.8			19.1	19.1					12.9	12.9	17.6	17.6
France			25.5	14.2					21.5	14.6			39.4	29.9		
Germany			8.8[2]	1.3							14.8	6.2	15.9	8.5		
Greece			20.6[2]	15.5					46.9[3]	19.5			48.9	18.9[2]	56.3	13.5
Ireland			13.9	0.0			13.9	0.0					24.3	1.5		
Italy	12.7	9.6	13.6	10.2							37.6	32.1	51.8	31.0		
Latvia													6.4[2]	0.0		
Luxembourg			12.3[2]	1.5							14.7	1.6	16.6	1.5		
Netherlands			30.9	17.0	26.6	15.5			11.7	10.1			30.0	13.6		
Portugal			11.8[2]	11.8			9.4	9.4					26.1	14.4	20.0	9.4
Slovakia			7.2	5.6	5.9	5.1			19.7	4.6			19.2	3.6		
Slovenia	7.2	0.0	2.9[2]	0.0			1.8	0.0					2.2[2]	0.0		
Spain			0.0	0.0			0.0	0.0					0.0	0.0		

Notes: [1]. A party is considered anti-euro in accordance with its attitude toward the euro in 2014; [2]. European elections instead of the national elections of that year; [3]. Data refer to the first election in the year.

Table 9.3 – Votes for anti-euro parties (national elections; 2008–2015)

Country	Year	%	Country	Year	%
Austria	2008	28.2	Greece	2015a	13.5
	2013	29.8		2015b	17.0
	2017	26.0	Italy	2008	9.6
Belgium	2010	10.7		2013	32.1
	2014	7.4		2018	60.5
Estonia	2011	0.4	Luxembourg	2009	1.4
	2015	0.2		2013	1.6
Finland	2011	19.1	Netherlands	2010	15.5
	2015	17.6		2012	10.1
France	2012	14.6		2017	13.1
	2017	14.4	Portugal	2009	9.1
Germany	2009	1.5		2011	9.4
	2013	6.2		2015	9.4
	2017	12.6	Slovakia	2010	5.1
Greece	2009	13.5		2012	4.6
	2012a	19.5		2016	8.6
	2012b	13.3			

Table 9.4 – Votes for anti-euro parties (European elections; 2009 and 2014)

	2009				2014			
	R	L	N	Tot.	R	L	N	Tot.
Austria	17.3			17.3	21.4		2.8	24.2
Belgium	15.7	1.0		16.7	5.4	3.5		8.9
Estonia					1.3			1.3
Finland	9.8			9.8	12.9			12.9
France	8.1	6.1		14.2	28.7	1.2		29.9
Germany	1.3			1.3	8.5			8.5
Greece	7.1	8.8		15.9	12.1	6.8		18.9
Ireland							1.5	1.5
Italy	10.2			10.2	9.8		21.2	31.0
Luxembourg	1.5			1.5		1.5		1.5
Netherlands	17.0			17.0	13.6		0.3	13.9
Portugal		11.8		11.8		14.4		14.4
Slovakia	5.6			5.6	3.6			3.6

Legenda: Right-wing (R), Left-wing (L), Not classified (N)

This explanation shows some limitations and at least requires further specifications. The fifth cleavage approach implies that almost all the most important new parties cited above are populist parties and share some characteristics traditionally identified in this party typology. One of these characteristics deals with the education level of party supporters (Kriesi et al. 2012; Hakhverdian et al. 2013; Hooghe and Marks 2017). The usual representation of these supporters as poorly educated people fits poorly the case of these new parties, including the anti-euro ones. On the other hand, dialectic building and the proposed policy solutions require a particular ability to manage (often in a misleading way) complex themes such as the monetary economy, history and economic theory. This means that, notwithstanding these new parties lack well-educated ruling groups,[4] their supporters have sufficient elaboration capabilities to join complex debates and to collect information.

Another element to consider deals with the influence of the other cleavages in shaping attitudes toward transnationalism. Some of these parties (mainly right oriented) define themselves as "sovereignists" and emphasise the nationalistic nature of their political objectives. So they call for support from former electors of traditional extreme-right parties and other parties raised by different cleavages than the valorial one. Also, the characterisation of these parties as populist (in particular for the national-sovereignist ones) connects their roots to fascist parties in the inter-war period and the cleavages that caused their rise. So a re-elaboration of the traditional cleavages is needed to understand their influence on the national-sovereignist populism. Also, the national-sovereignist attitude, usually not declared, exists in left-wing-inspired populist parties too. In this case, hidden nationalist attitudes depend

[4] This was not the case for Alternative für Deustchland. See Grimm (2015).

on the nature of economic policy proposals, mainly inspired by past experiences in which national states had the power to raise public debts and adopt deficit spending policies. In other words, the implicit nationalism of left-wing populists derives mainly from a lack of originality in economic policy proposals instead of the influence of cleavages.

Finally, an adaptation of the materialist/post-materialist paradigm to the national/supranational cleavage underestimates the relevance of materialist interests in supporting European integration. Notwithstanding the relevance of pro-European education for supranationalist supporters, materialist interests concerning opportunities, careers and economic interests (personal or from a collective perspective) play a relevant role.

In summary, using the fifth cleavage approach to explain the rise of populist parties in Western Europe, in particular the anti-euro ones and those that appeared with the eurozone crisis, does not work so well. A fifth "socio-political" cleavage approach probably works better. This new cleavage, being a non-valorial one, fits better with the Lipset-Rokkan explanation of party families' genesis when combined with other evolutionary theories that explain the rise of the European Union and the transformations induced by European integration such as those proposed by Bartolini (2006) and Schimmelfennig (2010). So this new fifth cleavage depends both on the scission of the levels of government between national and supranational and the different sets of opportunities created by this transformation. The latter also reshaped in part some previous cleavages, such as those between capital and work or the centre-periphery ones, and oriented parties' and voters' attitudes in a different way toward the European integration process.

The cleavages/new cleavage approach is not the only way to see the rise of new parties in the 2000s. Another crucial element to consider regards the communication and socialisation channels and the rise of web politics. In fact, the diffusion of online political participation explains how populists built their approach toward complex issues such as monetary ones. The "unmediated" interaction between individual participants and the sources they find online structures the attitudes of populist supporters toward a specific topic and makes them confident in the apparent rationality of their thought. Moreover, circular hyperlinked references confirm and consolidate their beliefs, allowing unskilled people to deal with complex issues, at least in online debates. In this process, the level of education has lost its relevance because many populists are well-educated people but in non-social fields. So they combine their analytical skills and the opportunity to collect and elaborate information from the Web to join the political debates superseding the role of socialisation and political education traditionally played by political parties. Instead, they become sensitive to simplified and vulgarised political visions such as the populistic one.

5 – The politics of exiting the euro

Notwithstanding the "new media" approach rivals the new cleavage approach in explaining political support for populist parties, both approaches contribute to identifying some elements of the euro crisis impact on European and domestic policy. Also, all these approaches help to explain why monetary issues became so crucial in the political debate. However, the relevance assumed by monetary matters made the euro one of the primary targets for populists and magnified the potential electoral support for EMU exit solutions to the economic crisis and the constrictions created by the EMU.

The possibility of leaving the EMU was very real in Greece during the most dramatic phases of its internal crisis and the rise in power of the first Tsipras government. In France, the 2017 presidential election campaign saw the *ballotage* defeated candidate Marine Le Pen strongly oriented toward driving

France out of the EMU. In Italy, the first temptation for the so-called "Italexit" arose in 2011 during the Berlusconi government when the sovereign debt crisis became dramatic. Later, after the fall of the Centre-Right coalition led by Berlusconi and the rise in power of the Monti, Letta and Renzi governments, anti-euro parties gained growing support. In the 2018 elections, two of them, the Lega and the Movimento Cinque Stelle, obtained a parliamentary majority that ensured they would rise to power at the cost of moderation of extremely sensitive topics such as staying in the EMU. However, the subsequent tensions with the EU about respecting the SGP constraints resuscitated the anti-euro attitudes of the two parties, the Lega in particular. Finally, in Germany, the German exit option, supported by both the new rising party Alternative für Deutschland and the traditional extreme parties, was considered a relevant policy option by influential economists. This option was also supported abroad by the Nobel Prize winner Stiglitz as a means to save the eurozone by splitting it into two parts (Stiglitz 2017). So something considered impossible until the mid-2000s became a solid policy option widely discussed in the 2010s. This option profoundly influenced the political debate in some member states and worried the governments of the others, particularly Germany and the leading creditor countries. However, these two debates emphasised two different perspectives. The exit debate in potential outgoing countries centred on the domestic consequences of exiting and the way to minimise costs in finding arrangements with the EU partners. Instead, the European debate on exits (Grexit and Italexit in particular) focused on the systemic consequences of these events and the distribution of costs between exit and non-exit member countries. Brexit offered an opportunity to reflect on the ways of exiting, as well as the consequences of doing so and the arrangements required. However, as the UK is not part of the monetary union, many of the most sensitive matters were not relevant.

On the exit countries' side, apart from all the logistical problems due to the secrecy and timeliness required to avoid speculation and panic, the main problem concerns the common market and the economic relationship with the other member states. Juridically speaking, leaving the EMU requires leaving the EU in accordance with the Lisbon Treaty rules as in the case of Brexit. So exiting the euro is only possible by calling upon Article 50 and leaving the EU. However, this means starting a two-year-long negotiation in which financial turmoil will undoubtedly affect the value of bonds and the interest rates of the exiting country. In other words, secrecy and timeliness are incompatible with the exit procedure as depicted in the Lisbon Treaty. The only secret and sudden exit is an illegal unilateral abandonment of the EMU. This does not match the friendly attitude of the other EMU members and makes the next negotiation to stay in the common market very difficult.

On the other hand, in the *acquis communautaire*, there are no procedures for expelling a member country from the EU or excluding it from the common market. So the apparent consequence of a sudden exit from the EMU by a member country, if it does not abandon the common market voluntarily, is a juridical vacuum that can be faced only with aggressive informal governance measures by the European institutions and the remaining member states. Insufficient room remains for cooperative arrangements because the exit of an important country, a debtor one in particular, risks creating a domino effect that makes EMU membership less and less sustainable and increases the risk proportionally of creditor countries facing costs for debtor countries' devaluations and defaults. Moreover, the hostility of creditor countries to EMU exit plans also depends on the TARGET2 credits and the arrangements required for setting them with exiting countries. Governor Draghi indicated the Italian TARGET2 debtor balance as a proxy for the costs Italy had to pay for exiting the EMU, notwithstanding this indicator regards just the debt the country has with the ESCB system and does not include all the indirect costs derived from interest rate increases, exclusion from the common market, inflation and other items. So a possible exit event of an EMU member state can create a legal and political stalemate capable of destroying the whole EU.

Conclusion

In this book, consolidating theories, explanations and beliefs about European integration and economic policies to face the crisis has been criticised implicitly and explicitly. It is time to stress how evidence proposed in this book supports these criticisms and what this implies for the debate on the integration process and its future. In addition, many chapters touch on themes that go beyond the limits of the topic discussed here, notwithstanding they are crucial for understanding the whole process of European monetary integration and its implications. This conclusion provides the opportunity to recover some elements that emerged and touched on those themes, and to include them in the debate on monetary integration. Finally, after the introductory chapter, we proposed some questions about the rationale of monetary integration and the future of the common currency and the whole European Union that it is now time to answer.

1 – Rethinking theories of European integration

The first set of questions posed by this book regard the theoretical approach to monetary integration in the broader framework of European integration theories. Some of the assumptions adopted in this work to explain the path of monetary integration and its effects challenge the most diffused and appreciated theoretical approaches to the whole integration process. More specifically, these theoretical challenges touch on three crucial elements of the theoretical debate on European integration: its origins, its objectives and its path.

All these three elements are connected with the theoretical literature by the so-called "European mythology" that inspired theories, beliefs and political behaviours. It was the way in which integration was explained and justified by its initial supporters (mainly scholars and politicians) that generated the European mythology that shaped theories, choices and attitudes concerning European integration. For decades, scholars had believed in solidarity, freedom, economic growth, democracy and equality among peer member states as the inspiring and complementary values of integration. They diffused this vision among their students, readers and citizens with the help of EU officers and institutions interested in supplying a simple, shareable and attractive view of integration, a vision that many EU officers and politicians shared too. So a strict connection arose among the European integration origins as perceived by political actors and citizens, its objectives as declared by the European founding fathers, its path as a consequence of the interaction between objectives perceived or pursued by scholars, citizens and politicians, and the constraints imposed by the international structure.

These connections explain the success of both neo-functionalist and intergovernmental approaches, at least until the end of the 20th century. The apparent coherence between objectives and progress toward "an ever closer union" and the enlargement of integrational sectors "converging" toward the communitarian solution suggested that neo-functionalist mechanisms worked in driving integration in the right and expected direction. On the other hand, the predominant role of governments, as well as the tensions and the limitations to integration generated by their contrasts, reinforced the intergovernmental belief in the "neo-realist" explanation of European integration. So "converging evidence" generated by "convergent integrations" fostered a debate completely focused on integration as a complete and independent process unbound by wider processes in terms of space (international constraints and exogenous shocks) and time (long-term transformations of political and economic structures). Also, both theories suffered the "Europeanist attitude" of the early context in which theories and policies regarding European integration appeared. This attitude suggested the creation of a united

Europe as the primary objective and the logical conclusion of the integration process and supported the widely shared idea of the predominance of political integration in the integration process.

This book demonstrates, hopefully unequivocally, that some assumptions of the Grand Theories on European integration were wrong or questionable. First, European integration was not independent of external constraints and not confined to the strict limits of the post-World War II period. Instead, there are pieces of evidence of relevant steps toward integration generated by reactions to external shocks. Meanwhile, European integration in the monetary field is more satisfactorily understood with a long-term approach that found its origins in the collapse of the international payment system in the early 1930s, rather than the "choice for Europe" in the 1950s.[1] Second, European integration mostly depended on economic factors and short-term objectives instead of an ambitious political design for creating the United States of Europe. So politics was not the predominant factor in determining integration. However, the political dimension of economic choices explains some crucial passages of European integration better than economic rationality. Third, the crucial actors identified by the Grand Theories in institutions, governments or interest groups were less continuously relevant than claimed. In fact, their influence (in terms of monetary integration at least) changed over time, and none of them was predominant forever as implicitly suggested by the most rigid approaches until the 1990s. Rather, most actors gained and lost influence at different times and, most importantly, in some cases had to react to external stimuli generated by the mechanisms of the international system and that escaped entirely European actors' control. So the central assumption of the most diffused theories on European integration, which derived from traditional approaches to international relations studies and focused on the primacy of politics and interna-

[1] Similarly, a long-term approach was proposed by Bartolini (2004 and 2006) who saw European integration as the sixth phase of European political evolution that started with the formation of the nation state.

tional institutions, works poorly or only occasionally for monetary integration. Finally, Grand Theories were static and lost the evolutionary nature of European integration because they were formulated in the early phases of the process, or derived from theories proposed at that time. This induced theorists of the 1950s–1970s to build their theories on the few elements that had already emerged from such a long and complicated process as European integration. In the monetary integration case, this short-term perspective bias is particularly evident.

These conclusions are challenging but not innovative. From the 1990s, the "Grand Theory" approach was under attack from new findings and analysis proposed mainly by historians and political scientists. The groundbreaking work of Alan Milward demonstrated that "the founding fathers of European unity" were much more pragmatic than believed and more interested in solving economic problems crucial to national interests and the balance of power in post-war Europe than creating Europe (Milward 1992). Scholars of international political economy such as Henning showed the relevance of exogenous factors in addressing European choices and the path of integration (1998). On the other hand, new studies on European integration and the functioning of the European Union emphasised the relevance of mid-range theories to explain parts of the integration process, implicitly proposing a fragmented vision of the same process their predecessors saw as a continuum of consequential events activated by a single engine such as the neo-functionalist mechanisms or intergovernmental negotiations (Hooghe and Marx 2009; Schimmelfennig 2010; Bickerton, Hodson and Puetter 2015a). So the existence of a single engine for integration became in doubt when the acceleration of European integration and its effects started to be explained by other, more specific engines. Later, the insertion of European integration into the framework of a long-term transformation of the whole European structure as proposed by Bartolini dismantled a crucial assumption of the Grand Theory, namely its temporally restricted dimension (2006). Finally, the rising hostility against European integration that followed the Maastricht Treaty and skyrocketed after the early years of the euro dismantled the oversimplified views of the formation of national preferences as an elitist and governmental process as proposed by many theories, particularly intergovernmentalist and liberal intergovernmentalist ones. On the other hand, the impact of integration on member states' politics and its negative feedback emerged as a new, previously unobserved, unexpected and unavoidable structural mechanism of the integration process. It was mostly monetary integration that activated and fed this mechanism, and it was monetary integration that was targeted by opponents of further sovereignty surrender.

2 – Explaining explanations of European integration

Some of this book treats European mythology and the Grand Theories from a challenging perspective. However, its aim is not to dismiss previous approaches to European integration or deny their value at the time they emerged. Rather, this book proposes a "theory of integration theories" that barely explains their origins. Were ideals, beliefs and political declarations on European integration just illusions and propaganda? Were Grand Theories wrong? These seem to be implicit questions derived from the approach and hypothesis adopted in this book. However, they had not been explicitly proposed because the matter is much more complicated than that. The construction of ideals and beliefs is not just the result of abstract thinking or propaganda. Many intellectuals drew their theories from evidence and interpreted the processes they studied on the basis of that evidence. They saw in European integration a single, continuous and temporally delimited phenomenon because it was *such* a phenomenon at that time. They anticipated its evolution because evidence suggested the soundness of the premises they adopted and because politicians' declarations anticipated policy choices that made the supposed evolution realistic. The obsolescence of neo-functionalism was caused by the insurgence of constraints, sometimes unpredictable, that changed the nature of the integration process. However, its survival resulted in a path-dependent process that induced scholars to react to the demonstrated incongruence of some conclusions regarding that theoretical approach, re-elaborating instead of abandoning it. The intergovernmental approach, though, became problematic when the evidence of the influence of external constraints and the ineffectiveness of governments' action emerged, undermining the assumption of the predominance of governmental actors in addressing the process. The disclosed relevance of systemic influences and non-governmental actors' action reduced the explicative capabilities of the intergovernmental approach. So the original neo-realist-inspired intergovernmentalism required adaptation to the newly emerged level of complexity, and the reformulation of the central assumption of the intergovernmental approach in the liberal intergovernmental theory. In this case too, as happened with neo-functionalism, the heritage of the past theoretical debate shaped its evolution and saved some assumptions that could be useful, dismissing, in particular, the emphasis on the predominance of the political side and the obsessive focus on intergovernmental negotiations.

On the politicians' side, it is probable that most of the founding fathers and those other politicians and officers that worked on integration and contributed to creating the European mythology believed in European integration, its desirability and the soundness of all those argumentations they used to justify their work and choices. In the early stages of European integration, the creation of the European mythology was substantially instrumental in supporting the legitimacy of European construction. It was impossible to explain to unskilled citizens the complexity of the process and the reasons for integration, in particular those technical details poorly understood even by many politicians involved in the integration politics and later undervalued or ignored by scholars only focused on the political side of integration. This meant that the European mythology was a policy tool, not a trick or a misunderstanding. Later, many of those who succeeded the founding fathers were "victims of themselves" in a circular process of diffusion and absorption of propagandistic views that fed the consolidation of their beliefs and their methods of communication. Such a perverse mechanism of perception oriented both the active and passive actors of integration, i.e. politicians and officers on one side and member states' citizens on the other. This mechanism meant that European identity entered into crisis when the divergence between the expected outcomes and practical results of the integration process became evident. Monetary integration was explosive in this sense, and this makes its study a crucial step toward understanding the complexity of today's EU crisis, avoiding the simplistic explanations that generated the anti-European shift of parties and electors as well as the disenchantment of many scholars and intellectuals. Also, understanding this complexity stresses the communicative and perceptive relevance acquired by monetary integration and shows that its impact on European integration, on the whole, is not confined to the economic and monetary field. Rather, monetary integration had a crucial role in dismantling the communication strategy based on the European mythology as well as influencing the political attitudes, behaviours and communication focus in member states about European integration.

3 – Monetary integration, the euro crisis and the misunderstandings of the EU responsibilities

The analysis of the monetary integration process and the explanation offered for the different actors' behaviours and policy choices revealed many incongruencies and some crucial misunderstandings in the foremost criticisms against the EU that emerged in political and academic debates.

One of them regards the linkage between the euro crisis and the austerity policies imposed or induced by the EU. We have stressed that many misunderstandings resulted in confusion about the objective of the EU institutions and those of the member states and their citizens. The core of these misunderstanding results from the erroneous perception and the imperfect knowledge of the EU prerogatives and institutional mission as well as the political strategies of the EU actors. These limits are widely diffused among citizens and politicians, in particular among those who rarely participated in the EU decision-making process. However, many academics and intellectuals share these misunderstandings because of the influence of the European mythology on their cultural background or the inability to distinguish between what the EU has to do and what they want the EU to do. In other words, many of the academics and politicians that criticise the European Union for its choice of policies do not distinguish clearly enough between the EU's duties as defined by the treaties and what they maintain it is necessary to do in the face of the crisis and many other problems that affect the EU area.

The case of austerity policies is a relevant example of this misunderstanding. The policy of austerity was not imposed by the EU on member states in trouble. Rather, austerity was the unavoidable consequence of the EMU architecture that the member states decided upon and approved through signing treaties after Maastricht. Also, austerity resulted in the inability or lack of will in the most troubled countries to make drastic reforms to restructure the state budget before and after the crisis. So the primary sin of the EU was its inability to impose these reforms before or immediately after the start of the EMU. In other words, austerity was not a policy choice the EU adopted to face the crisis. Rather, it resulted from applying the EU rules the EU institutions are obliged to apply because they derived from the treaties agreed by the member states and that constitute the basis of EU law and legitimacy.

Tensions and criticisms of the EU institutions for their policy of austerity also derived from another misunderstanding that this book aims to dissolve. Many opponents of the EU's economic and monetary policy misinterpret the nature of the EU. More specifically, they see in the EU institutions a political actor instead of a policy actor. So they assign to the EU a political role, decisional autonomy and political objectives that the EU does not have. Thus, they expect the EU to implement anti-crisis policies that are beyond its legal duties and that the EU cannot arrogate by itself. Defining, adopting and implementing anti-crisis economic policies were not tasks the EU institutions had to carry out. It was a duty of the national governments to face the impact of the crisis. They proved to be unable to deal with such a challenge, and it became impossible for member states alone to fulfil this mission. However, this does not mean the EU had to do it. Member states decided years before the EU institutions have not this power. Neither with the 2008 crisis they assigned this function to the EU. Again, a governance gap explains the EU policy much better than ideological and conspiracy views that inspired many criticism against the EU.

Moreover, the EU institutions have their own survival and self-defence needs. In Chapters 5 and 7, the logic of the European Central Bank stabilisation policy is explained. The ECB was the EU institution most capable of using its powers to counter the mounting crisis in Europe in the early 2010s. However, the rationale of the ECB action was inspired by survival objectives. It was capable of acting because at the core of the European System of Central Banks the ECB has to save and consolidate immediately and as a matter of priority. Only after this rescue and only after this system granted the ECB the formal and informal powers needed to do "whatever it takes" to save the EMU did the ECB act to support the EU economy and the most troubled member states.

In summary, the way in which the EU institutions acted during the crisis, the policy choices they made, and the limits of these choices and policies mainly depended on the rules that shape the EU structures and institutional architecture as well as on the internal dynamics generated by the nature of the policy actor assumed by the EU institutions. However, the rules and powers assigned to the EU had been decided by member states that remain the chief engineers of their destiny. So, paradoxically, those sins attributed to the EU by populists, sovereignists and national Marxists resulted from choices that the member states made. This happened mainly within an intergovernmental negotiation environment that represented the negotiation context they implicitly asked for in claiming the return to sovereign national states, notwithstanding decades of integration caused a transcendence of national frontiers that made national governments incapable of fully controlling the consequences of their integrative choices (Bartolini 2004, p. 172–3).

4 – The gamble for Europe. Was monetary integration a far-sighted choice or an epochal mistake?

In this book, we have adopted the explanation that saw the Maastricht Treaty and the choice for the euro as a political act inspired by the need to face external challenges to member states' economies, the national interests of the different member states and as the realisation of the French strategy for Europe. This means rejecting neo-functionalist views of monetary integration as the obvious consequence of economic and market integration as well as the liberal intergovernmentalist emphasis on negotiation. As a consequence, monetary integration has been depicted here as a political choice, while creating the euro in the 1990s is not considered to have been unavoidable. This raises the question of the adequacy of the creation of the common currency.

Many of those who are reading this book probably started this intellectual voyage with this question in mind and are still searching for an answer. The analysis proposed in the previous chapters depicts monetary integration in a grey-light perspective as a "second-best option" in the face of international monetary instability, a political choice to contain the German economic power, a conglomerative solution to many different national problems and intergovernmental tensions. In other words, opting for the euro was a gamble in which member states bet for a communitarian solution to commercial and financial problems out of blind faith rather than the certainty that it would all end happily. So it is inappropriate to consider the creation of the EMU a far-sighted decision.

Today this choice is represented by many people as a mistake, an epochal one capable of annihilating the whole European construction. The truth probably lies somewhere in the middle. This book suggests that adopting the euro was an inappropriate choice for some EU member countries. Southern European countries, Greece and Italy in particular, suffered from structural problems and political and administrative weaknesses that made the common currency constraints extremely difficult to sustain. So for EMU sustainability and the economic competitiveness of the most troubled countries, it may have been a better choice to have stayed out of the common currency, notwithstanding the immediate gains that admission guaranteed them in terms of the reduction of interest. An alternative solution with a view to admitting all EMU applicants could have been to have reinforced the economic governance of the common currency from the beginning. However, this would have been a challenging mission. The dynamics determining the creation of the EMU suggest that the costs of keeping the most troubled countries of Southern Europe out of the EMU were acceptable, and the solution more straightforward to implement than introducing a stricter and more invasive EMU governance from the start. So a smaller and better working EMU was probably the preferable mix of economic and political choices.

This conclusion does not imply that the whole EMU creation was a mistake or, worse still, that dismantling the EMU as suggested by someone is a solution to today's problems. Also, our study does not suggest that single countries exiting is a working solution for those countries or the EMU. We have seen that pressing problems and the costs of international monetary instability required a communitarian solution. Also, the intention to proceed toward the famous even closer union (or at least toward more integrated markets) required an integrated framework of economic and financial cooperation that sooner or later had to get ready for the jump to unification. Unfortunately, the "window of opportunity" that opened in the early 1990s appeared too early for some member countries to converge toward an integrated economy capable of working with a single currency. The political strategy prevailed, but monetary integration was a gamble that only a few players could win. Today, the latter are still waiting for victory and realise that losers embarking on the euro ship reduced their chances of winning. So what is the solution to the inefficiency of the EMU and the unsustainability of EMU burdens for most troubled countries?

5 – Exiting the euro or solving EMU problems?

This book uses the case study of monetary integration to support a different vision of the whole integration process based on the idea of "different but convergent European integrations" determined by structural and international constraints to the European nation state that shaped its evolution in the long term. Monetary integration is one of these integrations, not a fragment of a wider and fully comprehensive process that started in the 1950s. So this book supports the most innovative findings in the European integration literature of the last 30 years, particularly the long-term approach to integration proposed by Bartolini, and some elements of historical institutionalism and post-functionalism that explain the impact of integration on its path and on member states' politics. More specifically, this book uses an unusual perspective based on a specific sector, namely monetary integration, to stress how different forms of integration converged toward a single and almost unified process. A monetary history approach shows how external constraints and "technical needs" played a relevant role in generating the most successful and controversial part of the whole integration process. Finally, the constructivist concept of perception is recovered here to explain the asymmetry between the ideals and outcomes of the integration process that generated the actual identity crisis of the European Union and the political reaction led by populist parties.

The result is the most innovative theoretical proposal offered by this book. It is not just the view of European integration as a sum of integrations, but the idea that monetary integration and its needs since the end of the 2000s prevailed on other sectors of integration and shaped the future of the process. However, the convergence of integration processes is more similar to a crash of monetary integration in other integrative processes, rather than a merging. Nothing indicates that this crash had a positive or a neutral effect on integration and that it will help to reach deeper integration. Rather, there are definite possibilities that monetary integration will destroy the whole European integration process if working solutions for combining economic governance and member states' politics are not found. This can only happen if structural imbalances are solved.

Literature and political debates suggest at least three solutions to the EMU problems. The first is to dissolve the EMU. This seems the preferred solution for anti-Europeanists, populist parties and sovereignists in particular. The second solution is the exit from the EMU of those countries incapable of sustaining the constraints of the common currency. Grexit, Italexit, Spainexit and similar will purge the EMU of its more problematic members, returning them their sovereignty and the economic independence to devalue their currency and reorganise their economies. The third solution proposed is splitting the EMU into two parts, sometimes referred to as a "hard euro area" and a "soft euro area". Germany and the stronger economies of Central and Northern Europe will stay in the hard euro area while Southern European countries will create a soft euro area with their own common currency that they can devalue toward the hard euro to keep their economies competitive in the integrated European market (Stiglitz 2017).

The analysis carried out in this book suggests that none of these proposals seems to be a working solution for the EMU. Dismantling the EMU would recreate the problematic contexts that led to the idea of monetary unification. The main difference with the 1990s is that most of the economic structures and many of the firms of that time have disappeared in the most troubled countries, and they will not return just because of the euro abandonment. Since the 1990s it is not only the monetary regime that has changed. The international trade pattern, technology, preferences, the industrial structures of the EMU member countries and the effects of monetary integration on member countries' economies have changed today's context dramatically compared with the 1990s. Also, the massive amounts of TARGET2 balances will engulf the intra-European relations for decades.

The same is also true for single countries' exits. In this case, additional problems made this solution even more problematic than the full dissolution of the EMU. In fact, exiting the EMU means exiting the EU. So Italy, Greece, Spain and all the other potential exiting countries will also exit from that common market where they aim to regain competitivity. Also, exiting the euro will feed interest rate divergence, charging the exiting countries' economy and state budget with further costs capable of making the economic conditions worse than before.

The Stiglitz proposal does not work politically either. In fact, the single market grants access to all EMU members. Consequently, the hard euro-soft euro exchange rate will determine the success or the bankruptcy of firms in the two monetary areas. This will require monetary coordination, which has already failed in the past. Moreover, none of the governments in the two monetary zones will accept relevant losses in national economic competitiveness and will fight fiercely against this eventuality for obvious electoral reasons. So the environment in which the European Union without the single currency and its member states would work is entirely different and will affect the latter's economies unpredictably.

The Stiglitz proposal has the advantage of saving the euro and making monetary integration more flexible. However, this solution pays inadequate attention to the political dimension of the transformations required. Having two euros would duplicate all the political incongruences, tensions and governance gaps of the single currency. So coordination inside each of the two euro areas would still be problematic, particularly in the soft euro area. Also, coordination between the two areas risks being problematic because they would become the main arenas for economic supremacy in the EU. So splitting the euro areas risks becoming the first step toward EU dissolution.

Of course, there are further and more generic solutions. The most widely acclaimed is reforming the EMU. However, this solution is just a meta-solution because the reforms proposed or supposed are many and conflicting. So each set of reforms is a proposed solution. On the other hand, the unique solution proposed by the EU is reforming member states and making them fit the EMU structure and an empowered governance system it seems too late to be successful. A mixture of EU and member state reforms is the only feasible solution, or at least the least dangerous one to adopt.

The TARGET2 balances are probably the most important indicator of EMU structural imbalances, the most problematic issue to face, and a crucial instrument for solving the EMU's problems. If one or more countries leave the EMU to pay their debts or collect their credits this will be a very complicated matter, in particular for the largest debtors (Italy and Spain) and creditors (Germany). On the other hand, the existence of massive imbalances in the TARGET2 system creates anxiety in creditor countries about the risk of debtors' non-compliance after exiting the EMU and justifies a potentially positive attitude of creditors toward solutions capable of reducing the TARGET2 balances. However, it is only by reversing the structural trade deficit of debtor countries that TARGET2 balances can be reduced. In other words, the problem remains to induce creditor countries to increase consumption and buy more from debtor countries.

Seemingly, exiting the EMU and devaluing their new national currencies would allow debtor countries to sell more to the euro area and repay their debts to the TARGET2 system. This is the solution implicitly proposed by the supporters of euro-exiting solutions. However, there are elements that undermine such a simple option. In fact, the TARGET2 imbalances depend on the financial and commercial predominance of creditor countries, Germany in particular. This predominance has been consolidated over the 20 years of the life of the euro and has resulted in the crisis or obsolescence of the debtor countries' productive structures. Exiting the euro will not resuscitate and modernise the industrial sectors that have been dismantled or declined in debtor countries. Also, a broad devaluation of exiting countries' new currencies will help them to improve their trade balances only if they maintain access to the single market. Unfortunately, this will create an unacceptable disadvantage for those industrial sectors in the EMU countries touched by the exiting countries' concurrence. So the exit option is politically unsuitable at the EU level.

An inside solution is more viable than the exit one. In this case, a European industrial policy can reorganise existing instruments such as cohesion funds, research grants and production quotas to rebuild the industrial sectors of the debtor countries, drawing them toward new products and industrial sectors not in concurrence with the creditor countries' industries. This policy can draw resources from the existing budget, redirecting funds from the less developed countries outside the eurozone to the more unbalanced ones in the EMU. Also, light taxation of the TARGET2 creditor balances can help in collecting resources to be used for solving the North-South divide in the EMU without penalising those industries and countries that have gained predominance in certain sectors of the European economy. Such a plan can give the EU institutions terrific power in terms of the macroeconomic conditionality that the actual plans for economic governance empowerment cannot obtain, being focused mainly on macroeconomic stabilisers and shock absorption instead of structural reforms. Of course, such a strategy will enlarge the widening cleavage between the EMU area and non-EMU countries, i.e. the most probable line of fracture for the EU in the future.

6 – *Euro without Europe? Monetary integration and the future of the European Union*

This book shows how monetary integration activated mechanisms and processes with uncertain outcomes that can be addressed and managed only if certain conditions are respected. It also supports the idea that monetary integration can survive for a while (but not forever) the lack of a European state. It suggests, too, that it is improbable that European integration could survive the dismantling of the EMU. In fact, if such an enormous and expensive collective effort fails, no trust could be rebuilt for further integration.

EMU collapse is a remote eventuality, but it is less remote today than in the early 2000s. Some authors consider it unavoidable and support their conclusion with theories that suggest the common currency is unsustainable without specific conditions or a European state. This book, however, explains the EMU's difficulties with initial poor governance, the delayed introduction of increasingly stringent rules and the resistance of some member state governments to changing their government style in accordance with European standards. So the problem is not the unsustainability of the euro but the lack of governance and the damages derived from its delayed and weak implementation. Some of these issues could be faced and resolved through political will and stricter cooperation. This "governance gap theory" suggests that European integration needs "more and better governance" rather than the "more Europe" often proposed as the only solution to the EU crisis. Unfortunately, the right time for further sovereignty surrender and the adoption of better and more stringent governance has passed.

Rising anti-Europeanism and poor political coordination make further integration and governance enhancement unacceptable to a large proportion of European electors. The way in which monetary integration was realised generated an obstruction to further integration that made it almost impossible today to propose further steps or ameliorative measures for integration. Paradoxically, only in technicalities and in "already discredited fields" such as banking integration does some space still exist for government coordination. However, the gradual fall of pro-EU governments restricts drastically any space for further integration or just the correction and amelioration of EU and EMU governance. So a European state is destined to remain a remote possibility for years, and the EMU has to survive for a long while without "Europe" to make it possible. This is the crucial challenge today for European integration.

The need to keep the EMU working to avoid the collapse of the EU, combined with the need to consolidate and improve the EU's economic governance, cannot be faced with "more Europe" or with a "united Europe". Rather, it is likely that searching for a better Europe will have to be done in a "less Europe" context, or at least within a European context, thereby losing coordination, coherence and legitimacy. Then, the risk is that the euro will not only have to survive without Europe, but that it will remain in a limbo in which the EMU's limitations and problems are evident and understood, but unsolvable because of a frozen decisional framework that cannot do anything more than survive and resist disaggregation. So stalemate rather than the dissolution of the EMU and EU is the most dangerous risk for Europe in the near future.

Works cited

1. Official Documents

Commission of the European Communities (1969), *Commission Memorandum to the Council on Co-ordination of Economic Policies and Monetary Co-ordination within the Community*, COM (69) 150, Brussels (Barre Plan I).

Commission of the European Communities (1970), *Commission Memorandum to the Council on Preparation of a Plan for the Phased Establishment of an Economic and Monetary Union*, COM (70) 300, Brussels (Barre Plan II).

Commission of the European Communities (1970), *Commission Memorandum and Proposals to the Council on the Establishment by Stages of Economic and Monetary Union*, COM (70) 1250, Brussels (Barre Plan III).

Commission of the European Communities (1970), *Report to the Council and the Commission on the Realisation by Stages of Economic and Monetary Union in the Community*, Brussels (Werner Report).

Commission of the European Communities (1975, *Report of the Study Group «Economic and Monetary Union 1980»*, Brussels (Marjolin report).

Commission of the European Communities (1976), *Optica Report 75. Toward Economic Equilibrium and Monetary Integration in Europe*, Brussels (Optica Report).

Commission of the European Communities (1977), *Report of the Study Group on the Role of Public Finance in European Integration*, Brussels (MacDougall report).

Committee for the Study of Economic and Monetary Union (1989), *Report on Economic and Monetary Union in the European Community Presented April, 17, 1989*, Brussels (Delors report).

Committee for the Study of Economic and Monetary Union (1989), *Collection of Papers Submitted to the Committee for the Study of Economic and Monetary Union*, Brussels (Delors report papers).

European Central Bank (2010), *Reinforcing Economic Governance in the Euro Area*, Frankfurt.

European Commission (2010a), *Enhancing Economic Policy Coordination for Stability, Growth and Jobs – Tools for Stronger EU Economic Governance*, COM(2010) 367/2.

European Commission (2010b), *Reinforcing Economic Policy Coordination*, Bruxelles, 12 May, COM (2010) 250 final.

European Commission (2012a), *A Blueprint for a Deep and Genuine Economic and Monetary Union. Launching a European Debate*, Bruxelles, 30-11, COM (2012) 777 final/2.

European Commission (2012b), *Toward a Genuine Economic and Monetary Union*, Bruxelles (Van Rompuy Report).

European Commission (2014), *Communication on the Guidelines on the Application of the Measures Linking Effectiveness of the European Structural and Investment Funds to Sound Economic Governance According to Article 23 of Regulation (EU) 1303/2013*, COM (2014) 494 final.

European Commission (2015), *Completing Europe's Economic and Monetary Union*, Bruxelles (Five Presidents Report).

European Commission (2017a), *White Paper on the Future of Europe. Reflections and scenarios for the EU27 by 2025*, Bruxelles, COM(2017) 2025.

European Commission (2017b), *Reflection Paper on the Deepening of the Economic and Monetary Union*, Bruxelles, COM (2017) 291.

European Council (2011), *European Council 24-25 March 2011: Conclusions*, (Euro Plus Pact).

House of Lords European Union Committee (2014), *Genuine Economic and Monetary Union and the Implication for the UK*, Authority of the House of Lords, London.

Task Force on Economic Governance (2010), *Strengthening Economic Governance in the EU. Report of the Task Force to the European Council*, Bruxelles.

Aeschimann, É and Riché P (1996), *La Guerre de Sept Ans. Histoire secrète du franc fort 1989-1996*, Calmann-Lévy, Paris.

Aldcroft, DH (1977), *From Versailles to Wall Street, 1919–1929*, Berkeley, University of California Press.

Aliber, RZ (1982), 'The Evolution of Currency Areas: a Speculation on Monetary History' in RN Cooper et al. (eds.), *The International Monetary System Under Flexible Exchange Rates: Global, Regional and National*, Ballinger Publishing Co., Cambridge (Mass.).

Apel, E (1998), *European Monetary Integration 1958-2002*, London, Routledge.

Arndt, HW (1944), *The Economic Lessons of the 1930's*, London, Frank Cass.

Arzheimer, K (2015), 'The AfD: Finally a Successful Right-Wing Populist Eurosceptic Party for Germany?',*West European Politics*, vol. 38, no. 3, pp. 535–556.

Bagnai, A (2012), *Il Tramonto dell''euro. Come e perché la fine della moneta unica salverebbe democrazia e benessere in Europa*, Reggio Emilia, Imprimatur.

Bakker, R, Edwards, E, Hooghe, L, Jolly, S, Marks, G, Polk, J, Rovny, J, Steenbergen, M and Vachudova, M (2014), *2014 Chapel Hill Expert Survey version 2015.1.* available on chesdata.eu. Chapel Hill, NC: University of North Carolina, Chapel Hill, 2015.

Bakker, R, Edwards, E, Hooghe, L, Jolly, S, Marks, G, Polk, J, Rovny, J, Steenbergen, M and Vachudova, M (2015), 'Measuring Party Positions in Europe: The Chapel Hill Expert Survey Trend File, 1999-2010', *Party Politics*, vol. 21, no. 1, pp. 143-152.

Bartolini, S (2004), 'Tra formazione e trascendenza dei confini. Integrazione europea e stato-nazione', *Rivista italiana di scienza politica*, vol. XXXIV, no. 2, pp. 167-195.

Bartolini, S (2006), *Restructuring Europe*, Oxford University Press, Oxford.

Basch, A (1944), *The Danube Basin and the German Economic Sphere*, Columbia University Press, New York.

Baster, ASJ (1929), *The Imperial Banks*, P.S. King & Son, London.

Baster, ASJ (1935), *The International Banks*, P.S. King & Son, London.

Bell, PW (1956), *The Sterling Area in the Post-war World: Internal Mechanism and Cohesion 1946-1952*, Oxford University Press, Oxford.

Berbuir, N, Lewandowsky, M and Siri, J (2015), 'The AfD and Its Sympathisers: Finally a Right-Wing Populist Movement in Germany?', *German Politics*, vol. 24, no. 2, pp. 154–178.

Bergsten, CF (1975), *The Dilemma of the Dollar: The Economics and Politics of United States International Monetary Policy*, M.E. Sharpe, Armonk (NY).

Bickerton, CJ, Hodson, D, and Puetter, U (2015a), *The New Intergovernmentalism: States and Supranational Actors in the Post-Maastricht Era*, Oxford University Press, Oxford.

Bickerton, CJ, Hodson, D, and Puetter, U (2015b), 'The New Intergovernmentalism: European Integration in the Post-Maastricht Era', *Journal of Common Market Studies*, vol. 53, no. 4, pp. 703-722.

Bindseil, U and König, PJ (2011), *The Economics of TARGET2 Balances*, Humboldt-Universität zu Berlin, School of Business and Economics, Discussion Paper 2011-035.

Bistis, G (2013), 'Golden Dawn or Democratic Sunset? The Rise of Far Right in Greece', *Mediterranean Quarterly*, vol. 24, no. 3, pp. 35-55.

Blavoukos, S and Pagoulatos, G (2008), 'The Limits of EMU Conditionality: Fiscal Adjustment in Southern Europe', *Journal of Public Policy*, vol. 28, no. 2, pp. 229-53.

Block, FL (1977), *The Origins of International Economic Disorder: A Study of United States International Monetary Policy From World War II to the Present*, University of California Press, Berkeley.

Blyth, M (2013), *Austerity: The History of a Dangerous Idea*, Oxford University Press, New York.

Bonefeld, W (2012), 'Freedom and the Strong State: On German Ordoliberalism', *New Political Economy*, vol. 17, no. 5, pp. 633-56.
Börzel, TA (2018), 'Researching the EU (Studies) into demise?', *Journal of European Public Policy*, vol. 25, no. 3, pp. 475-485.
Brown, B (2004), *Euro on Trial. To Reform or Split Up*, Palgrave, Basingstoke.
Brunsden, J (2017), *Germany stands firm against EU bank deposit guarantee plan*, Financial Time online, https://www.ft.com/content/58c9a172-ae7d-11e7-beba-5521c713abf4.
Buchanan, JM (1967), *Public Finance in Democratic Process: Fiscal Institutions and Individual Choice*, The University of North Carolina Press, Chapell Hill.
Buchanan, JM and Tullock, G (1962), *The Calculus of Consent: Logical Foundations of Constitutional Democracy*, University of Michigan Press, Ann Arbor.
Buchanan, JM and Wagner, RE (1977), *Democracy in Deficit: The Political Legacy of Lord Keynes*, Academic Press, New York.
Burley, AM and Mattli, W (1993), 'Europe before the Court: A Political Theory of Legal Integration', *International Organization*, vol. 47, no. 1, pp. 41-76.
Capoccia, G and Kelemen, RD (2007), 'The Study of Critical Junctures: Theory, Narrative, and Counterfactuals in Historical Institutionalism', *World Politics*, vol. 59, no. 3, pp 341-369.
Cheneval, F and Schimmelfennig, F (2013), 'The Case for Demoicracy in the European Union', *Journal of Common Market Studies*, vol. 51, no. 2, pp. 334-350.
Christiansen, T and Piattoni, S (eds) (2003), *Informal Governance in the European Union*, Edward Elgar, Cheltenham (UK).
Christiansen, T and Neuhold, C (2013), 'Informal Politics in the EU', *Journal of Common Market Studies*, vol. 51, no.6, pp. 1196–1206.
Chwieroth, JM (2013), 'The Silent Revolution:' How the Staff Exercise Informal Governance over IMF Lending', *The Review of International Organizations*, vol. 8, no. 2, pp. 265–290.

Clayes, G, Leandro, A, and Mandra, A (2015), *European Central Bank Quantitative Easing: The Detailed Manual*, Bruegel Policy Contribution, 2015/02.

Cohen, B (1994), 'Beyond EMU: The problem of sustainability', in B Eichengreen and J Frieden (eds), *The Political Economy of European Monetary Unification*, Westview, Boulder (CO), pp. 149-165.

Conan, AR (1961), *The Rationale of the Sterling Area*, Macmillan, London.

Connolly, B (1997), *Rotten Heart of Europe: The Dirty War for Europe's Money*, Faber & Faber, London.

Conrad, B (2006), 'Informal Politics', *Hamburg Review of Social Science*, vol. 1, n. 3, pp. 256–72.

Coombs, CA (1976), *The Arena of International Finance*, John Wiley and Sons, New York.

Coultrap, J (1999), 'From Parliamentarism to Pluralism: Models of Democracy and the European Union's Democratic Deficit', *Journal of Theoretical Politics*, vol. 11, no. 1, pp. 107-35.

Cowles, MG, Caporaso, JA, and Risse, T (eds.) (2001), *Transforming Europe. Europeanization and Domestic Change*, Cornell University Press, Ithaca (NY).

Crombez, C (2003), 'The Democratic Deficit in the European Union: Much Ado About Nothing?', *European Union Politics*, vol. 4, no. 1, pp. 101-120.

Crowley, P (ed.) (2002), *Before and Beyond EMU. Historical Lessons and Future Prospects*, Routledge, New York.

Crum, B (2013), 'Saving the Euro at the Cost of Democracy?', *Journal of Common Market Studies*, vol. 51, no. 4, pp. 614–630.

Dahl, RA (1999), 'Can International Organizations be Democratic? A Sceptic's View', in I Shapiro and C Hacker-Cordon (eds), *Democracy's Edges*, Cambridge University Press, Cambridge, pp. 19-37.

De Beus, J (2001), 'Quasi-National European Identity and European Democracy', *Law and Philosophy*, vol. 20, no. 3, pp. 283-311.

De Cecco, M (1984), *The International Gold Standard: Money and Empire*, Pinter, London.

Decker, F (2002), 'Governance Beyond the Nation-state. Reflections on the Democratic Deficit of the European Union', *Journal of European Public Policy*, vol. 9, no. 2, pp. 256-272.

Degryse, C (2012), *The New European Economic Governance*, European Trade Union Institute working paper, 2012.14.

Dehousse, R (2003), *The Open Method of Coordination: A New Policy Paradigm?*, Les Chaiers Européens de Sciences Po, n. 3, Centre d'Ètudes Européennes at Sciences Po, Paris.

Dellas, H and Tavlas, GS (2009), *An Optimum-Currency-Area Odyssey*, Bank of Greece, Athene.

Della Sala, V (2010), 'Political Myth, Mythology and the European Union', *Journal of Common Market Studies*, vol. 48, no. 1, pp. 1–19.

Dinan, D (2014), 'Governance and Institutions: The Unrelenting Rise of the European Parliament', *Journal of Common Market Studies*, vol. 52, S 1, pp. 109-124.

Di Quirico, R (1998), 'Financing Italian Growth: Italian Banks and the New York Financial Market During the Inter-War Period', *Essays in Economic and Business History*, vol. XVI, pp. 53-73.

Di Quirico, R (1999), 'The First Phase of Italian Banks' Expansion Abroad: 1900-1931' *Financial History Review*, vol. 6, n. 1, pp. 7-24.

Dor, E (2016), *Explaining the Surge of TARGET2 Liabilities in Italy: Less Simple Than the ECB's Narrative*, IESEG School of Management, Lille.

Dornbusch, R (1996), 'Euro Fantasies. Common Currency as Panacea', *Foreign Affairs*, vol. 75, no. 5, pp. 110-124.

Drummond, IM (1972), *British Economic Policy and the Empire 1919-1939*, George Allen and Unwin, London.

Dutzler, B and Hable, A (2005), 'The European Court of Justice and the Stability and Growth Pact: Just the Beginning?' *European Integration Online Papers*, vol. 9, no. 5.

Dyson, K and Featherstone, K (1999), *The Road to Maastricht. Negotiating Economic and Monetary Union*, Oxford University Press, Oxford.

Dyson, K, Featherstone, K and Michalopoulos, G (1996), 'Italy and EMU as Vincolo Esterno: Empowering the Technocrats, Transforming the State', *South European Society and Politics*, vol. 1, no. 2, pp. 272-299.

Eberlein, B and Grande, E (2005), 'Beyond Delegation: Transnational Regulatory Regimes and the EU Regulatory State', *Journal of European Public Policy*, vol. 12, no. 1, pp. 89-112.

Eichengreen, B (2008), *Globalizing Capital. A History of International Monetary System*, Princeton University Press, Princeton.

Einaudi, L (2001), *Money and Politics: European Monetary Unification and the International Gold Standard (1865-1873)*, Oxford University Press, Oxford.

Ellinas, AA (2013), 'The Rise of Golden Dawn: The New Face of the Far Right in Greece', *South European Society and Politics*, vol. 18, no. 4, pp. 543-565.

Ellinas, AA (2015), 'Neo-Nazism in an Established Democracy: The Persistence of Golden Dawn in Greece', *South European Society and Politics*, vol. 20, no. 1, pp. 1-20.

Ellis, HS (1941), *Exchange Control in Central Europe*, Harvard University Press, Cambridge (Mass.).

Falco, G and Storaci, M (1977), 'Il ritorno all'oro in Belgio, Francia e Italia: stabilizzazione sociale e politiche monetarie (1926-1928)', *Italia contemporanea*, no. 126, pp. 3-43.

Featherstone, K (2011), 'The Greek Sovereign Debt Crisis and EMU: A Failing State in a Skewed Regime', *Journal of Common Market Studies*, vol. 49, no. 2, pp. 193–217.

Feldstein, M (1992), 'The Case Against EMU', *Time Magazine*, 13 June.

Feldstein, M (1997), *The Political Economy of the European*

Economic and Monetary Union: Political Sources of an Economic Liability, NBER Working Paper Series, no. 6150.

Feldstein, M (2000), 'Europe Can't Handle the Euro', *The Wall Street Journal*, 8 February.

Fernandes, S (2014), *Who Calls for the Shots in the Euro Area: 'Brussels' of the Member States?*, Notre Europe, Policy paper 111.

Fforde, J (1992), *The Bank of England and Public Policy, 1941-1958*, Cambridge University Press, Cambridge.

Flora, P, Kuhnle, S and Urwin, D (eds.) (1999), *State Formation, Nation-building, and Mass Politics in Europe: The Theory of Stein Rokkan*, Oxford University Press, Oxford.

Fodor, G (1986), 'The Origin of Argentina's Sterling Balances 1939-43', in G Di Tella and DCM. Platt (eds), *The Political Economy of Argentina 1880-1946*, MacMillan, Basingstoke.

Follesdal, A and Hix, S (2006), 'Why There is a Democratic Deficit in the EU: A Response to Majone and Moravcsik', *Journal of Common Market Studies*, vol. 44, no. 3, pp. 533–562.

Franchino, F (2004), 'Delegating Powers in the European Community', *British Journal of Political Science*, vol. 34, no. 2, pp. 269-293.

Franchino, F (2005), 'A Formal Model of Delegation in the European Union', *Journal of Theoretical Politics*, vol. 17, no. 2, pp. 217-47.

Franchino, F (2007), *The Powers of the Union*, Cambridge University Press, Cambridge.

Frankel, JA and Rose, A (1996), *The Endogeneity of the Optimum Currency-Area Criteria*, NBER Working Paper Series, no. 5700.

Franzosi, P, Marone F and Salvati, E (2015), 'Populism and Euroscepticism in the Italian Five Star Movement', *The International Spectator: Italian Journal of International Affairs*, vol. 50, no. 2, pp. 109-124.

Gardner, RN (1980), *Sterling-Dollar Diplomacy in Current Perspective: The Origins and Prospects of Our International Economic Order*, Columbia University Press, New York.

Georgiou, GC (2013), 'Cyprus's Financial Crisis and the Threat to the Euro', *Mediterranean Quarterly*, vol. 24, no. 3, pp. 56-73.
Gocaj, L and Meunier, S (2013), 'Time Will Tell: The EFSF, the ESM, and the Euro Crisis', *Journal of European Integration*, vol. 35, no. 3, pp. 239–53.
Goetschy, J (1999), 'The European Employment Strategy: Genesis and Development', *European Journal of Industrial Relations*, vol. 5, no. 2, pp. 117–37.
Gowa, J (1983), *Closing the Gold Window. Domestic Politics and the End of Bretton Woods*, Cornell University Press, Ithaca.
Gorjão, P (2012), 'Portugal and the Straitjacket of the European Financial Crisis', *The International Spectator: Italian Journal of International Affairs*, vol. 47, no. 4, pp. 64-68.
Grimm, R (2015), 'The Rise of the German Eurosceptic Party Alternative für Deutschland', *International Political Science Review*, vol. 36, no. 3, pp. 264-278.
Haas, EB (1958), *The Uniting of Europe. Political, Social and Economic Forces, 1950-57*, Stanford University Press, Stanford.
Haas, EB (1964), *Beyond the Nation-state. Functionalism and International Organization*, Stanford University Press, Stanford.
Haas, EB (1975), *The Obsolescence of Regional Integration Theory*, University of California, Berkeley.
Haberler, G (1977), 'The International Monetary System after Jamaica and Manila',*Weltwirtschaftliches Archiv*, vol. 113, no 1, pp. 1-30.
Habermas, J (2001), 'Why Europe Needs a Constitution', *New Left Review*, no. 11, pp. 5-26.
Hakhverdian, A, van Elsas, E, van der Brug, W and Kuhn, T (2013), 'Euroscepticism and Education: A Longitudinal Study of 12 EU Member States, 1973–2010', *European Union Politics*, vol. 14, no. 4, pp. 522-541.
Heinisch, R (2016), 'The Austrian Freedom Party: Organizational Development and Leadership Change', in R. Heinisch and O. Mazzoleni (eds.), *Understanding Populist Party Organisation.*

The Radical Right in Western Europe, Palgrave Macmillan, Basingstoke.

Heipertz, M and Verdun, A (2004), *The Dog that Would Never Bite? What We Can Learn from the Origins of the Stability and Growth Pact*, CGPE Working Paper 04-06, January.

Heipertz, M and Verdun, A (2010), *Ruling Europe. The Politics of the Stability and Growth Pact*, Cambridge University Press, Cambridge.

Held, D (1987), *Models of Democracy*, Stanford University Press, Stanford.

Helleiner, E (1994), *States and the Reemergence of Global Finance. From Bretton Woods to the 1990s*, Cornell University Press, Ithaca (NY).

Helmke, G and Levitsky, S (2004), 'Informal Institutions and Comparative Politics: A Research Agenda', *Perspectives on Politics*, vol. 2, no. 4, pp. 725-740.

Henning, RC (1998), 'Systemic Conflict and Regional Monetary Integration: The Case of Europe', *International Organization*, vol. 52, no. 3, pp. 537-573.

Henshaw, PJ (1996), 'Britain, South Africa and the Sterling Area: Gold Production, Capital Investments and Agricultural Markets, 1931-1961', *The Historical Journal*, vol. 39, no. 1, pp. 197-223.

Hertz, F (1947), *The Economic Problem of the Danubian States: A Study in Economic Nationalism*, Gollancz, London.

Hirowatari, K (2015), *Britain and European Monetary Cooperation, 1964–1979*, Palgrave Macmillan, Basingstoke.

Hirschman, AO (1945), *National Power and the Structure of Foreign Trade*, University of California Press, Berkeley.

Hobza, A and Zeugner, S (2014), *The 'Imbalanced Balance' and its Unravelling: Current Accounts and Bilateral Financial Flows in the Eurozone*, Economic Papers 520, European Commission, Bruxelles.

Hodson, D (2015), 'Eurozone Governance: Deflation, Grexit 2.0 and the Second Coming of Jean-Claude Juncker', *Journal of Common Market Studies*, vol. 53, S1, pp. 144–161.

Hoffman, S (1966), 'Obstinate or Obsolete? The Fate of the Nation State and the Case of Western Europe', *Daedalus*, vol. 95, pp. 862-915.

Hooghe, L and Marks, G (2009), 'A Postfunctionalist Theory of European Integration: From Permissive Consensus to Constraining Dissensus', *British Journal of Political Science*, vol. 39, no. 1, pp. 1-23.

Hooghe, L and Marks, G (2017), *Cleavage Theory Meets Europe's Crises: Lipset, Rokkan, and the Transnational Cleavage*, The Euengage Working Paper Series.

Höpner, M and Spielau, A (2018), 'Better Than the Euro? The European Monetary System (1979–1998)', *New Political Economy*, vol. 23, no. 2, pp. 160-173.

Hopkin, J (2012), 'A Slow Fuse: Italy and the EU Debt Crisis', *The International Spectator: Italian Journal of International Affairs*, vol. 47, no 4, pp. 35-48.

Horvath, J (2003), *Optimum Currency Area Theory: A Selective Review*, Bank of Finland, Institute for Economies in Transition, Helsinki.

Howarth, DJ (2000), *The French Road to European Monetary Union*, Palgrave, Basingstoke.

Hurrelmann, A (2015), 'Demoi-cratic citizenship in Europe: an impossible ideal?', *Journal of European Public Policy*, vol. 22, no. 1, pp. 19-36.

Inglehart, R (1977), *The Silent Revolution: Changing Values and Political Styles among Western Publics*, Princeton University Press, Princeton.

Ingram, JC (1969), 'Comment: The Currency Area Problem', in RA Mundell and AR Swoboda (eds), *Monetary Problems of the International Economy*, The University of Chicago Press, Chicago, pp. 95-100.

Jabko, N (2003), 'Democracy in the Age of the Euro', *Journal of European Public Policy*, vol. 10, no. 5, pp. 710-739.

Jabko, N (2010), 'The Hidden Face of the Euro', *Journal of European Public Policy*, vol. 17, no. 3, pp. 317-733.

Jensen, T (2009), 'The Democratic Deficit of the European Union', *Living Reviews in Democracy*, vol. 1, pp. 1-8.
Jones, E (2012), 'Italy's Sovereign Debt Crisis', *Survival*, vol. 54, no. 1, pp. 83-110.
Jones, G (1995), *British Multinational Banking 1830-1990*, Oxford University Press, New York.
Jonung, L and Drea, E (2009), *The Euro: It Can't Happen, It's a Bad Idea, It Won't Last. US Economists on the EMU, 1989 – 2002*, European Commission, Directorate-General for Economic and Financial Affairs Publications, Brussels.
Jouen, M (2015), *The Macro-Economic Conditionality, the Story of a Triple Penalty for Regions*, Policy Papers 131, Notre Europe, Paris.
Kaplan, JI and Schleiminger, G (1989), *The European Payments Union. Financial Diplomacy in the 1950s*, Oxford University Press, Oxford.
Karagiannis, Y (2016), 'The Origins of the Common Market: Political Economy vs. Hagiography', *Journal of Common Market Studies*, vol. 54, no. 2, pp. 233–248.
Katsikas, D (2012), 'The Greek Crisis and the Search for Political Leadership', *The International Spectator: Italian Journal of International Affairs*, vol. 47, no. 4, pp. 49-56.
Kenen, PB (1969), 'The Theory of Optimum Currency Areas: An Eclectic View', in R. Mundell and A. Swoboda, (eds), *Monetary Problems of the International Economy*, Chicago University Press, Chicago, pp. 59-77.
Keynes, JM (1913), *Indian Currency and Finance*, MacMillan, London.
Kindleberger, CP (1973), *The World in Depression 1929-1939*, Allen Lane, London.
King, WTC (1936), *History of the London Discount Market*, Frank Cass, London.
Kioupkiolis, A (2016), ''Podemos: the Ambiguous Promises of Left-Wing Populism in Contemporary Spain', *Journal of Political Ideologies*, vol. 21, no. 2, pp. 1–22.
Kleine, M (2013), 'Knowing Your Limits: Informal Governance

and Judgment in the EU', *Review of International Organizations*, vol. 8, no. 3, pp. 245-264.

Koheler, M (2014), 'European Governance and the European Parliament: From Talking Shop to Legislative Powerhouse', *Journal of Common Market Studies*, vol. 52, no. 3, pp. 600-615.

Kølvraa, C (2016), 'European Fantasies: On the EU's Political Myths and the Affective Potential of Utopian Imaginaries for European Identity', *Journal of Common Market Studies*, vol. 54, no. 1, pp. 169–184.

Kösters, W, Neumann MM, Ohr R and Vaubel R (1998), 'Der Euro kommt zu früh', *Frankfurter Allgemeine Zeitung*, February 9.

Kriesi, H (2007) 'The Role of European Integration in National Election Campaigns', *European Union Politics*, vol. 8, no. 1, pp. 83–108.

Kriesi, H (2014) 'The Populist Challenge', *West European Politics*, vol. 37, no. 2, pp. 361-378.

Kriesi, H, Grande, E, Lachat, R, Dolezal, M, Bornschier, S, and Frey T (2006), 'Globalization and the Transformation of the National Political Space: Six European Countries Compared', *European Journal of Political Research*, vol. 45, no. 6, pp. 921–56.

Kriesi, H, Grande, E, Lachat, R, Dolezal, M, Bornschier, S, and Frey, T (2008), *West European Politics in the Age of Globalization*, Cambridge University Press, Cambridge.

Kriesi, H, Grande, E, Dolezal, M, Helbling, M, Höglinger, D, Hutter, S, and Wüest, B (2012). *Political Conflict in Western Europe*, Cambridge University Press, Cambridge.

Krozewski, G (1993), 'Sterling, the 'Minor' Territories, and the End of Formal Empire, 1939-1958', *Economic History Review*, vol. XLVI, no. 2, pp. 239-265.

Krugman, PR (1998), 'The Euro: Beware of What You Wish For', *Fortune*, December.

Krugman, PR (2013), *Revenge of the Optimum Currency Area*, NBER Macroeconomics Annual 2012, vol. 27

Kunstein, T and Wessels, W (2013), *The New Governance of the Economic and Monetary Union: Adapted Institutions and Innovative Instruments*, Istituto Affari Internazionali, Roma.

Lanzone, ME and Ivaldi, G (2016), 'From Jean-Marie to Marine Le Pen: Organizational Change and Adaptation in the French Front National', in R Heinisch and O Mazzoleni (eds.), *Understanding populist party organization: a comparative analysis*, Palgrave Macmillan, Basingstoke, pp. 131-158.

Lanzone, ME, Ivaldi, G and Woods, D (2017), 'Varieties of Populism across a Left-Right Spectrum: The Case of the Front National, the Northern League, Podemos and Five Star Movement', *Swiss Political Science Review*, vol. 23, no. 4, pp. 354-376.

Lapavitsas, C, Kaltenbrunner A, Lindo D, Michell J, Painceira JP, Pires E, Powell J, Stenfors A and Teles N (2010), 'Eurozone Crisis: Beggar Thyself and Thy Neighbour', *Journal of Balkan and Near Eastern Studies*, vol. 12, no. 4, pp. 321-373.

Lavington, F (1929), *The English Capital Market*, Methuen & Co. Ltd, London.

League of Nations (1926a), *The Financial Reconstruction of Austria*, League of Nations, Geneva.

League of Nations (1926b), *The Financial Reconstruction of Hungary*, League of Nations, Geneva.

League of Nations (1944), *International Currency Experience: Lessons of the Inter-War Period*, League of Nations, Geneva.

Lindberg, LN (1963), *The Political Dynamics of European Economic Integration*, Stanford University Press, Stanford.

Lipset, SM and Rokkan S (eds.) (1967), *Party Systems and Voter Alignments: Cross-National Perspectives*, Free Press, New York.

Lord, C and Beetham, D (2001), 'Legitimizing the EU: Is there a 'Post-Parliamentary Basis' for its Legitimation?', *Journal of Common Market Studies*, vol. 39, no. 3, pp. 443-462.

Madden, JT and Nadler, M (1968), (reprint of the 1935 edition), *The International Money Markets*, Greenwood Press, New York.

Magnusson L and Stråth B (eds.) (2001), *From the Werner Plan to the EMU, In Search of a Political Economy for Europe*, Peter Lang, Brussels.

Maier CS (1975), *Recasting Bourgeoise Europe. Stabilisation in France, Germany and Italy in the Decade after World War I*, Princeton University Press, Princeton.

Majone, G (1998), 'Europe's 'Democratic Deficit': The Question of Standards', *European Law Journal*, vol. 4, no. 1, pp. 5-28.

Majone G (2002), 'The European Commission: The Limits of Centralization and the Perils of Parliamentarization', *Governance*, vol. 15, n. 3, pp. 375–392.

Majone, G (2006), 'The Common Sense of European Integration', *Journal of European Public Policy*, vol. 13, no. 5, pp. 607-626.

Malinvaud, E, Flemming, JS, Phelps, ES, Solow, RM, Atkinson, AB, Blanchard, O. and Fitoussi JP (1992), *La désinflation compétitive, le mark et les politiques budgétaires en Europe*, OFCE and Éditions du Seuil, Paris.

Marks, G, Hooghe, L and Blank, K (1996), 'European Integration since the 1980s: State Centric versus Multi-Level Governance', *Journal of Common Market Studies*, vol. 34, no. 3, pp. 343-378.

Marsh, D (2009), *The Euro. The Battle for the New Global Currency*, Yale University Press, New Haven (Conn).

März, E (1984), *Austrian Banking & Financial Policy. Creditanstalt at a Turning Point 1913-1923*, St. Martin Press, New York.

Matthijs, M (2017), 'Integration at What Price? The Erosion of National Democracy in the Euro Periphery', *Government and Opposition*, vol. 52, no. 2, pp. 266–294.

McKinnon, R (1963), 'Optimum currency areas', *American Economic Review*, vol. 53, no. 4, pp. 717-725.

McNamara, K (1998) *The Currency of Ideas: Monetary Politics in the European Union*, Cornell University Press, Ithaca (NY).

Meade, JE (1957), 'The Balance of Payments Problem of a European Free Trade Area', *Economic Journal*, vol. 67, no.267, pp. 379-396.

Meny, Y (2002), 'De la democratie en Europe: Old Concepts and New Challenges', *Journal of Common Market Studies*, vol. 41, no. 1, pp. 1-13.

Meyer, FV (1952), *Britain, The Sterling Area and Europe*, Cambridge University Press, Cambridge.

Milward, AS (1981), 'The Reichsmark Bloc and the International Economy' in L Kettenacker (ed.), *Der Führerstaat. Mythos und Realität*, Klett-Cotta, Stuttgart, pp. 377-411.

Milward, AS (1987), *The Reconstruction of Western Europe, 1945-51*, Routledge, London (first edition 1984).

Milward, AS (1992), *The European Rescue of the Nation State*, Routledge, London.

Minenna, M, Boi, GM and Verzella, P (2016) *The Incomplete Currency. The Future of Euro and Solutions for the Eurozone*, John Wiley and Sons LTD, Chichester (UK).

Moggridge, DE (1972), *British Monetary Policy 1924–1931: The Norman Conquest of $4.86*, Cambridge University Press, Cambridge.

Moravcsik, A (1999), *The Choice for Europe*, Routledge, London.

Moravcsik, A (2002), 'In Defense of the 'Democratic Deficit': Reassessing Legitimacy in the European Union', *Journal of Common Market Studies*, vol. 40, no. 4, pp. 603–624.

Moravcsik, A (2008), 'The Myth of Europe's Democratic Deficit', *Intereconomics: Journal of European Public Policy*, vol. 43, no. 6, pp. 331-340.

Moravcsik, A and Schimmelfennig, F (2009), 'Liberal Intergovernmentalism', in Wiener, A and Diez, T (eds), *European Integration Theory*, Oxford University Press, Oxford, pp. 67-87.

Moreau, P (2018), 'Le national-populisme en Autriche et en Allemagne: approche comparative de l'AfD et du FPÖ', *Revue d'Allemagne et des pays de langue allemande*, vol. 50, no 1, pp. 159-182.

Mortensen, J (2013), *Economic Policy Coordination in the Economic and Monetary Union. From Maastricht via the SGP to the Fiscal Pact*, CEPS Working Paper, n. 381.

Mourlon-Druol, E (2012), *A Europe Made of Money: The Emergence of the European Monetary System*, Cornell University Press, Ithaca (NY).
Mundell, R (1961), 'A Theory of Optimum Currency Areas', *American Economic Review*, vol. 51, no. 4, pp. 657-665.
Needham, D (2014), *UK Monetary Policy from Devaluation to Thatcher, 1967–82*, Palgrave Macmillan, Basingstoke.
Nedergaard, P and Snaith, H (2015), 'As I Drifted on a River I Could Not Control': The Unintended Ordoliberal Consequences of the Eurozone Crisis', *Journal of Common Market Studies*, vol. 53, no. 5, pp. 1094–1109.
Newton, CCS (1984), 'The Sterling Crises of 1947 and the British Response to the Marshall Plan', *Economic History Review*, vol. 37, no. 3, pp. 391-408.
Nicolaidis, K (2013), 'European Demoicracy and Its Crisis', *Journal of Common Market Studies*, vol. 51, n. 2, pp. 351–369.
Niemann, A and Ioannou, D (2015), 'European Economic Integration in Times of Crisis: a Case of Neofunctionalism?', *Journal of European Public Policy*, vol. 22, no. 2, pp. 196-218.
Pagoulatos, G and Triantopoulos, C (2009), 'The Return of the Greek Patient: Greece and the 2008 Global Financial Crisis', *South European Society and Politics*, vol. 14, no. 1, pp. 35-54.
Paiva Abreu, M. de (1990), 'Brazil as a creditor: sterling balances, 1940-1952', *Economic History Review*, vol. 43, issue 3, pp. 450-469.
Palpant, C (2006), *European Employment Strategy. An Instrument of Convergence for the New Member States?*, Policy Paper no. 18, Notre Europe, Paris.
Papadopoulos, Y (2010), 'Accountability and Multi-level Governance: More Accountability, Less Democracy?', *West European Politics*, vol. 33, n. 5, pp. 1030-1049.
Parrini, CP (1969), *Heir to Empire: the United States Economic Diplomacy, 1916-1923*, University of Pittsburgh Press, Pittsburgh.
Pierson, P (1995), 'Fragmented Welfare States: Federal Institutions

and the Development of Social Policy', *Governance*, vol. 8, no. 4, pp. 449-478.

Pierson, P (1996), 'The Path to European Integration: A Historical Institutionalist Analysis', *Comparative Political Studies*, vol. 29, no. 2, pp. 123-163.

Pollack, MA (2009), The New Institutionalisms and European Integration, in A Wiener, and T Diez (eds), *European Integration Theory*, Oxford University Press, Oxford, pp. 137-156.

Powell, ET (1966), (reprint of the 1915 edition), *The Evolution of the Money Market 1385-1915*, Cass &Co., London.

Puetter, U (2004), 'Governing Informally: the Role of the Eurogroup in EMU and the Stability and Growth Pact', *Journal of European Public Policy*, vol. 11, no. 5, pp. 854-870.

Puetter, U (2012), 'Europe's Deliberative Intergovernmentalism: The Role of the Council and European Council in EU Economic Governance', *Journal of European Public Policy*, vol. 19, no. 2, pp. 161-78.

Radaelli, C (2003), *The Open Method of Coordination: A New Governance Architecture for the European Union*, Swedish Institute for European Policy Studies, Stockholm.

Ránky, G (1983), *Economy and Foreign Policy. The Struggle of the Great Powers for Hegemony in the Danube Valley, 1919-1939*, Columbia University Press, New York.

Raveaud, G (2007), 'The European Employment Strategy. Towards More and Better Jobs?', *Journal of Common Market Studies*, vol. 45, no. 2, pp. 411–443.

Redwood, J (1997), *Our Currency, Our Country: the Dangers of European Monetary Union*, Penguin Books, London-New York.

Rees, GL (1963), *Britain and the Postwar European Payments Systems*, University of Wales Press, Cardiff.

Ritshl, AO (2001), 'Nazi Economic Imperialism and the Exploitation of the Small: Evidence from Germany's Secret Foreign Exchange Balances, 1938-1940', *Economic History Review*, vol. LIV, no. 2, pp. 324-345.

Ritterberger, B (2014), 'Integration without Representation? The European Parliament and the Reform of Economic Governance in the EU', *Journal of Common Market Studies*, vol. 52, no. 6, pp. 1174–1183.

Rittberger, B and Blauberger, M (2017), 'Introducing the debate section: 'The EU in crisis: EU studies in crisis?', *Journal of European Public Policy*, vol. 25, no. 3, pp. 436-439.

Rodrik, D (2011), *The Globalization Paradox: Democracy and the Future of the World Economy*, W.W. Norton, New York.

Rombi, S (2016), 'European Voters in the Face of Crisis: the Prominence of Unemployment', *Rivista italiana di Scienza politica*, vol. 46, no. 2, pp. 151-173.

Rothschild, KW (1947), *Austria's economic development between the two World Wars*, Frederick Muller, London.

Ruggie, JG (1982), 'International Regimes, Transactions, and Change: Embedded Liberalism in Post-War Economic Order', *International Organisation*, vol. 36, no. 2, pp. 379-415.

Sadeleer, N De (2012), 'The New Architecture of the European Economic Governance: a Leviathan or a Flat-Footed Colossus?', *Maastricht Journal of Comparative and EU Law*, vol. 19, no. 3, pp. 354-383.

Salines, M, Glöckler, G and Truchlewski, Z (2012), 'Existential Crisis, Incremental Response: The Eurozone's Dual Institutional Evolution 2007–2011', *Journal of European Public Policy*, vol. 19, no. 5, pp. 665-681.

Sartori, G (1976), *Parties and Party Systems. A Framework for Analysis*, Cambridge University Press, Cambridge.

Sbragia, A (2001), 'Italy Pays for Europe: Political Leadership, Political Choice, and Institutional Adaptation', in MG Cowles, JA Caporaso and T Risse (eds), *Transforming Europe. Europeanization and Domestic Change*, Cornell University Press, Ithaca (NY), pp. 79-96.

Scharpf, FW (1970), *Demokratietheorie zwischen Utopie und Anpassung*. Universitätsverlag, Konstanz.

Scharpf, FW (1997), 'Economic Integration, Democracy and the

Welfare State', *Journal of European Public Policy*, vol. 4, no. 1, pp. 18-36.

Scharpf, FW (1999), *Governing in Europe: Effective and Democratic?*, Oxford University Press, Oxford.

Scharpf, FW (2009), 'Legitimacy in the Multilevel European Polity', *European Political Science Review*, vol. 1, no. 2, pp 173-204.

Schenk, CR (1994), *Britain and the Sterling Area. From Devaluation to Convertibility in the 1950s*, Routledge, London.

Schenk, CR (2010), *The Decline of Sterling. Managing the Retreat of an International Currency, 1945–1992*, Cambridge University Press, Cambridge.

Schimmelfennig, F (2010), 'The Normative Origins of Democracy in the European Union: Toward a Transformationalist Theory of Democratization', *European Political Science Review*, vol. 2, no. 2, pp. 211-233.

Schimmelfennig, F (2015a), 'Liberal Intergovernmentalism and the Euro Area Crisis', *Journal of European Public Policy*, vol. 22, no. 2, pp. 177-195.

Schimmelfennig, F (2015b), 'What's the News in 'New Intergovernmentalism'? A Critique of Bickerton, Hodson and Puetter', *Journal of Common Market Studies*, vol. 53, no. 4, pp. 723–730.

Schimmelfennig, F, Leuffen, D, and Rittberger, B (2015), 'The European Union as a System of Differentiated Integration: Interdependence, Politicization and Differentiation', *Journal of European Public Policy*, vol. 22, no. 6, pp. 764-782.

Schmitt-Beck, R (2017), 'The 'Alternative für Deutschland in the Electorate': Between Single-Issue and Right-Wing Populist Party', *German Politics*, vol. 26, no. 1, pp. 124-148.

Schmitter, PC (1971), 'A Revised Theory of Regional Integration, in Regional Integration: Theory and Research', L.N. Lindberg and S.A. Scheingold (eds), *Regional Integration: Theory and Research*, Harvard University Press, Cambridge (MA), pp. 232-264.

Schmitter, PC (2000), *How to Democratize the European Union… And Why Bother?*, Rowan and Littlefield, Lanham (MD).

Schmitter, PC (2003), 'Making Sense of the EU. Democracy in Europe and Europe's Democratization', *Journal of Democracy*, vol. 14, no. 4, pp. 71-85.
Schmitter, PC (2009), 'On the Way to a Post-Functionalist Theory of European Integration', *British Journal of Political Science*, vol. 39, no. 1, pp. 211-215.
Schubert, A (1990), *The Credit Anstalt Crisis of 1931*, Cambridge University Press, Cambridge.
Scitovsky, T (1957), 'The Theory of the Balance of Payments and the Problem of a Common European Currency', *Kyklos*, vol. 10, no. 1, pp. 18-44.
Shambaugh, JC (2012), 'The Euro's Three Crises', *Brookings Papers on Economic Activity*, vol. 43, no. 1, pp. 157-211.
Sinn, HW (2014a), *The Euro Trap. On Bursting Bubbles, Budgets, and Beliefs*, Oxford University Press, Oxford.
Sinn, HW (2014b), Europe's Brush with Debt, Project Syndicate, https://www.project-syndicate.org/commentary/eurozone-debt-mutualization-or-individual-liability-by-hans-werner-sinn-2014-10?barrier=true
Skidelsky, R (2009), *Keynes: The Return of the Master*, Public Affairs, New York.
Solomon, R (1999), *Money on the Move. The Revolution in International Finance since the 1980s*, Princeton University Press, Princeton.
Spiro, DE (1999), *The Hidden Hand of American Hegemony. Petrodollar Recycling and International Markets*, Cornell University Press, Ithaca (NY).
Spourdalakis, M (2014), 'The Miraculous Rise of the 'Phenomenon SYRIZA'', *International Critical Thought*, vol. 4, no. 3, pp. 354-366.
Stavrakakis, Y and Katsambekis G (2014), 'Left-wing Populism in the European Periphery: The Case of SYRIZA', *Journal of Political Ideologies*, vol. 19, no. 2, pp. 119-142.
Steil, B (2013), *The Battle of Bretton Woods. John Maynard Keynes, Harry Dexter White, and the Making of a New Order*, Princeton University Press, Princeton.

Stiglitz, JE (2017), *The Euro: How a Common Currency Threatens the Future of Europe*, W. W. Norton & Company, New York.
Stillman, PG (1974), 'The Concept of Legitimacy', *Polity*, vol. 7, no. 1, pp. 32-56.
Stone, RW (2013), 'Informal Governance in International Organizations: Introduction to the Special Issue', *The Review of International Organizations*, vol. 8, no. 2, pp. 121–136.
Storaci, M (1993), 'L'Italia e il blocco dell'oro (1933-1935)' in *Ricerche per la storia della Banca d'Italia*, vol. III, Laterza, Bari, pp. 441-486.
Storaci, M and Tattara, G (2001), 'Kingdom of Italy's External Borrowing and Domestic Monetary Policy Between the Two World Wars', *Financial History Review*, vol. 8, no. 1, pp. 49-72.
Streeck, W and Thelen, K (eds) (2005), *Beyond Continuity: Institutional Change in Advanced Political Economies*, Oxford University Press, Oxford.
Streeck, W (2014), *Buying Time: The Delayed Crisis of Democratic Capitalism*, Verso, New York.
Suchman, M (1995), 'Managing Legitimacy: Strategic and Institutional Approaches', *Academy of Management Review*, vol. 20, no. 3, pp. 571–610.
Talani, LS (ed.) (2008), *Between Growth and Stability. The Demise and Reform of the European Union's Stability and Growth Pact*, Edward Elgar, Cheltenham (UK).
Toloudis, N (2014), 'The Golden Dawn: The Financial Crisis and Greek Fascism's New Day', *New Labor Forum*, vol 23, no.1, pp. 38–43.
Unfried, M (2000), 'The Cardiff Process: The Institutional and Political Challenges of Environmental Integration in the EU', *Review of European Community & International Environmental Law*, vol. 9, no. 2, pp. 112–119.
Varoufakis, Y (2017), *Adults in The Room: My Battle with Europe's Deep Establishment*, Bodley Head, London.
Verdun, A (2015), 'A Historical Institutionalist Explanation of the EU's Responses to the Euro Area Financial Crisis', *Journal of European Public Policy*, vol. 22, no. 2, pp. 219-237.

Verhelst, S (2011), *Linking Cohesion Policy to European Economic Governance: An Idea Up for Improvement*, European Policy Brief 3, Royal Institute for International Relations, Brussels.

Vilpišauskas, R (2013) 'Eurozone Crisis and European Integration: Functional Spillover, Political Spillback?', *Journal of European Integration*, vol. 35, no. 3, pp. 361-373.

Weiler, JHH, Haltern, UR and Mayer, F (1995), 'European Democracy and its Critique: Five Uneasy Pieces', *West European Politics*, vol. 18, no. 3, pp. 4-39.

Wiener, A and Diez, T (eds) (2009), *European Integration Theory*, Oxford University Press, Oxford.

Willet, TD (1999), 'A Political Economy Analysis of the Maastricht and Stability Pact Fiscal Criteria', in AH Hallet, M Hutchison and S Jensen, (eds), *Fiscal Aspects of Monetary Integration*, Cambridge University Press, Cambridge, pp. 37-66.

Willet, TD (2000), 'Some Political Economy Aspects of EMU', *Journal of Policy Modelling*, vol. 23, no. 3, pp. 379-389.

Williams, D (1963), 'London and the 1931 financial crisis', *Economic History Review*, vol. 15, no. 3, pp. 513-528.

Williams, D (1968), 'The Evolution of the Sterling System' in CR Wittlerey and JS Wilson (eds), *Essays in Money and Banking in Honour of R.S. Sayers*, Oxford University Press, London, pp. 266-297.

Wolfe, M (1951),*The French Franc Between the Wars, 1919-1939*, Columbia University Press, New York.

Wright, KM (1954), 'Dollar Pooling in the Sterling Area, 1939-1952', *The American Economic Review*, vol. 44, no. 4, pp. 559-576.

Wylie, L (2002), 'EMU: a Neoliberal Construction', in A Verdun (ed.), *The Euro. European Integration Theory and Economic and Monetary Union*, Rowman and Littlefield Publishers, Lanham, pp. 69-89.

Young, B and Semmler, W (2011), 'The European Sovereign Debt Crisis: Is Germany to Blame?', *German Politics & Society*, vol. 29, no. 1, pp. 1-24.

Zimmerman, H (2001), 'The Euro Under Scrutiny: Histories and Theories of European Monetary Integration', *Contemporary European History*, vol. 10, no. 2, pp. 333-341.

Zweifel, TD (2002), 'Who is Without Sin Cast the First Stone: The EU's Democratic Deficit in Comparison', *Journal of European Public Policy*, vol. 9, no. 5, pp. 812-40.

Index

www.ingramcontent.com/pod-product-compliance
Lightning Source LLC
Chambersburg PA
CBHW051402240926
51852CB00005B/91/J
* 9 7 8 8 8 8 3 9 8 0 9 7 8 *